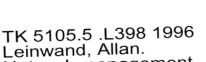

Network Management

A Practical Perspective

Second Edition

Allan Leinwand
Cisco Systems

Karen Fang Conroy
Cisco Systems

▲
▼▼
ADDISON-WESLEY
An imprint of Addison Wesley Longman, Inc.
Reading, Massachusetts • Harlow, England • Menlo Park, California
Berkeley, California • Don Mills, Ontario • Sydney
Bonn • Amsterdam • Tokyo • Mexico City

This book is in the **Addison-Wesley UNIX and Open Systems Series**
Series Editors: Marshall Kirk McKusick and John S. Quarterman

Senior Editor: Thomas Stone
Associate Editor: Deborah R. Lafferty
Production Supervisor: Juliet Silveri
Production Services: Susan Geraghty
Marketing Manager: Bob Donegan
Senior Manufacturing Manager: Roy Logan
Cover Design Supervisor: Barbara Atkinson

Library of Congress Cataloging-in-Publication Data

Leinwand, Allan.
  Network management / Allan Leinwand, Karen Fang Conroy. — 2nd ed.
    p.   cm.
  Includes bibliographical references and index.
  ISBN 0-201-60999-1
  1. Computer networks—Management.   I. Conroy, Karen Fang.
  II. Title
  TK5105.5.L398   1996
  004.6—dc20   95–23029
                                                              CIP

Access the latest information about Addison-Wesley books from our
World Wide Web page:

http://www.aw.com

The programs and applications presented in this book have been included
for their instructional value. They have been tested with care but are not
guaranteed for any particular purpose. The publisher does not offer any
warranties or representations, nor does it accept any liabilities with respect
to the programs or applications.

Many of the designations used by manufacturers and sellers to distinguish
their products are claimed as trademarks. Where those designations appear
in this book, and Addison-Wesley was aware of a trademark claim, the
designations have been printed in initial caps or all caps.

5 6 7 8 9 10 MA   01 00 99 98

5th Printing March, 1998

To our families and friends who learned with
us that it is less painful the second time around

UNIX AND OPEN SYSTEMS SERIES

Programming under Mach	Joseph Boykin David Kirschen Alan Langerman Susan LoVerso
Practical Internetworking with TCP/IP and UNIX	Smoot Carl-Mitchell John S. Quarterman
Frontiers of Electronic Commerce	Ravi Kalakota Andrew Whinston
Network Management: A Practical Perspective, 2nd Edition	Allan Leinwand Karen Fang Conroy
The Internet Connection: System Connectivity and Configuration	John S. Quarterman Smoot Carl-Mitchell
UNIX, POSIX, and Open Systems: The Open Standards Puzzle	John S. Quarterman Susanne Wilhelm
A Quarter Century of UNIX	Peter H. Salus
Casting the Net: From ARPANET to Internet and Beyond	Peter H. Salus
Network Programming in Windows NT™	Alok Sinha

Series Editors
Marshall Kirk McKusick
John S. Quarterman

OTHER RELATED TITLES

The E-Mail Frontier: Emerging Markets and Evolving Technologies	Daniel J. Blum David M. Litwack
The ISDN Literacy Book	Gerald L. Hopkins
Internet System Handbook	Daniel C. Lynch, Editor Marshall T. Rose, Editor

Preface

What is network management? Probably anyone who has had contact with a data network has a different conception of the subject. Depending on the size and complexity of the data network, this form of management could be as simple as having one person check the PCs on the local area network once a week or as involved as having a staff of fifty people armed with beepers and protocol analyzers on 24-hour call. From one network to another, priorities can differ dramatically.

We hope that this book will help the network engineer obtain a clearer view of network management in his or her individual environment. Because network engineers have different expectations and viewpoints, our first goal is to define all the pieces that make up network management. The five categories of network management as defined by the International Organization for Standardization Network Management Forum are the framework for this book. These categories are fault management, configuration management, performance management, security management, and accounting management.

OBJECTIVES

This book is intended for readers interested in the field of network management, whether beginners in networking or seasoned network engineers. To help explain the many concepts in network management, this book is divided into four parts, each with a separate objective.

Part 1: Overview of Network Management is designed to familiarize the reader with network management systems and the five areas of network management. Experienced network managers may want to skim or skip over the first few chapters, as they are fairly basic. The goal is to introduce people who are new to network management to key terminology, definitions, and concepts. Chapter 1 introduces the basic concepts of a network management system and the five areas of network management. Chapter 2 explores network management systems and potential architectures. Chapters 3–7 delve into the five areas of network management in depth, giving the reader insight into accomplishing network management tasks and evaluating tools for a network management system. We also wanted to provide the engineer with a practical means of designing or evaluating a network management system for his or her particular networking environment. Accordingly, for each category of network management, we describe simple, complex, and advanced tools. Although we realize that some of these tools might not exist today, we included them because an engineer could determine that a particular functionality would be useful and might want to pursue its development.

Note: We specifically do not mention products that are on the market today, for several reasons. Given the nature of the technology, announcements of new companies, new products, and enhancements to current network management applications happen almost daily. We prefer to help with the right questions to ask when looking at or evaluating a network management application, leaving the selection as an exercise for the reader. Any products or applications mentioned in the book are examples of what is currently available, and no recommendation is meant or implied.

Part 2: Network Management Protocols describes the two predominant network management protocols in use today. Chapter 8 explains the inner workings of the Simple Network Management Protocol (SNMP), versions 1 and 2. These protocols are the most widely deployed network management protocols on networking devices. Chapter 9 talks about the Common Management Information Services/Common Management Information Protocol (CMIS/CMIP). CMIS/CMIP is the OSI network management protocol and essentially has the same goals, but different implementation details, as SNMP.

Part 3: Management Information Bases is dedicated to all those network engineers who have stared uncomprehendingly at MIB variables such as:

iso.org.dod.internet.mgmt.mib.ip.ipNetToMediaTable.ipNetTo.Media Entry.Type (1.3.6.1.2.1.4.22.1.4)

Sometimes the easiest part of network management is getting information from the network devices. The problem is knowing how to analyze that information. Chapters 10 and 11 describe in detail two standard Management Information Bases (MIBs). A MIB defines all of the possible pieces of information available on a network device. Chapter 10 explains how to use the data in RFC 1213 MIB-II, which is supported on nearly every SNMP-compatible device. Chapter 11 illustrates how to use information found in RFC 1757, the Remote Network Monitoring Devices (RMON) MIB. RMON is becoming prevalent on many networks.

Part 4: Productivity Tools for Network Management introduces advanced ideas for network management systems. Chapter 12 looks at further productivity tools that you would want to see on a complete network management system.

INTENDED AUDIENCE

This book is intended for a broad range of readers interested in network management techniques and technologies:

- *Network designers and consultants*: Part 1 of this book gives a technical overview of network management.

- *Network managers, engineers, and administrators*: This book provides an introduction to the many aspects of network management, with an emphasis on tools and protocols in Parts 1 and 2.

- *Network management software developers*: All parts of this book will give you insight to the problems network management can solve and details on using network management protocols and MIBs.

- *Students and other communications professionals*: As a thorough introduction to the concepts of network management, all four parts of the book will help you understand this complex topic.

ACKNOWLEDGMENTS

We would like to acknowledge all the people who spent time and effort reviewing our manuscript:

Michael L. Barrow
Wayne Hathaway
Colin Kincaid
Donald Lafferty
Bob Natale
Barbara O'Toole
Cathy Putnam
Richard Weiss

Our special appreciation goes to Debbie Lafferty and Tom Stone for coercing us into this second edition and keeping the faith we would get it done. Also, thanks to everyone else behind the scenes involved with publishing this book.

If you have comments or questions about network management or this book and would like to contact us, you can reach Allan through electronic mail at leinwand@cisco.com and Karen at conroy@cisco.com. You can also reach both of us at Cisco Systems by calling (408) 526-4000.

San Jose, California   A.L.
                                                                                        K.F.C.

Contents

PART 1

Overview of Network Management

Chapter 1

Network Management

*The first sight Chris saw that morning was at least 100 yellow notes stuck to the terminal, the answering machine message light blinking out of control, and a line of people surrounding the office space. In unison they all groaned, **"The network is down!"***

So starts another day in the life of a network engineer. Chris flew past the people and started typing furiously on a keyboard. Sure enough, there was no access to Chicago, Singapore, New York, San Francisco, or Paris. Major portions of MegaNet, *the company wide international network, seemed to have disappeared into a black hole. Chris sighed and glanced at the "Don't Panic" button stuck to the wall. In the direction of the customer service group a faint voice was heard saying, ". . . I'm sorry, can you call back later, the computer is down. . . ." To the right, people in the order processing department were involved in a rousing game of bridge as they waited to input orders to the computer at Corporate. The Research and Development department chair races originally scheduled for 5:00 P.M. were in full swing. It seemed that only Chris and upper managers crowding around the office were concerned.*

Chris immediately knew how the day would proceed: Isolate the problem, fix the problem, and print out copious reports and graphs for management, showing what happened and why it will not happen

again. And with a little bit of luck, maybe even a cup of coffee to drink.
Before grabbing a screwdriver and heading for the computer room,
Chris added another yellow note to the pile on the computer screen:
"Investigate network management systems ASAP!"

This is a familiar scenario to many people. Data networks have become common and accepted in our daily lives, although we may not always be aware of them. Data networks allow us 24-hour access to our bank accounts and enable retail stores to approve our credit card purchases immediately. Research and development centers use data networks to keep abreast of rapidly changing technologies, and companies of all sizes rely on them to perform necessary day-to-day business operations.

Data networks provide exceptionally rapid and efficient access to vast quantities of information. We have come to depend on data networks so much that disruption of a network can mean disruption of business and our daily lives, resulting in, for example, frustrated users and customers, delays in receipt of critical data, possible loss of business revenue, or inability to reach much-needed funds outside of normal banking hours. Therefore keeping a data network in good working order is critical. This is where data network management comes in.

In this chapter we define a data network and briefly describe how to implement one. We introduce the network engineer/network manager as a key player in creating and managing networks. Next we present the idea of network management and briefly describe its five components—fault management, configuration management, security management, performance management, and accounting management—which form the bulk of discussion in this book.

1.1 DEFINITION OF A DATA NETWORK

A *data network* is a collection of devices and circuits for transferring data from one computer to another. It enables users at different locations to share the resources of a computer stationed elsewhere.

Most people use a data network every day and never realize it. A common example of a data network is the automated teller machine, or ATM.[1] An ATM processes bank and credit card transactions, such as your withdrawal of money from your checking account or your request for a cash advance on a credit card.

---

[1] In the data networking field the acronym ATM has taken a new meaning: asynchronous transfer mode, a high-speed, cell-switched protocol. We will discuss the "new" ATM later in the book, but for this example we are using the "old-fashioned" definition.

For customer convenience, ATMs operate at *remote sites*, that is, at locations separate from the main computer that contains the information about your accounts. These remote sites do not possess the full customer data that the main computer does; to do so would be redundant, costly, and a security concern. Instead, an ATM uses a data network to establish a communication link to the main computer. The ATM uses this link to send information about your transaction, such as the account number and the amount to be withdrawn or advanced, to the main computer, which in turn checks your account to ensure that you have sufficient funds or available credit line to cover the withdrawal or advance. If you do, the computer then sends along the communication link the necessary signals that trigger the ATM to dispense your money (see Fig. 1.1).

The *information superhighway* is a term gaining acceptance throughout the world to describe a global data network that allows everyone to access multimedia information. Although the term tends to have a unique definition depending on the person or organization explaining it, such a network promises an individual easy access to vast quantities of information, convenience, entertainment, and communication abilities. Although these promises are yet unfulfilled, the prospect of data networks penetrating all aspects of our lives seems inevitable.

Although data networks will undoubtedly continue to affect our daily lives, they have had a remarkable influence on business in the past decades. For example, a scientist at a research lab in Chicago wants to run a program

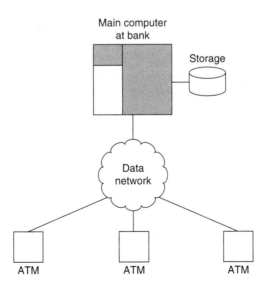

Figure 1.1 The data network provides the communication link between the bank's main computer and the ATMs.

that will take eight hours to complete on the local lab computer. But that local computer also connects by data network to a supercomputer in Miami, which can run the program in only three hours. Thus using a data network to access the supercomputer saves five hours of computing time, giving the scientist the program results much more quickly.

As another example, consider an organization that provides banking facilities throughout a large geographic region. A mainframe computer at a central site holds most of the information about customers' accounts. A minicomputer at each bank branch keeps banking records for a single day, uploading the data over a network to the central site nightly. Without the use of this data network, the transfer of data from the branch offices to the central offices would be far less timely.

As you can see, linking computers through a data network allows organizations to share the information resources of other computers. Thus those organizations become more informed, efficient, and productive.

1.2 ROLE OF THE NETWORK ENGINEER

Due to the importance of a functioning data network, usually one or more *network engineers* have responsibility for installing, maintaining, and troubleshooting the network. For these technical experts, the solution to a network problem could be as simple as answering a confused user's question or as complicated as identifying and replacing failed or malfunctioning equipment or initiating disaster-recovery procedures following a catastrophic event.

As a network expands, so too do the size and number of potential problems and the scope and complexity of the network engineer's job. Engineers need to know large amounts of information about the data network. The sheer volume of this information can quickly become unmanageable, particularly as the network grows and changes. To help the engineers do their jobs, the concept of network management evolved. The overall goal of network management is to help network engineers deal with the complexity of a data network and to make sure that data can go across it with maximum efficiency and transparency to the users.

1.3 IMPLEMENTATION OF A DATA NETWORK

Implementing a data network does not automatically guarantee that everyone in an organization will be able to share computing resources. The primary goal of the data network is to meet the organization's communication needs. To achieve this, the engineer must develop a comprehensive plan.

As an analogy, consider the U.S. highway system, a (somewhat) logical planning, designing, and building of the nation's major highways, developed by the government, usually with the goal of providing access between metropolitan areas. Just as highway engineers work to provide roadways to help the typical driver, the network engineer works to produce a data network that satisfies the needs of the typical user of a computer system. Obviously, a thorough analysis of these users' requirements regarding that system will heavily influence the design plan of the data network.

When developing a plan, network engineers often survey the user community. The design may include adding pieces to an existing network to give access to new locations, providing redundancy to guard against isolation given the failure of a single circuit, or increasing the bandwidth of a network link. Frequently this process incorporates an examination of the applications and protocols used on the network.

After developing the network plan, the engineer performs the following tasks to implement the data network:

1. Build

2. Maintain

3. Expand

4. Optimize

5. Troubleshoot

Using the network plan, the engineer should first determine the desired connectivity and the pieces of software and hardware required. Two main types of technology provide communication connectivity between points on a data network: the local area network (LAN) and the wide area network (WAN). A *LAN* ties together hosts at speeds ranging from 4 Mbps to 155 Mbps (megabits per second), with the goal of providing connectivity over relatively short distances. A *WAN* usually operates at speeds ranging from 9.6 Kbps (kilobits per second) to 45 Mbps and beyond to provide connectivity over relatively long distances. Also, many engineers elect to build networks that use WAN technology to interconnect LANs transparently to a user of the data network.

After building the network, the network engineer will need to maintain the network. Regardless of how much care the engineer has taken while building the network, it still will need maintaining. For example, software running on devices may change, pieces of the network will require upgrades, or equipment will develop faults and need replacing.

Changes in users' needs usually will affect the overall network plan, triggering the third task for the engineer: providing for expansion. Because expanding the existing network is often preferable to redesigning and build-ing an entirely new one, the engineer needs to apply the correct networking solution to accommodate these changes.

Fourth, the network engineer needs to optimize the data network—no sim-ple task. Considering that a typical network may have hundreds of devices, each with its own peculiarities and all of which must work together in har-mony, only through careful planning can the engineer ensure that these de-vices contribute optimally to a well-functioning data network. For example, the announcement of a new product or technology may lead to the replace-ment of an existing piece of equipment for better service. The engineer would need to plan the deployment of this device carefully. Knowing which para-meters on the device need setting and which are irrelevant to the existing sit-uation, the engineer can achieve optimum network performance.

By performing each of these steps, the network engineer can minimize net-work troubles. Of course, since no network is infallible, problems will in-evitably occur. Therefore the need for the fifth task—troubleshooting—will always exist.

1.4 OVERVIEW OF NETWORK MANAGEMENT

Organizations invest significant amounts of time and money in building com-plex data networks. Rather than a company's dedicating one or more net-work engineers to maintenance alone, it would be more cost-effective if the system could look out for itself for the most part and, in the process, perform routine tasks for the engineer. This arrangement would free the engineer to work on the future development of the network.

From this need was born the concept of network management. *Network man-agement* is the process of controlling a complex data network to maximize its efficiency and productivity. To better define the scope of network manage-ment, the International Organization for Standardization[2] (ISO) Network Management Forum[3] divided network management into five functional areas:

- Fault management

- Configuration management

- Security management

---

[2] This international organization was founded to promote cooperation in technological devel-opments, particularly in the field of communications. Members are "the national body most rep-resentative of standardization in its country." ANSI—the American National Standards Institute—is the ISO representative in the United States.

[3] This international consortium promotes the implementation of network and systems manage-ment.

- Performance management

- Accounting management

Fault Management

Fault management is the process of locating problems, or faults, on the data network. It involves the following steps:

1. Discover the problem.

2. Isolate the problem.

3. Fix the problem (if possible).

Using fault management techniques, the network engineer can locate and solve problems more quickly than could be done without them.

For example, in a typical setup a user logs into a remote system by way of several network devices. Suddenly the connection drops. The user reports the problem to you, the network engineer. You would begin by isolating the problem. Without an effective fault management tool, you first would want to determine whether the problem results from a user error, such as entering an invalid command or trying to access an unreachable system. If you find no user errors, you then would have to check each device between the user and the remote system, beginning with the device closest to the user. Let's say that you find no connectivity on this first device, as shown in Fig. 1.2. En-

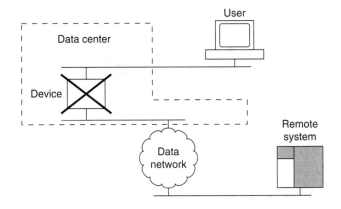

Figure 1.2 An effective fault management tool can help the network engineer isolate a problem that results from a failed device on the data network.

tering the data center, you find that all the lights on the device are off. Investigating further, you notice signs of construction in the area and that the plug for the device is on the floor. You conclude that someone must have unplugged the device accidentally. After reinserting the plug, this time into a wall outlet away from the construction area, you then would verify that the device now is working normally.

With the aid of a fault management tool, you could have isolated the problem much more quickly. In fact, such a tool might have enabled you to isolate and fix the problem before the user reported it.

Configuration Management

The configuration of certain network devices controls the behavior of the data network. *Configuration management* is the process of finding and setting up (configuring) these critical devices.

Assume that a quirk in version A of the software in an Ethernet bridge is causing network performance problems. To fix the anomaly, the bridge manufacturer has released a software upgrade, version B, that will require your installing new firmware in each of the 100 bridges on the network. Accordingly, you have planned a phased deployment to bring all the bridges on the network to version B. First, however, you would need to determine the current software version installed at each bridge. But lacking an effective configuration management tool, you would have to physically inspect each bridge.

A configuration management tool could provide a list of all bridges, showing you the current software version for each, thus making it easier for you to locate which need new software (see Fig. 1.3).

Configuration management information	
Bridge name	Software version
Corporate 1	A
Site 23	B
Site 62	B
Corporate 8	A
*	*
*	*
*	*
*	*
*	*

Figure 1.3 A configuration management tool can help the network engineer determine which software versions are installed on the data network.

Security Management

Security management is the process of controlling access to information on the data network. Some information stored by computers attached to the network may be inappropriate for all users to view. Such sensitive information may include, for example, details about a company's new products or its customer base.

Suppose that an organization decides to use security management techniques to allow remote access to its network through dialup lines on a terminal server for a group of engineers, as seen in Fig. 1.4. Once engineers connect to the terminal server, they can log in to their computer to do their work.

After a few weeks, the administrator of one of the payroll computers on the network comes to you with a report showing many unsuccessful remote login attempts originating from the terminal server used by the engineers. The terminal server does allow access to any computer on the network—leaving the destination host security preventing the access to sensitive information. Thus no engineers have gained access to the payroll computer, but the mere fact that someone is trying is a security concern.

Your first step may be to use a configuration management tool to limit the computer's accessibility from the terminal server. However, to discover who is attempting to gain access to this payroll computer, you will have to periodically log in to the terminal server and record which engineers are using it. Ideally, you can correlate the times at which the unsuccessful remote login attempts are being made with who is logged in on the terminal server.

Security management would give you a way to monitor the access points on the terminal server and record which engineer is using the device on a periodic basis. Security management also could provide you with audit trails and sound alarms to alert you of potential security breaches.

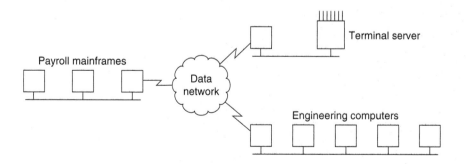

Figure 1.4 A security management tool allows the network engineer to monitor which computers the users on the terminal server are attempting to access.

Performance Management

Performance management involves measuring the performance of network hardware, software, and media. Examples of measured activities are overall throughput, percentage utilization, error rates, and response time. Using performance management information, the engineer can ensure that the network will have the capacity to accommodate the users' needs.

Suppose that a user complains about poor file transfer performance to a site across the network. Without a performance management tool, you would first have to look for network faults. If you find no fault, your next step would be to evaluate the performance of each link and device between the user's terminal and the destination across the network. During your investigation, you might discover that the average utilization of one link is very close to its capacity. You might then decide that the solution to the file transfer performance problem is to upgrade the current link or to install a new one to add capacity (see Fig. 1.5). If a performance management tool had been available, you might have been able to detect early on that the link was nearing capacity, perhaps even before the performance was impacted.

Accounting Management

Accounting management involves tracking each individual and group user's utilization of network resources to better ensure that users have sufficient resources. It also involves granting or removing permission for access to the network.

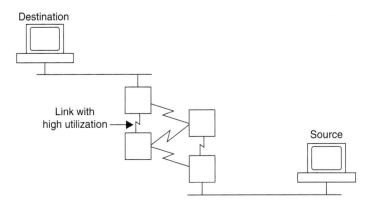

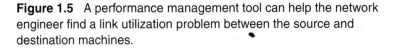

Figure 1.5 A performance management tool can help the network engineer find a link utilization problem between the source and destination machines.

Suppose that you need to upgrade a department file server's network interface because it reached its packet-processing capacity. Without an accounting management tool, you would not know which users have clients that access the file server. Thus you ask the users to see who has client computers that access the file server on a regular basis. As a result of your investigation, you discover that the departmental documentation group has many clients who use a desktop publishing system on the file server. After some rudimentary analysis, you conclude that this traffic contributes nearly half of the load on the file server's network interface.

You might decide that giving this documentation group its own file server would alleviate a large amount of the network traffic that this interface card has to handle, removing the need to upgrade the interface card and allowing the rest of the department to remain unchanged. Further, you might decide to locate the new file server on the same network segment as the documentation group, which could reduce network traffic throughout the department. With an accounting management tool, however, you would quickly learn that the documentation group accesses the file server with many clients on a regular basis—so you would have been able to handle the situation sooner (see Fig. 1.6).

1.5 NETWORK MANAGEMENT PROTOCOLS

An essential factor in achieving the goals of network management is the ability to acquire information from and effect change to network devices. In the chapters where we talk about the various network management areas, such as fault or configuration, we also describe tools, ranging from simple to ad-

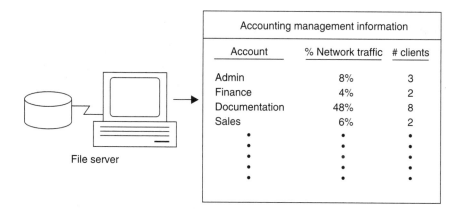

Accounting management information		
Account	% Network traffic	# clients
Admin	8%	3
Finance	4%	2
Documentation	48%	8
Sales	6%	2

File server

Figure 1.6 An account management tool can help the network engineer determine the dominant file server user.

vanced. Likewise, the requirements in network management protocols could fall into those categories. A *simple* network management protocol would define common data formats and parameters and allow for easy retrieval of information. A *more complex* network management protocol would add some change capability and a security mechanism to protect the information requested and to prevent just anyone from making these changes. An *advanced* network management protocol would be able to remotely execute network management tasks, similar to a remote procedure call, and be totally independent of network protocol layer, so all networking devices, regardless of the protocol, are manageable.

So where is the technology today? Much work has gone into developing a standardized set of network management protocols to help extract the necessary information from all network devices. The most common network management protocols are SNMP (Simple Network Management Protocol) and the newer SNMPv2 (version 2) and CMIS/CMIP (Common Management Information Services/Common Management Information Protocol). A quick answer is that SNMP is a bit beyond the simple tool, with adequate monitoring capabilities and some change capabilities. SNMPv2 greatly enhances the SNMP feature set. CMIS/CMIP approaches the advanced tool, but implementation issues have limited its use. The bounded nature of the standard network management protocols today is a key point in the development of network management applications. Many of the applications that we describe do exist today, but the limitations of the current standardized network management protocols have precluded the development of some of the more advanced tools. Much work is being done to improve both technology and network protocols, so you should expect to see more advanced network management applications in time.

Note that these protocols do not state how to accomplish the goals of network management. They simply give methods to monitor and configure network devices. The challenge to analyze the information from network management protocols in an effective manner rests on the shoulders of software engineers writing network management applications. We give suggestions for such applications throughout this text.

SUMMARY

Data networks help us perform our jobs efficiently, give us easier access to money and goods, and provide information and entertainment. Both private and public organizations use data networks for the transfer of information.

Because of the increasing importance and complexity of data networks, many organizations employ experts in data network management to be specifically responsible for them. These network engineers implement the data network—that is, build, maintain, expand, optimize, and troubleshoot it—and must know about both LAN and WAN technologies when performing these steps.

Once a data network is in place, efficient management will maximize its potential. The process of network management consists of five functional areas as defined by the International Organization for Standardization (ISO) Network Management Forum: fault management, configuration management, security management, performance management, and accounting management.

Network management protocols can monitor, acquire information from, and effect change to devices in the network. Some standardized network management protocols exist, including the Simple Network Management Protocol (SNMP) versions 1 and 2 and the Common Management Information Services/Common Management Information Protocol (CMIS/CMIP).

FOR FURTHER STUDY

Alder, J., "Bits and Bytes—The Challenge of Network Management," *Data Communications Magazine*, December 1990.

Black, U., *Data Networks: Concepts, Theory and Practice*, Englewood Cliffs, NJ: Prentice-Hall, 1989.

Halsall, F., *Data Communications, Computer Networks and Open Systems*, Reading, MA: Addison-Wesley, 1992.

Tannenbaum, A., *Computer Networks*, Englewood Cliffs, NJ: Prentice-Hall, 1988.

Chapter 2

The Network Management System

In This Chapter:

Chris spent the morning finishing the reports on the major network outage that had occurred a few weeks ago. While Chris was clearing the computer screen of the omnipresent yellow notes, one fluttered down to the floor. Scrawled on the note was, "Investigate network management systems ASAP!"

Because MegaNet seemed to be relatively stable and there were no fires to fight at the moment, Chris decided to do just that. Reaching over and grabbing a few magazines from the top of the in-tray, the network engineer settled down to read about network management.

Hours later, Chris realized that there was more to network management systems than just turning things red or green on a map.

In this chapter we examine the network management system in detail. We start by looking at two major elements of the system: the network management platform and accompanying applications. It is important to understand the difference between these two pieces, because they have unique goals.

Next, we look at three possible architectures of a network management platform: centralized, hierarchical, and distributed. The goal of this chapter is to help you choose the proper network management platform and applications for your networking environment, so we outline a practical approach for choosing a network management system for your particular environment and data network. To tie everything together, the chapter closes with a description of the Open Software Foundation[1] Distributed Management Environment (OSF DME), an open architecture for building network management systems.

2.1 THE NETWORK MANAGEMENT PLATFORM

Historically network management revolved around multiple systems, each managing one specific set of components on the data network. A typical network management center could have a separate system for managing modems, multiplexers, hubs, bridges, routers, and other types of network components. Restrictions of money, physical space, and technical expertise all led to the desire to have the network components managed by a single system that would also show their interconnections on a network map. Out of this need came the network management platform.

A network management platform is a software package that provides the basic functionality of network management for many different network components. The goal of the network management platform is to provide generic functionality for managing a variety of network devices (see Fig. 2.1). This basic functionality includes:

- A graphical user interface (GUI)

- A network map

- A database management system (DBMS)

- A standard method to query devices

- A customizable menu system

- An event log

The GUI is useful for a variety of reasons, including giving the user easier access to the features of the platform. The GUI should conform to a common

---

[1] The Open Software Foundation was originally formed by vendors trying to create a standardized UNIX operating system. The scope grew to include most mechanisms needed for a useful distributed computing environment—including window systems, remote procedure calls, file systems, and more.

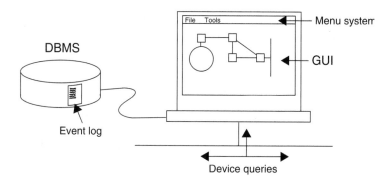

Figure 2.1 The basic components of a network management platform.

look-and-feel standard, such as Microsoft Windows, OSF Motif, or Sun Microsystems OpenLook. By using a standard GUI, the platform will behave in a manner that is documented and conformed to by different vendors. As we will discuss in the next section, the overall network management system will most likely comprise a platform and applications from a variety of vendors. If all vendors build their applications using a common look and feel, it makes the system easier to use and manipulate.

The map is useful for nearly every area of network management. Fault management tools can help isolate the cause of the fault, using colors on the map. Configuration management tools can show the physical and logical configuration of the network pictorially. Performance management tools can graphically show the current performance of devices and links by color or different pictures. If the network management platform provides a way to automatically discover the devices in the network (called autodiscovery) and then draw the network graphically (called automapping), this is an added benefit.

The standard method to query devices is essential because the platform must be able to gather information from many different vendor components. A customizable menu system is needed so that extensions to the platform appear seamless to the user.

A database management system helps in many network management tasks. Applications can use the database for information storage. Relationships can be built between data items, which help in network diagnosis and maintenance. Many database management systems allow users to generate customized reports and perform automated backup.

The last essential feature a network management platform should have is an event log. This log records each network event chronologically in a readable format. The platform writes information to the log about any known network events and can generate its own network events. Also, network devices may send asynchronous messages that could be interpreted as network events. Regardless of how the platform learns of network events, it should provide an event log to help the network engineer keep abreast of network conditions.

Additionally, the basic functionality of the network management platform should have the following features to be considered a strategic solution:

- Graphing tools
- Application programming interface (API)
- System security

The network management platform should give network engineers the ability to produce graphs, such as line, bar, or pie chart, of data. Also, the ability to merge graphs into reports is beneficial, since managers often like to see information represented on a graph instead of raw data or text reports. Graphs of current network traffic and errors can help in fault and performance management, and graphs of historical data help isolate network trends.

An API is a library of programming procedures and functions allowing access to information kept within the network management platform. Only through the API can external programs use the network map, integrate into the menu system, store and retrieve information from the database, send messages to the event log, and so forth. Thus the API is important for two reasons: It allows for integration of vendor applications, and it allows network engineers to write custom programs for their environments. Without an API, the network management platform is essentially a "black box" that allows only third-party extensions or local customization. The API also needs to be standardized across multiple network management platforms. Without a standard API, an application that communicates with the platform will need to be changed if the organization decides to change platforms. The OSF DME is an example of a specification for a standard API for network management platforms.

Another important feature of the network management platform is to have a security mechanism for itself. The network management platform and associated applications contain a wealth of information about the network, the configuration of the component devices, network and applications security, performance, and accounting methods. This information is useful for any network cracker trying to compromise network security. The security for the platform must be additional to that provided by the operating system on which it resides. In many cases the security of the operating system does not exist at all (as on many types of DOS), or another organization is responsible for setting it up.

These basic functions of a network management platform should enable a network engineer to accomplish all the functional areas of network management. The network engineer could query all devices for information through the platform and then use this data in many ways. For example, a network engineer wanting to produce a graph of serial link utilization on all links throughout the network would have to follow these steps:

1. Decide what information is needed from each network component (usually bytes sent or received per interface)

2. Gather the appropriate information, using the network management platform

3. Put the queried numbers in a spreadsheet or similar package to produce the desired graphs

The first step is the most difficult. Although the network management platform can use a standard method to query each network component, each component may have the data kept in a unique manner. In today's environment many pieces of information are kept in a standard management information base (MIB) format. This means that you would learn one piece of information that would work on all devices. However, as we will see in Part 3, the MIB usually contains hundreds of unique pieces of information, which still makes figuring out what information to look at a challenge in many cases.

Numerous network management platforms exist in the market today. Some examples include SunConnect SunNet Manager, HP (Hewlett-Packard) OpenView, IBM (International Business Machines) Netview/AIX, and AT&T (American Telephone and Telegraph) StarSentry. Each of these platforms provides the necessary features, as well as some additional features. For example, IBM Netview/AIX, which is based on HP OpenView, has a Rolodex index system that allows users to keep track of current outstanding network problems. SunConnect SunNet Manager allows users to customize three-dimensional graphs of network information. Regardless of product differentiation, however, the goal of any network platform is to provide generic functionality for overall network management.

2.2 NETWORK MANAGEMENT ARCHITECTURES

A network management platform can use various architectures to provide functionality. The three most common network management architectures are:

- Centralized

- Hierarchical

- Distributed

There is no "best" architecture; each type has specific features that work well in certain environments. It is a good rule of thumb to choose a network management architecture that most closely resembles your corporate organizational structure. In many cases the network will be structured in a similar manner.

Centralized Architecture

A *centralized* architecture has the network management platform on one computer system, at a location that is responsible for all network management duties, as shown in Fig. 2.2. This system uses a single centralized database. For full redundancy, this system is backed up to another system at regular intervals. Although the central system is the focal point for network management, it can allow access and can forward events to other consoles throughout the network. The single location of a centralized architecture is used as follows:

- For all network alerts and events

- For all network information

- To access all management applications

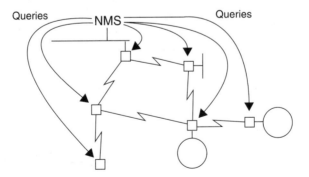

Figure 2.2 In a centralized architecture the single network management is responsible for all management duties on all network devices.

Using a centralized approach, a network engineer can have a single location to view all network alerts and events, which is useful for troubleshooting and problem correlation. Having one place to access all of the network management applications and information provides convenience, accessibility, and security for the network engineer. By virtue of having only a single management location, security is much easier to maintain. Physically, the network management station can be located in a locked and restricted access area, and the system can be set up to allow only certain users.

However, having all of the network management functions depend on a single system is not redundant or fault tolerant. Full backups should be maintained—ideally, at another physical location. As network elements are added, it may be difficult and expensive to scale a single system to handle the necessary load. A significant disadvantage to this architecture is having to query all network devices from a single location. This puts traffic load on all network links connected to the management site and throughout the network. If the connection from the management station to the network gets severed, all network management capabilities are lost. Locating the network management station in a central spot in the network would help this problem, but the ideal location for the network management platform may not be the ideal place for the network engineers to reside.

An example of a centralized network management architecture on the market today is IBM's Netview, which runs on a single host and performs all network management activities for a Systems Network Architecture (SNA) network. Users can have multiple access points to the central system; these access points allow queries and can receive network events, called Netview consoles.

Hierarchical Architecture

A *hierarchical* network management architecture uses multiple systems, with one system acting as a central server and the others working as clients (see Fig. 2.3). Some of the functions of the network management platform reside within the server; others run on the clients. For example, network engineers could configure separate client systems to monitor and poll different portions of the network.

The platform could use client/server database technology. The clients would not have separate database systems but would use the central server database accessed through the network. Because of the importance of the central system in the hierarchy, it will require backups for redundancy (a good idea in any case).

A hierarchical architecture for the network management platform has the following key features:

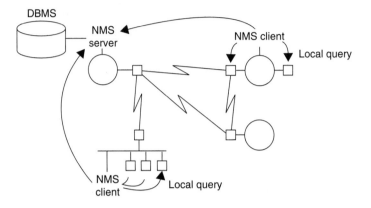

Figure 2.3   In a hierarchical architecture the NMS clients perform local management queries and use the NMS server for database storage.

- Not dependent on a single system

- Distribution of network management tasks

- Network monitoring distributed throughout network

- Centralized information storage

The hierarchical approach helps to alleviate one of the problems in a centralized approach by distributing network management tasks between the central system and the clients. Network engineers can distribute network monitoring on the clients, saving valuable bandwidth resources throughout the data network. Also, since keeping network monitoring close to the end systems is most critical to save bandwidth, the clients may not need the entire functionality of the central server. As we will see later, an RMON (remote network monitoring device) client is one example of this approach. Many network management tasks require the retrieval of information about many facets of the network. Therefore it is often beneficial to have a centralized location for data. Even though some of the management tasks are on clients using the hierarchical approach, this architecture still provides for a single place to store information about the network.

Because the hierarchical architecture uses multiple systems to manage the network, there is no longer a single centralized location for management of the entire network. This may make information gathering a bit more difficult and time consuming for the network engineer. Another issue is that the list of devices managed by each client needs to be logically predetermined and manually configured. Unless done carefully, this can often lead to both the central system and a client or two monitoring or polling the same device. One possible result of this problem is the consumption of twice as much bandwidth on the network for network management purposes.

Some of the more popular platforms on the market are SunConnect Sun-Net Manager, HP OpenView, IBM Netview/AIX, and AT&T StarSentry. Each of these platforms allows a network engineer to set up concurrently running platforms that operate in a hierarchical manner.

Distributed Architecture

The *distributed* architecture combines the centralized and hierarchical approaches, as shown in Fig. 2.4. Instead of having one centralized platform or a hierarchy of central/client platforms, the distributed approach uses multiple peer platforms. One platform is the leader of a set of peer network management systems; each individual peer platform can have a complete database for devices throughout the entire network, which allows it to perform various tasks and to report the results back to a central system.

Because the distributed platform combines the centralized and hierarchical approaches, it also has the advantages of both, including:

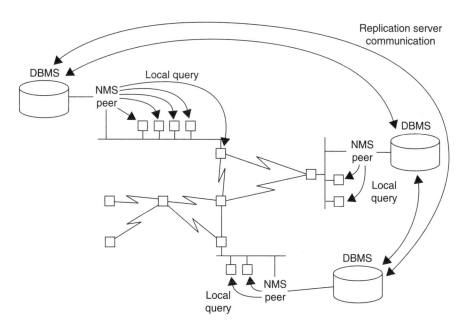

Figure 2.4 In a distributed architecture multiple peer network management systems have complete databases.

- Single location for all network information, alerts, and events
- Single location to access all management applications
- Not dependent on a single system
- Distribution of network management tasks
- Distribution of network monitoring throughout the network

Database replication server technology is extremely useful to this platform. A replication server keeps multiple databases on different systems completely synchronized, not a trivial task. The replication server technology for the database system is complex. In fact, the overhead associated with this synchronization can consume significantly more network resources than database client/server technology.

2.3 NETWORK MANAGEMENT APPLICATIONS

The network management platform provides generic functionality for all managed devices. In contrast, the design of network management applications is to help the network engineer manage a specific set of devices or services. The relationship between the network management platform and applications is shown in Fig. 2.5. Many network management applications are developed by network device vendors to help customers manage their devices.

For example, the manufacturer of a network device, such as a modem, a hub, or a bridge, would build a suite of applications to work in conjunction with the network management platform in providing a cohesive set of tools for the network engineer. Using this strategy, a network engineer would need to purchase only the tools necessary to manage a specific set of devices. If you are trying to manage a network of hubs and file servers, for example, you could ask the vendors if they have a set of specific applications that work in

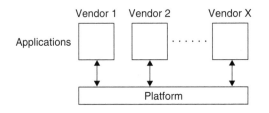

Figure 2.5 The relationship between a network management platform and applications.

conjunction with a network management platform. You could then have a network management system that provides all of the generic functionality of the platform and applications to manage specific features on the hubs and file servers using the same map, having the same look and feel (GUI), accessible through the same menu system, and querying the same database system.

The network management applications have the following goals:

- Effectively manage a specific set of devices

- Avoid functionality overlap with the platform

- Integrate with a platform through the API and menu system

- Reside on multiple platforms

A network management application tries to effectively manage a specific set of devices. For example, a hub manufacturer could build an application that shows the physical connectors on the hub when a user selects the hub on the network map. This application could allow the user to configure features of the hub, turn ports on or off, or monitor error rates and throughput. This application could help accomplish configuration and performance management tasks for the hub.

Network management applications strive not to incorporate functionality that overlaps with the platform. Overlap would result in multiple ways to accomplish the same result on the platform, perhaps providing a confusing interface for the user. Also, producing features that exist on the platform could be a waste of development effort for the application developers.

The only exception to this rule is when the platform does not provide a feature that applications need. For example, if the platform provides the ability to produce line graphs but an application needs to display pie charts, the application may provide this feature. If multiple applications (possibly written by different vendors or organizations) each produce their own pie charts and associated interfaces, the application developers may urge the platform vendor to incorporate this feature to avoid possible user confusion.

A network management application also has the goal of interfacing with the platform through the API and menu system. This allows the user to view the applications and platform as one uniform network management system. The API allows for a programmatic interface to the platform; the menu system allows for the invocation of application programs from the same menu system the user sees on the platform. On many platforms integrating an application with the menu system requires no more than editing a text file. If the application executes as a separate process, menu integration is usually a fairly trivial task. If all of the applications the network engineer uses on the platform coexist with the platform in this manner, it is possible for a wealth of features to be available to help perform network management.

An application that is available only on a single platform forces the network engineer to use this platform for network management tasks. This is not an ideal situation because the single platform may not have the necessary features or support other needed applications. *MegaNet* uses products made by the *Zippy Switching Company* and *ConnectAll Hubs*. If *Zippy* has a series of applications that integrates only with SunConnect SunNet Manager and if *ConnectAll Hubs* has a product that works only with IBM Netview/AIX, it is a difficult task to manage both types of devices from a single platform. It is a goal of network management applications to work with all of the popular platforms. However, integration requires careful planning to keep things current as platforms change and evolve and as new platforms appear.

Although applications that work in conjunction with the platform make significant strides in accomplishing network management, this approach currently has one significant drawback: Applications do not share information. For example, suppose that a *MegaNet* workstation is connected using 10baseT to a hub. The hub has another 10baseT connection to an Ethernet bridge, which connects the hub to the rest of the data network. One day the hub port connected to the bridge fails due to excessive errors. The application managing the workstation says that it has become unavailable. Another application managing the hub shows it off the network as well. A third application monitoring the bridge reports a failure on an interface. In this case the platform gets three entries in the event log for the network engineer to decipher. Depending on the tracking system (and who is available), three engineers may get dispatched to work on each separate "problem." To help avoid this duplication of effort, the platform needs an intelligent application monitoring the event log. If a fault management application took the events and computed the topology of the network from information stored in the relational database, it possibly could have deduced that the problems had a common cause. This application would need to understand the hierarchy of the devices involved in the events and conclude that the workstation is unavailable because the hub port connecting to the bridge is down.

2.4 A PRACTICAL APPROACH TO CHOOSING A NETWORK MANAGEMENT SYSTEM

A network management system is built from two major components: the platform and the accompanying applications. By choosing these pieces carefully, we can build a system to help network engineers perform the functional areas of network management. A practical approach to choosing a network management system follows these steps:

1. Perform device inventory

2. Prioritize the functional areas of network management

3. Survey network management applications

4. Choose the network management platform

The first step in choosing a network management system is to identify the devices on the data network. Often these include workstations, personal computers, front-end processors, controllers, gateways, switches, routers, bridges, hubs, printers, and modems. You will need to discover whether each of these devices is manageable by any network management protocols, either standard or proprietary. If a device cannot be managed by a standard network management protocol, do not eliminate it from the inventory; gateway software may be available to provide translation between the device protocol and a standard protocol. Once you have a list of devices, you need to prioritize the mission-critical devices. For example, although it may be desirable to manage all printers on the network, perhaps managing these devices takes a lower priority than managing the front-end processors that provide access to a mainframe computer.

The next step is to prioritize the functional areas of network management for your organization. In many cases the most important area of network management is fault management. However, your organization could require that security management or configuration management take first priority. This step is essential because you need to be able to pick the most important network management applications for the devices.

The third step is to find network management applications that help perform your key areas of network management for your devices. Network management applications help you accomplish the functional areas of network management. Without these applications, you have only the generic functionality of the network management platform to help you accomplish network management. Using applications designed to manage the devices you prioritized allows you to spend resources actively managing the network instead of building applications to allow you to perform network management.

The last step in choosing a network management system is to select the network management platform. Ideally, the applications you selected all work on at least one common platform. If they work together on only one platform, your choice of a platform is straightforward. If you have a choice of platforms, you should choose the one with the architecture that closely resembles the way your organization plans to manage the network. For example, if your organization plans to have one centralized network management center with no network engineers at other sites, a centralized or hierarchical platform may be best. If your organization plans to have multiple redundant network management centers throughout the network, a distributed platform makes more sense.

Another criterion when selecting a platform is the hardware available to run the software on. For example, if the ideal platform for your data network runs on hardware that your organization does not have or know how to support, a less than ideal platform selection may be better. The network management platform needs hardware to run, and if this hardware is continually broken or troublesome, it makes the job of performing network management difficult. Today network management platforms do exist on a variety of hardware systems, including mainframes, workstations, and personal computers, and many platforms are supported on multiple hardware systems.

In choosing a network management system, organizations tend to perform these steps out of order. Many times the selection of the network management platform comes first; only later is it discovered that there are no applications that run on the platform to manage the important devices on the network. If you follow the steps presented here, you can choose a network management system that works well for your data network and organization.

2.5 THE OSF DME

The Open Software Foundation (OSF) is an organization that explores technologies for use throughout the computer industry. One of these technologies is the Distributed Management Environment (DME), which tackles the problem of managing distributed network devices. The OSF DME defines standard methods for accomplishing some of the functionality of network management systems and applications. If all network management platforms and applications follow these standards when implementing features, a uniform approach to the functional areas of network management could be accomplished. This approach leads to greater flexibility and open products for network engineers.

In July 1990 the OSF issued an RFT (Request for Technology), allowing any organization to submit a solution to any part of the overall DME architecture. Twenty-five organizations submitted proposals; in September 1991 the OSF chose the implementations to be included in the production of the DME, among them those from IBM, HP, Tivoli Systems, and Bull Data Systems.

From this vast overall goal and set of technologies, the OSF built the structure of the DME (see Fig. 2.6). The first piece of this structure is the DME framework. This framework specifies two approaches a network management platform could use: the traditional framework for traditional client/server network management applications and platforms and the object-oriented framework for object-oriented technology. The second piece of the structure, called the Distributed Services, is made up of all services that are helpful in

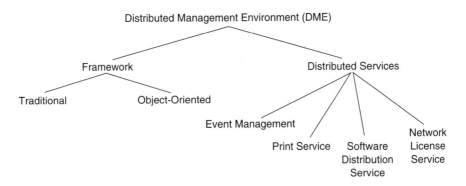

Figure 2.6 Structure of the DME.

the management of a distributed environment, such as event management, print service, methods for software distribution, and network license service.

The Traditional Framework

The DME *traditional framework* accommodates a variety of network devices and protocols existing on the majority of data networks today (see Fig. 2.7). The client/server methods in this framework use existing, established technology. The network management system is the server; the network devices are seen as clients. The traditional framework specifies a standard for the following features provided by a network management platform and associated applications:

- A graphical user interface (GUI)

- A method for acquiring data from the network

- A way for applications to understand management information

- An application programming interface (API)

X11 Motif was chosen for the GUI portion of the traditional framework architecture. This specification allows for a wealth of functionality and has a well-defined set of specifications for use. Software engineers can use it to write applications, and it is supported on many varieties of workstations and personal computers.

The traditional framework can use two schemes to gather data from the network: SNMP and CMIS/CMIP. Thus this architecture can manage all of the devices that currently support SNMP and those that may support CMIS/CMIP in the future.

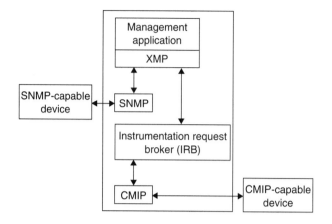

Figure 2.7 The DME traditional management framework.

X/Open's XMP was chosen for the application programming interface. This interface provides access to both the SNMP and CMIS/CMIP. However, these two protocols have different rules for governing their Structure of Management Information (SMI), forcing XMP to use two different ways to access each protocol. This means that applications must decide which protocol to use for data gathering. XMP provides direct access for applications to SNMP. However, another level of abstraction, called the Instrumentation Request Broker (IRB), allows XMP to access CMIS/CMIP. The IRB attempts to provide a simplified interface to CMIS/CMIP that allows application developers to view network devices as managed objects. This level of abstraction allows the CMIS/CMIP object-oriented design to work within the traditional framework.

The IRB allows applications to view network devices as objects. An object is a software-defined entity having its own properties, methods, and internal workings. The internal structure of an object is not known outside of the object. Applications that use an object simply need to know its properties and methods. Objects hide complexity and make it easier to build a complex application by breaking the many facets of the application into smaller, indivisible components.

For example, imagine an object that defines the *engine* of an automobile, as seen in Fig. 2.8. The object has certain internal properties: number of cylinders, horsepower, fuel injection, torque, and so on. The engine object offers these methods: start, stop, accelerate, and coast. From outside the engine object, only these four methods can be accessed. The internals of the object are hidden.

Now picture a software application that is trying to simulate an *automobile* object. Instead of writing separate code to simulate an engine, the application simply uses the previously defined engine object. Furthermore the automobile itself is an object and will have some methods similar to the engine

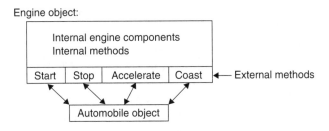

Figure 2.8 An engine object and its relationship to an automobile object.

methods: start, stop, accelerate, coast. So when an application tells the automobile object to start, the automobile object may invoke the engine method to start. This is called building a hierarchy of objects.

Let's go back to the IRB. Consider an application written to produce a report showing the up-time percentage of all serial links throughout a data network. A serial link could be an object with its own properties and methods. A serial link object might have the properties of bandwidth, end points, propagation delay, errors/sec, bits/sec, up time, and circuit identifier. The methods available on a serial link object may include up time, bandwidth utilization, and error utilization. If an application wanted to produce a report showing the up-time percentage of all serial link objects over the past month, it might follow these steps:

1. Request all objects of type serial link.

2. Invoke the method up time on all serial link objects.

3. Calculate percentage up time over the last month

As you can see, objects allow the application to produce the desired results without knowing the physical location of all the serial links. Also, knowing which network devices have serial links is not a prerequisite. The OSF uses the power of objects further in the object-oriented framework.

The Object-Oriented Framework

The DME *object-oriented framework* makes extensive use of object-oriented technology for the purposes of network management. Instead of using a classic client/server architecture, this framework allows the network management system and network devices to appear as peer objects. A network management application, which is an object, communicates with network devices by using their associated methods. Likewise, the network devices communicate with the network management system by calling its methods. These methods are invoked when an operation is received by an object. This structure is similar to the remote procedure call (RPC) function programmers use. The OSF Distributed Computing Environment (DCE) defines the RPC mechanism that the framework uses.

The Management Request Broker (MRB) is the object-oriented framework's version of the IRB seen in the traditional framework. One major difference is that the MRB acts as the interface to operations on remote network devices and to all management applications. The MRB, in turn, communicates to the remotely managed objects through the DCE RPC. Through the use of the DCE RPC, one managed object can invoke a method on another peer-managed object. The DCE RPC mechanism has a rigorous security system and a way to locate network objects. Although these tasks may be too numerous for a network device to accomplish, they could easily be accomplished by a system. Therefore the object-oriented framework will most likely be first used for systems management. However, this does not preclude this framework from ever being used for network management.

The Management User Interface (MUI) is the GUI of the object-oriented framework. The MUI is based on the X11 Motif look and feel, providing a common graphical interface for all management applications. In an object-oriented sense, the MUI is another managed object that provides methods for accessing elements of the display on the network management system.

An *adaptor* is another component of the object-oriented framework. OSF realizes that there should be a way for existing technology to be incorporated into the DME. This makes transition to this framework easier and does not require a potential upgrade on all network management applications and devices overnight to support object-oriented technology. An example may be an adaptor for SNMP. The adaptor could translate between the basic SNMP operations and DME methods. This could enable SNMP-managed devices to be seen as objects with appropriate methods.

Distributed Services

In addition to the management frameworks, the OSF has decided to provide a few essential applications with DME. These applications include:

- Event services
- Print services
- Network license services
- Software distribution services

The event services give a way to log, filter, and forward relevant network events in a distributed environment. The print services provide distributed print service throughout the network. Control and maintenance of software licenses are handled by the network license service. The software distribution services help install applications for distributed use.

Although these types of applications will help in the management of a distributed network, they do not rely on the DME framework. Each of these applications uses the structure described by the OSF DCE. Because of this separation between the distributed services and the framework, OSF has released the DCE components separately from the DME framework.

The Future of DME

The DME architecture for network management systems encompasses a wealth of technology and functionality. The traditional framework can work well for managing network objects using existing protocols and standards. The object-oriented framework uses newer technology and holds promise for building complex network management applications. Based on technology and architecture, it appears that the DME has a strong future in the world of network management.

Unfortunately DME has one significant problem: If all network management platform vendors adopt the DME framework, they could lose their differentiating features. For example, if SunNet Manager, HP OpenView, and IBM Netview/AIX all have the same GUI, protocols, API, and so on, the bargaining position of these platforms based on unique abilities may be lost. Of course, the applications provided with each platform may be different and could be a differentiation factor. However, platform vendors have not made a major effort to conform to the DME framework. In fact, the future of whether to implement DME is currently being considered by many major network management platform vendors. The people who lose because of this issue include the network management application writers who have to continue to support multiple APIs on different network management platforms and the network engineers who have to manage data networks and would like a standard platform for all management activities.

SUMMARY

In our examination of the network management system, we began by describing a network management platform as the basic management system, providing a generic set of functionality for all network devices. The components of a platform consist of a graphical user interface (GUI), a hierarchical map, the ability to query network devices, a database management system, a customizable menu system, and an event log.

We then looked at three possible architectures for the network management platform: centralized, distributed, and hierarchical. Next, we examined network management applications, which are part of the overall network management system and communicate directly with the platform through an application programming interface (API).

We described a practical approach to choosing a network management system. The approach recommends surveying the network, prioritizing the network management tasks for your environment, surveying the applications available for the network devices you deploy, and then choosing a network management platform to accommodate the applications.

The OSF DME is an example of a network management architecture. The OSF framework describes two approaches: the traditional framework and the object-oriented framework. The traditional framework uses technology widely available today, whereas the object-oriented framework uses newer technology.

FOR FURTHER STUDY

Chappell, D., "The OSF Distributed Management Environment," *ConneXions*, October 1992.

Kauffels, F., *Network Management: Problems, Standards, and Strategies*, Reading, MA: Addison-Wesley, 1992.

Klerer, S.M., "The OSI Management Architecture: An Overview" *IEEE Network*, March 1988.

Chapter 3

Fault Management

In This Chapter:

> *"The main goal of a network management system is to make the network engineer's life easier," Chris thought. "What would make running* MegaNet *easier?" The network engineer decided to start a list of the tasks that made up the job. The phone rang, and the person on the other end of the line started listing various networking woes that had to be fixed immediately. Chris put "firefighting" at the top of the list.*

Fault management is the process of locating and correcting network problems, or *faults*. Of the many tasks involved in network management, comprehensive fault management is probably the most important. It consists of identifying the occurrence of a fault on the data network, isolating the cause of the fault, and correcting the fault (if possible).

In this chapter we explore the benefits of fault management and discuss the three steps involved in accomplishing it for a data network. We describe three possible tools that you can use and explain the methods available for a fault management system to report faults.

3.1 BENEFITS OF THE FAULT MANAGEMENT PROCESS

Fault management increases network reliability by giving the network engineer tools to quickly detect problems and initiate recovery procedures. This is important, because many people rely as heavily on a data network to do their jobs effectively as they do on a telephone network. Users usually expect both networks to be available to them continuously, yet it is unrealistic to expect either network to function perfectly. When a data network experiences a loss of a device or a link, it is the job of the network engineer to maintain at least the *illusion* of complete and continuous connectivity between the users and the network. Doing this helps reinforce the reliability of the system in the eyes of users.

Unfortunately, engineers on many data networks spend too much time "firefighting," that is, fixing one crisis after another. Although managing a network in this manner may keep it going in the short run, it leaves no time for improvements. Fault management offers a variety of tools to provide the necessary information about the network's current state. Ideally, these tools can pinpoint exactly when a problem occurs and can relay that information immediately to the engineer, who then can begin to work on the fault and possibly solve it without users ever becoming aware it existed. Using fault management to break the cycle of one disaster after another will increase both the effectiveness of a network and the productivity of its engineer.

3.2 ACCOMPLISHING FAULT MANAGEMENT

Fault management is a three-step process:

1. Identify the fault.

2. Isolate the cause of the fault.

3. Correct the fault, if possible.

To illustrate, consider a DECnet node named *Cheers* that has only a single connection between it and the main data network (see Fig. 3.1). One day this connection fails. The first thing a network management system should tell you is that *Cheers* is no longer reachable. To accomplish this step the network management system could periodically poll *Cheers* to see whether it is still reachable; or another device on the network (physically closer to *Cheers*) may relay a message to the system. The tool next should isolate the cause of the problem—that *Cheers* is not reachable because the serial line connection from

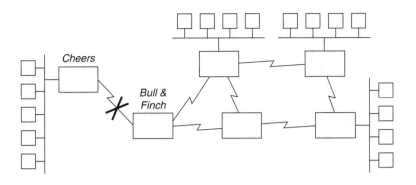

Figure 3.1 The single connection from *Cheers* to the main data *Bull & Finch* network has failed.

the node to the rest of the network has failed—through the use of another network connection. And third, the tool should help you correct the problem, if possible. In our example it could correct it by setting up another link between *Cheers* and the data network. As you can see, properly implemented fault management could correct a problem with no significant down time.

Obviously, the first task—identifying a problem—depends on your knowing when a problem exists. Next, you need to know if an identified problem is one you want to worry about; that is, you need to decide the most important problem to concern yourself with, as not all problems will have the same priority.

Gathering Information to Identify a Problem

To learn that a problem exists, we need to gather data about the state of the network. We can use either or, preferably, both of the following methods: logging critical network events or occasionally polling network devices. Let's consider each of these methods in turn.

Critical network events are transmitted by a network device when a fault condition occurs. A critical network event is, for example, the failure of a link, the restart of a device, or the lack of response from a host. In most cases relying solely on such events will not provide all the information necessary for effective fault management. For example, if a network device fails completely, it cannot send an event. Thus fault management tools that rely solely on critical network events may not always have the up-to-date status of every network device.

Occasional polling of network devices can help find faults in a timely manner. However, there is a tradeoff using this method: You must weigh the degree of timeliness you want in finding problems versus the consumption of bandwidth involved; that is, the shorter the notification time desired, the greater the amount of bandwidth that probably will be consumed. Other factors to consider when deciding on a polling interval are the number of devices you want to poll and the bandwidth of the links.

For example, let's assume that each query and response is 100 bytes long, including data and header information. For a network of 30 devices, you would send 100 bytes for the query and receive 100 bytes for the response for each device. This would give a total of 6000 bytes ((100 bytes + 100 bytes) * 30 devices), or 48,000 bits (6000 bytes * 8 bits/byte) of bandwidth used for each polling interval. Polling every 60 seconds would average 800 bits/second (48,000 bits/60 seconds) of bandwidth and enable you to have up-to-the-minute status of each device. Over an hour this means 172,800,000 bits (48,000 bits * 60 seconds * 60 polls), or approximately 173 megabits of bandwidth are used for polling. Depending on the bandwidth available on the network, this may or may not be significant overhead. You could lengthen the polling interval to every 10 minutes, which would result in 17,280,000 bits (48,000 bits * 60 seconds * 6 polls), or about one-tenth the bandwidth. However, if an event occurred, you might not be informed for up to 10 minutes.

A protocol that simply verifies that a device is operational also can be used to poll devices. ICMP Echo and Echo Reply (ping), Appletalk Echo, Banyan Vines Echo, and SDLC Receiver Ready (RR) frames are examples of such protocols. Note that this method by itself provides information only to help identify a possible fault condition.

Deciding Which Faults to Manage

Not all faults have the same priority. Some you will want to know about; others you may want the system to handle without telling you or to ignore completely. You need to decide which faults must be managed, that is, the most important types of faults for your particular network environment.

You want to do this for several reasons. First, if the number of faults is high, you might not be able to handle the volume. Second, by limiting event traffic, you can reduce the transmission of redundant or useless information and minimize the waste of network bandwidth.

Consider, for example, the case of a workstation manufacturer that decides to generate a network event whenever a user logs on to a system. Although this event provides useful information for accounting, it is irrelevant for fault management. Now suppose that a department within an organization buys 100 workstations. The administrators of the workstations configure them not only with a default configuration but also with instructions to send to the central fault management tool all network events, which include every time a user logs on. These extraneous events could quickly fill up the database on the network management system. Additionally, the bandwidth used to send this information could better be used to carry user data. The solution: Enable the network engineer to configure each network device to generate a specific subset of valid events. If this is not possible, the network management system needs a way to filter the incoming events and alert the network engineer of only specific events.

Your determination of which faults to manage will be influenced by the following factors:

- The scope of control you have over the network, which will affect the amount of information you can obtain from network devices

- The size of the network

On many networks a central organization manages the network backbone, as shown in Fig. 3.2. This backbone may consist of a variety of devices, such as X.25 switches, IP routers, and bridges. In a common arrangement the central organization manages the critical network events for each of the backbone devices—those that may affect the entire network—thus freeing up the local administration to manage only those faults on their particular hosts and devices.

The size of the data network also will influence your decision. On a relatively small data network of, say, fewer than fifty devices, a network engi-

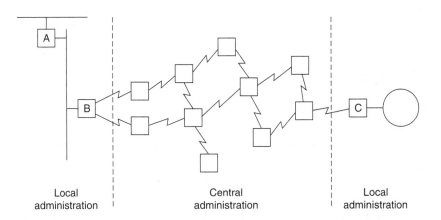

Figure 3.2 In this setup the dotted line divides local and central administration of the data network. The different administrations may choose to examine different critical network events.

neer may be able to manage every fault, including those dealing with hosts, routers, bridges, repeaters, and so forth. On a medium-sized network the engineer may be able to manage only those faults involving critical events for each host and network device. On a large data network the engineer may have time to examine only the critical events on the most important hosts and network devices.

In other increasingly common situations a central organization may be responsible for managing all devices on a large, geographically diverse data network. If you have scope to manage all of the faults on this large network, you should explore deploying a distributed or hierarchical management system. This method can help you condense the number of faults seen centrally and may even help filter and diagnose this information to help isolate the fault quickly. On internetworks today an RMON device may work well in these situations. (We explore RMON in detail in Chapter 11.)

SNMP defines seven critical faults, indicated by an SNMP "trap," that can provide a starting point for obtaining information from the data network. (Note, however, that more information on other faults, such as printer or disk drive failure, may be necessary to manage a network.) (We explore the traps further in Chapter 7.)

3.3 FAULT MANAGEMENT ON A NETWORK MANAGEMENT SYSTEM

After you decide which problems require management and determine how you will collect data on the state of the network, your next step is to implement the necessary fault management tools. The tool's effectiveness will rely heavily on the type of information the network devices provide.

A Simple Tool

The simplest tool would point out the existence of a problem but not indicate its cause. For example, a simple tool could send ICMP Echo messages (called "pings") to each host and device on the data network to test the connectivity up to the IP network layer. Many other network layer protocols, such as Novell IPX and Appletalk, also have an Echo-type message function. If the network protocol used does not have this capability, this test can be performed by having a program repeatedly attempt to connect to each host or device. On the *MegaNet* X.25 network, this test attempts to set up a virtual circuit to each X.121 destination address within the network. Failures to connect are noted for further investigation. This tool is particularly useful if the hosts or devices on the network are not sophisticated enough to send network events.

The output of this tool could be as simple as a log file or as complex as changing the colors on a hierarchical map. After a device has lost connectivity, the simple tool must alert the network engineer in a timely manner. It is possible to set up an implementation of this simple tool to access a pager directly and send the numeric message of the network address of the unreachable device.

In today's local network environments the LAN is a physical piece of cable and interconnection devices, such as repeaters, bridges, and hubs. Yet in the LANs being planned for the future a LAN may logically traverse several physical segments and network devices. This means that there may be a difference in the physical topology and the logical topology of the network. When the simple tool conveys information that a device or segment is unreachable, it will also have to depict the virtual LAN imposed on the physical LAN topology to help the network engineer diagnose the problem in a timely manner. For the simple tool, a host may be unreachable through a known router interface. If this occurs, the tool changes the color of the router interface to denote that a host attached to it is unreachable. In reality the router interface could connect to a virtual LAN, meaning that the unreachable host could be anywhere in the network topology. The simple tool isolates the problem to a given host existing on a virtual LAN, but finding the exact physical location of that device may not be as straightforward. Perhaps by selecting the device, the network engineer could bring up detailed information on its location from the network management systems database.

This type of simple tool exists within many network management platforms today. The platforms typically have a way to query the overall status of a device (see whether it communicates with the network) and to probe further into the status of the device. Many network management platforms initially just check the operational status of a device and then, if possible, check other vital statistics, such as the operation of each interface on the device. The platform can often find the operational status of each interface on the device even if the interface does not have a network address.

A More Complex Tool

If hosts and other devices on the network are sufficiently sophisticated to report network events, a more complex tool can be developed to take advantage of this capability. This tool would inform you when it detected a problem, by logging network events or by polling. Finding a fault through a critical network event also helps isolate the cause, or at least the reporting device. Flowchart 3.1 shows how this application could work.

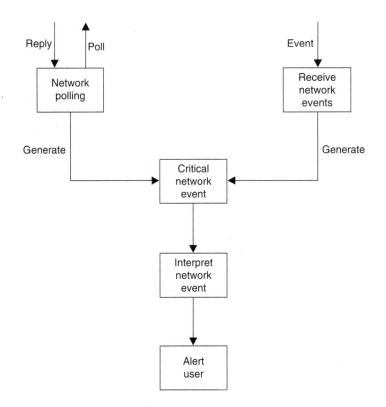

Flowchart 3.1 Flowchart of a more complex tool.

To further illustrate how such a tool might work, consider the *MegaNet* network management system shown in Fig. 3.3. A T-1 device in this system provides a circuit of 1.544 Mbps between two TCP/IP bridge/router (brouter) devices.

The T-1 device performs perfectly, but the circuit provided by the local phone company fails due to a hardware problem. In this case each brouter sends a critical network event to the network management system. The application then immediately relays this information to the network engineers.

The DECnet network shown in Fig. 3.4 provides a more complicated example of how the reporting capability of network devices could be used. This network includes a workstation, named *Sergeant*, that is a DECnet router with one megabyte of memory available for all networking processes and their buffer storage. Unknown to you, this is insufficient memory to cope with the recent network activity on the system. *Sergeant* has one LAN connection and a serial line to a similar DECnet router named *Pepper*, whose configuration assigns five megabytes of memory for networking. As indicated in the dia-

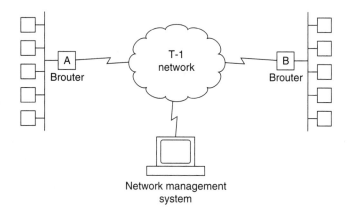

Figure 3.3 The T-1 network provides a 1.544 Mbps circuit between brouter A and brouter B.

gram, *Sergeant* resides at a small branch office, whereas *Pepper* is a concentrator node at a central location. The only way data from *Sergeant* can reach the rest of the company is through the serial link connecting the two routers. Now suppose that a sudden burst of traffic caused *Sergeant* to overflow its memory allocated for networking. This would result in a software error that would stop the DECnet routing process, which in turn would cause the system to crash. After a while, *Pepper* would recognize that the link had failed and would send a critical network event about the serial link failure to a central fault management tool. It now would be up to the tool to determine whether the physical link had indeed failed.

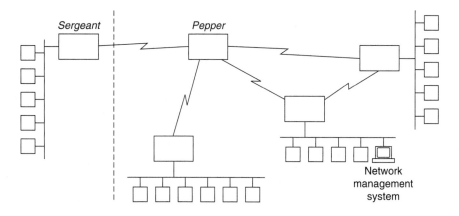

Figure 3.4 The DECnet network with *Sergeant* and *Pepper*.

The fault management tool would query *Pepper*, which had just sent the "link down" message. It may then determine whether the serial interface still has a *carrier signal*, a continuous wave that is modulated with information on a serial connection. The carrier signal tells a device that the link is operational. If the tool reported that *Pepper* had sent a "link down" message and that the carrier signal still existed on the link, it could then logically assume that the true cause of the fault might be the failure of *Sergeant*.

However, serial links do fail, even though both sides of the connection receive a carrier signal. The link drivers or modems used may send a continuous carrier signal to the brouter, whether the link is operational or not. To further isolate the fault, the fault management tool could test the link by putting the serial interface on *Pepper* in loopback and instructing the router to test its own interface. Doing this would test the hardware and connectivity on a portion of the link. If this test failed, the tool should report that although a carrier signal existed on the link in question, data did not traverse this link while in loopback. Additionally, if the link-level hardware that supported the link was accessible (a channel bank, DSU/CSU, T-1 multiplexer), the fault management tool could run some physical-level tests on the hardware to confirm its operation. Flowchart 3.2 shows how this application could function.

The network management application could now conclude that the fault was caused by a failure on either *Sergeant* or the link between *Sergeant* and *Pepper*. Considering the information supplied, this would be a reasonable conclusion. Still, you would have no idea what caused *Sergeant* to fail. So after resetting *Sergeant* to clear the problem, most likely the scenario would recur during subsequent heavy memory utilization on the DECnet router. Perhaps only after repeated router failures would it occur to you to examine the configuration of the memory assigned to networking and then to reconfigure *Sergeant* properly.

Recurrence of the fault might have been prevented at the time of the first event if *Sergeant* had sent a critical network event message to a fault management tool reporting that it was using 80 percent of its networking memory. Possibly, however, this type of event would not have generated an error message for you. But when the application concluded that the problem resided in the failure of *Sergeant*, it then could have scanned all recent events for any messages sent about that particular router. The additional information could have expedited the fault management process.

In practice, tools that perform each of these steps are rare, if they exist at all. Many individual tools can perform each specific part of the process for a set of common technologies (test for carrier signal, remotely put interfaces into loopback, check log files for recurring faults, and so on). But no single tool can do everything.

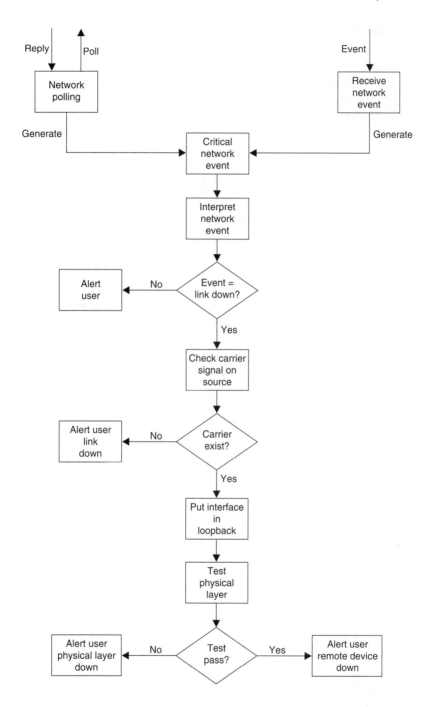

Flowchart 3.2   A fault management tool running some physical-level tests to confirm operation of hardware.

An Advanced Tool

The complex tool just described performs quite a bit of fault management, but it doesn't perform the final step: correcting the problem. In the following example we see how a fault management tool can resolve the lack of communication between two hosts.

Many faults on a data network result from the failure of a network device, yet the problem does not always lie within the networking hardware. Consider a situation in which two systems cannot communicate across a network. On *MegaNet* we have a user on *Hermes*, the source system, who has repeated unsuccessful attempts to send an electronic mail message to the destination system, *Zeus* (see Fig. 3.5). The fault management tool shows every piece of networking equipment to be operational, and no devices have sent any critical events, but it is apparent that part of the network is malfunctioning.

To solve a network problem, it is prudent to separate the task into smaller, distinct units. In this situation a reasonable approach is to first determine which devices provide the current connection between *Hermes* and *Zeus*. Next, we examine each step along the path, starting at the source. If at any step an error is found, you would examine that piece more closely until the problem is found. Let's look at this strategy in more detail.

The advanced tool would use a network management protocol to look at each device along the path, all the way up to the last device before *Zeus*. (We'll assume that both machines can communicate with each device on the path between them but not with each other.) (How this tool could determine the machines on the path between *Hermes* and *Zeus* is explained in Chapter 10.) Essentially, depending on the network protocol used, the method is to query

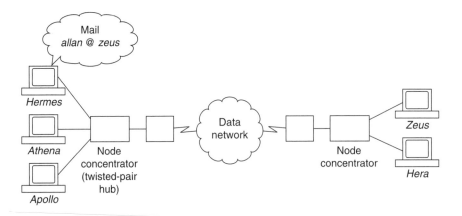

Figure 3.5 *Hermes* cannot send electronic mail to *Zeus*.

the routing table on each device, starting at the source for the route to the destination.

Back to the problem at hand. The tool discovers no faults on any of these devices on the path, yet the user still cannot send electronic mail through the network. At this point the tool would run a new set of tests on each device between the two machines that, although time consuming, would check for many possible problems.

One such test could check the error rates on each intermediary system and network device. Doing this may include sending data packets of various sizes from the source to the destination to see if an error occurred. A good way to test this is to find the MTU (maximum transmission unit) on the path and test in 100-byte increments until reaching the maximum packet size the network media will allow. In many protocols, such as IP, there are dynamic methods to discover the MTU along a path.

If this test proved inconclusive, the tool then could check the electronic mail process on both systems by attempting to send a message from *Hermes* to *Zeus* and then checking error logs. Most electronic mail systems, such as cc:Mail by Lotus or the Simple Mail Transport Protocol (SMTP), have standard error codes and messages the tool could be preprogrammed to understand. Or, the tool could try another network service to verify connectivity, such as file transfer, between the two machines.

Hermes attaches to the network by means of a twisted-pair hub. Using these additional tests, the tool discovers that large data packets that traverse this hub fail over 55 percent of the time. The electronic mail message the user was trying to send was quite large, and the application that broke this message into packets used a large packet size. Thus the tool has isolated the source of the problem.

Determining that the port on the hub could be the problem, the tool could move the port that attaches *Hermes* to the data network (if the software in the hub allows this action). Many newer hubs on the market allow for a software reconfiguration of a specific port within the hub (sometimes called a *virtual LAN* feature). Then the tool would rerun the test with large data packets. This time the connection from the hub to *Hermes* transmits 100 percent of the data without an error. The tool has corrected the problem. As a last step, the tool could produce a log of the procedure it used to find the problem so that you could fix the malfunctioning port.

Examples of this type of network management application are being developed. (We show you how to find a path through the network from the source to the destination address in Chapter 9.) Once all of these devices are known, the tool would need to determine if they could be set up remotely to run the appropriate tests, something fairly common in today's internetworking marketplace. Finally, physically switching the port a station attaches to a hub remotely is somewhat difficult, but the software to perform this task logically is being worked on in conjunction with ATM (asynchronous transfer mode) development.

3.4 IMPACT OF A FAULT ON THE NETWORK

A fault management tool must be capable of analyzing how a fault can affect other areas of the data network. Only then could it provide you with a complete fault analysis.

For example, consider a common situation in which a satellite connects an organization's DECnet and IBM SNA networks between Europe and the continental United States. If this link failed, the tool would inform you of the failure. The tool would even attempt to fix the problem and then may report it to you in a statement such as the following:

```
LINK FAILURE between Europe Node and United States Node
```

This information would be useful but wouldn't tell you that the failure is cutting off communication between Europe and the United States for DECnet and IBM SNA. With this additional information, however, you would know that the fault required immediate attention. Therefore an alternative version of the preceding statement could read like this:

```
LINK FAILURE between Europe Node and United States Node.
STOPS DECnet and IBM SNA traffic between Europe and United
States.
```

But now let's say that the data network for the organization also has a terrestrial link between the continental United States and Europe in addition to the satellite link, with both links servicing DECnet and IBM SNA traffic. Now when the fault management tool finds the satellite link down, the message might take this form:

```
LINK FAILURE between Europe Node and United States Node. Im-
pacts DECnet and IBM SNA traffic between Europe and United
States.
```

In this case traffic would be impacted but not completely stopped.

MegaNet has a substantial X.25 network with a large switch in New York that connects Boston, Buffalo, Newark, and Washington, D.C., to the rest of the network (see Fig. 3.6). If at some point the X.25 switch failed, the fault management tool could produce a message such as:

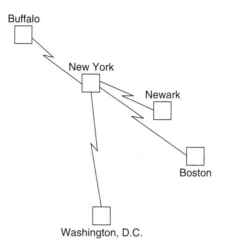

Figure 3.6 The *MegaNet* X.25 network topology.

```
SWITCH FAILURE in New York. NO ACCESS to Boston, Buffalo,
Newark, and Washington DC.
```

You know not only that there had been a failure but also how that failure affected network communication.

Designing a fault management tool that has the capability to report these types of faults and their implications is not an impossible task. As we see in the discussion of performance management in Chapter 6, information about the type of data traversing a network device can be stored by the network management system for use by fault management tools.

3.5 FORM OF REPORTING FAULTS

The form in which a fault is reported is nearly as important as the fault management process. The most common forms messages may take are text messages, graphical messages, and auditory signals.

Text messages are an appealing choice because they work on any type of terminal. However, a picture message is most effective. Note that to deliver this type of message, the fault management tool needs access to a color display capable of sophisticated graphics. As the tool ideally will reside on the network management system, this would probably not be a problem. Even without color, one method to catch the engineer's attention is to flash the picture of the device with the fault. An audible bell or noise has an advantage in that it will quickly call an engineer's attention to the tool if the engineer is working in another area. This method may be inadequate, however, if the tool is in a busy operations center with many people and monitoring systems. A combination of message forms may be best. For example, in the case of the failure of the X.25 switch, a picture of the fault could have shown New York as a failure site and the outlying sites as those affected. To clarify this graphical display, a text message could have been added.

Advantage of Color Graphics

Although other applications on the network management system may not require color graphics for their outputs, these graphics are particularly useful in fault management. For example, a display of mean time between failure for devices does not depend on the use of color; a text report would probably suffice for this network analysis application. Similarly, in accounting management and security management simple text displays usually are sufficient to report results.

However, graphics, even without color, will help indicate the status of a network device. Add color and the application can convey network status to you even more efficiently. To see how this might work, consider the following example. A graphical interface could show every device on a map drawn by the network management system. More complex networks might require a hierarchical map, with each node representing a building, a city, or even many cities. Each of these nodes could open into another map, with a finer granularity of nodes (see Fig. 3.7).

Finally, perhaps through many steps, each specific device on the network could be shown. To indicate the status of each device, a color scheme such as the following could be used:

- Green = device up with no errors

- Yellow = device may have an error

- Red = device in error state

- Blue = device up but was in error state

- Orange = device misconfigured

- Gray = no information on the device

- Purple = device being polled

According to this scheme, a green device would be one that had not experienced any critical network events, and a red device would be one known

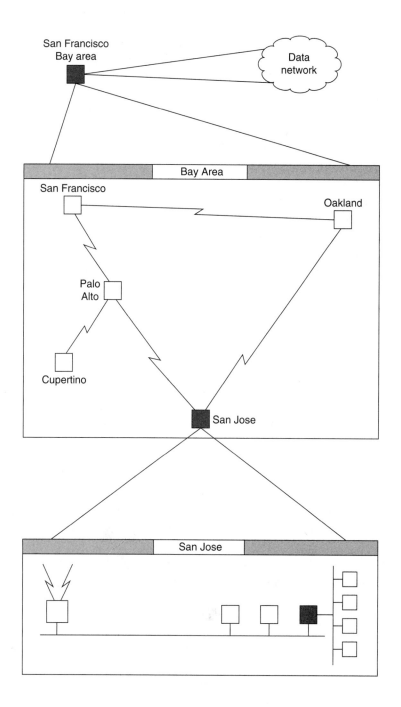

Figure 3.7 A hierarchical map used to isolate a fault.

to have a fault. A red device may be one that no longer answers polls because it does not hear them or it sends unintelligible replies. You could use yellow for those devices that did not respond to a *single poll sequence*—indicating that the device may have an error. In this case the fault management tool might show a device in a yellow status color until two poll intervals occurred without the device responding. Under this condition, you would know that when a device turned yellow, you should wait to see if a *second* poll interval occurred and failed, which would change the device to red and thus signal a situation needing your attention. Otherwise, if a device moved from green to red every time a single poll was lost or not answered, you might see devices go up and down frequently.

Yellow could also be used when a device has an automatic backup facility for some component that has failed for which the device has already compensated. For example, many devices, such as T-1 multiplexers, routers, and hubs, have backup power supplies. When one power supply fails, the other automatically takes over. Some devices have a similar feature for other hardware components, such as processors and interfaces. A yellow indication could mean that the device does have an error but that it is not critical yet.

Also, yellow could mean that the device has already corrected a network problem without manual intervention. Some devices have a capability called "dial-backup" to monitor a link and, if it fails, automatically bring up an alternate link. This usually requires a modem that speaks the Hayes command set or has V.24 capabilities.

If a device was in an error state and then returned to normal operation, the device would change to blue. Thus it would inform you that the device was now up but that it had recently experienced a fault.

A device that was orange, indicating it was misconfigured, could result from its having an incorrect password, network address, number of interfaces, or the like; you would know to check the configuration of orange devices. If no information could be found about a device, it would be colored gray, indicating that it could not be polled or never answered a poll. Finally, purple devices would be those currently being polled so the network engineer could see the progress of the tool.

Whether or not events that affect the devices would also change the color of the nodes higher in the network's hierarchical map would be determined by the network management system. However, in practical use the layer immediately above the one displayed would change accordingly in response to critical network events.

To see how a hierarchical map might work with the color assignments, picture the entire data network as a cloud. A green cloud would tell the network engineer that no critical events had occurred within the network. If this cloud turned red, the network engineer would know to inspect the graphic interface hierarchy to find a faulty device. Perhaps the cloud may explode into a map of the world on which one particular city was colored red. The network topology of the city could then be accessed with the faulty device shown in red. A report then could detail for the engineer the steps the system already had taken to correct the fault.

SUMMARY

The use of fault management tools on a data network provides greater efficiency for both the network engineer and the network. Fault management involves three major aspects: fault identification, cause isolation, and fault correction.

Identifying the fault includes determining how best to gather information about the network. One—or preferably both—of the following methods can be used: logging critical network events or occasionally polling network devices. Information gathering also involves determining which faults to manage for a particular data network. Network engineers should be guided in this determination by both the scope of control over the network, which affects the amount of information obtainable from network devices, and the size of the network.

A variety of tools, from simple to advanced, are designed to facilitate fault management. A simple tool would merely point out the existence of a fault but not identify its cause. A more complex tool would take advantage of the capability of hosts and devices to send critical network events, which would facilitate isolating the cause of the fault. An advanced tool would go one step further by correcting the fault.

We also stressed the impact a fault can have on other parts of the network. We noted the methods of reporting faults, giving particular emphasis on using color graphics to relay fault messages.

FOR FURTHER STUDY

Bosack, L., and Hedrick, C., "Problems in Large LANs," *IEEE Network Magazine* (2), January 1988.

Dauber, S., "Finding Fault, *Byte Magazine*, March 1991.

Chapter 4

Configuration Management

Chris looked with dismay at the electronic mail message. A vendor had just issued an advisory that due to a programming "feature," all devices with a certain configuration would need a software upgrade. According to the manufacturer, all devices shipped from the beginning of the month with a serial number greater than 2000–18829 had this upgrade. Sounded simple—find out how many of these devices were on MegaNet, *check the configuration of each one, check the serial number, upgrade if needed. Unfortunately this would take time. Catching sight of the list of things that would make the job easier, Chris decided to add "database." If all the information were consolidated, a single query would be enough to find out how many devices needed upgrading. Easy. Now doing the upgrades is another story. . . .*

Configuration management is the process of obtaining data from the network and using that data to manage the setup of all network devices. Configuration management involves gathering information about the current network configuration, using that data to modify the network configuration of the network devices, storing the data, maintaining an up-to-date inventory, and producing reports based on the data.

In this chapter we present the benefits of configuration management to the network engineer and discuss further the three steps involved. We then present three levels of configuration management tools for you to consider and review the various reports that can be obtained from configuration data.

4.1 BENEFITS OF THE CONFIGURATION MANAGEMENT PROCESS

Configuration management enhances the network engineer's control over the configuration of network devices by offering rapid access to vital configuration data about those devices. On more complex systems configuration management can also enable the engineer to compare the running configuration with that stored in the system and to change the configurations easily as needed.

For example, one aspect of configuration data is the current setup of each network device. Let's suppose that you are considering additional interfaces for a particular device. You would want to know first the number of physical interfaces already in the device, as well as the network addresses assigned to the interfaces, to help you configure the software on the device. With configuration management in place, you could locate this information easily because you would have a known location for storing this information.

In some cases a device may need to be modified. For example, consider an interface on a device that is causing errors on a LAN segment. Using a configuration management tool, you could remotely reconfigure the device to deactivate this interface. Let's say that you then examine the interface's configuration and notice that an incorrect software parameter is causing the errors. A configuration management tool could enable you to change the incorrect parameter to the proper setting and then reactivate the interface.

Configuration management can help a network engineer further by providing an up-to-date inventory of network components. Such an inventory can, for example, enable you to determine how many of a specific type of device exist on the network or aid in producing a report on all versions of an operating system that are in use (see Fig. 4.1) on devices throughout the network.

The inventory facility of configuration management need not be limited to tracking network devices. You could use it to record, among other things, vendor contact information, leased-line circuit numbers, or the quantity of network spares; the practicality of a comprehensive inventory cannot be overemphasized. For example, armed with data about the number of units purchased from a vendor, you may be in a position to negotiate volume discounts from that vendor. Or you could use inventory data showing that a leased line is opera-

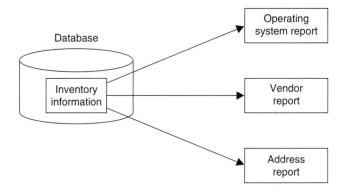

Figure 4.1 Network inventory data can be used to produce reports for network engineers.

tional only 50 percent of a given time period to check the number of circuits purchased from that vendor and press for better customer service.

Network inventory data should be considered confidential. In the hands of a malicious person, this type of data could harm the network in many ways. For example, suppose that someone learns about a software bug that can render a device inoperable. By getting the network inventory list and finding out how many of those devices are in the network, that person could cause a massive network failure by triggering the bug on all devices.

4.2 ACCOMPLISHING CONFIGURATION MANAGEMENT

Configuration management consists of the following steps:

1. *Gather information about the current network environment.* Failure to perform this step can result in the network engineer's wasting time on network problems caused by simple configuration errors. Collecting this information can be done manually by the engineer or automatically by the system.

2. *Use that data to modify the configuration of the network device.* Because a data network environment is continuously changing, the ability to modify its current configuration in real time is essential. Modification would be manual or automatic, depending on whether the collection method was manual or automatic.

3. *Store the data, maintain an up-to-date inventory of all network components, and produce various reports.*

Collecting Data Manually

Obtaining information from the network often begins with a manual effort. You may have to use remote login to reach each device on the network and then record the device's serial number in a notebook and its address assignments in a spreadsheet, flat ASCII file, or database. Although a manual effort will produce the desired result, using it to keep up-to-date records in an ever-changing data network environment can be difficult, error-prone, time consuming, and monotonous.

For example, suppose that you need to track in a table every network address assigned to a 5000-node network. This information may be sorted to facilitate easy address retrieval. With the addition of each new piece of equipment, you would have to acquire the pertinent data and then enter and re-sort it, obviously a tedious process when done manually.

Further, manual tracking of configurations works well only if you can find all the network devices. New systems added to the network by a user unbeknownst to you can be difficult to detect, especially if the data network is geographically dispersed. Even for those new systems you know about, obtaining the configuration information may involve your traveling to the system site or enlisting the aid of someone locally to gather the data.

The pitfalls of manual data collection can be avoided when you use automatic methods. For example, you could employ a network management protocol to obtain data about network devices regularly and to record the data automatically in the storage facility.

Another tool you can use is autodiscovery, which can produce a current listing of all devices on the network. Two common methods are used to implement autodiscovery. The first method is to send out a query, such as an ICMP Echo (ping) to every possible address on the network. When a device answers the query, ask for detailed information using a network management protocol. This approach has the advantage that it will discover every functioning device on the network but has the disadvantage of sending queries to nonexistent devices that consume some bandwidth. This approach also tends to take time to discover all devices, as queries sent to nonexistent devices need to time out. The second autodiscovery method is to find one device on the network and query it by means of a network management protocol to discover all of the devices it has communicated with recently. For each of these devices, perform a similar query, discovering devices in a breadth-first search manner. For each device, the tool can use the network management protocol to find all of the relevant information for the device. This mechanism has the advantage of working very quickly to discover devices on the data network but has the disadvantages of requiring the use of a network management protocol and failing to discover a device that has not communicated with any other device for a period of time.

Autodiscovery also can help produce a graphical map of the current data network, using a process called automapping, as seen in Fig. 4.2. Although you may need to modify a map produced by automapping before it fully reflects the geographic or functional layout of the network, the revised map is useful for showing the overall network configuration.

The amount of bandwidth an automatic configuration process consumes will, of course, influence your decision to use the method, although the benefits of automation should easily justify the costs. As in fault management, the frequency at which network devices are polled will affect the amount of bandwidth consumption. Accordingly, you would want to determine the appropriate frequency with which to gather this information; because network configurations usually change relatively infrequently, this polling may be as infrequently as once a week, thus keeping the amount of bandwidth consumption low.

Modifying Data

Once configuration management information has been obtained, it will usually need to be updated. Consider again the 5000-node network discussed earlier. If only 1 percent of these machines required an address assignment or change every week, you still would have to track 50 modifications a week. Moreover, network addresses are but one of many pieces of configuration management data. Any single device could have dozens of modifiable parameters to be tracked.

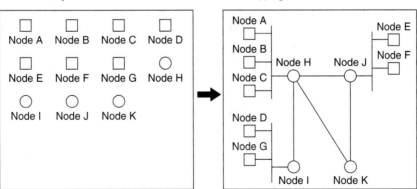

Figure 4.2 Autodiscovery finds devices on the network, whereas automapping produces useful configuration information in the form of a network map.

Obviously a manual method would be inefficient for this data process. Also, unless the engineer who did the manual configuration recorded his or her steps, a record of configuration changes would not be kept, which could lead to confusion when another network engineer examined the configuration of the changed device. In contrast, if the configuration management process allows the changing of the device configurations on the network management system, these changes could be recorded before they were sent to the device. As an added advantage, the network management system might be able to verify that the configuration changes were appropriate to the device and warn the engineer before inadvertently misconfiguring the device.

Storing Information

Configuration management should also provide a means for information storage. An efficient management system would store the entire configuration of a data network in a central location, thus placing configuration data within quick and efficient access by the network engineer. This single location could be a notebook or a PC-based spreadsheet in a network control center. Regardless of which method is used, the consistency and availability of data are invaluable to the network engineer.

Using an ASCII file is a common storage medium and has three advantages: ASCII is easy to read, is easily accessed from remote locations, and has a file structure that is usually easy to understand and administer. Therefore most application programs (regardless of the hardware platform) can read ASCII files. However, ASCII characters use considerable storage space in a computer system, and vast amounts of data stored in this manner can consume valuable disk space. Further, the uncomplicated structure of ASCII files may make for slow access during search procedures. But perhaps an even more important disadvantage is that ASCII files are unable to provide complex data relationships.

A more efficient alternative is a *database management system* (DBMS). A DBMS offers many advantages over ASCII files for data storage because it:

- Stores data efficiently, enabling large amounts to reside on a single computer

- Stores data in its own format, which allows for fast searching for specific data

- Can automatically sort stored data in various ways

- Usually can automatically restore lost data

- Enables the user to relate various types of data to one another

Perhaps the primary advantage of using a DBMS is that it enables the user to relate various types of information to one another. Figure 4.3 shows, for example, that configuration data for a particular device may direct the engineer to the device's vendor. This vendor data may in turn point to a specific person to contact in the vendor organization if a problem occurs on the device.

The flow of related information is not restricted to network devices; it can include all information necessary for configuration management. Thus using a DBMS for storage can help the network engineer in all aspects of the configuration management process.

Note, however, that a DBMS does have disadvantages: (1) it often involves a complex set of intricate administration procedures; (2) it uses its own language, which the engineer may not know; and (3) since a DBMS is much more complex, it is often tied to a particular operating system or hardware platform. This makes the data stored in the DBMS difficult to move from one system to another. Most DBMS vendors have solved this problem by allowing data in the DBMS to be put into ASCII format, thereby gaining the ease of transportability and use. The benefits a DBMS can provide, however, may very well offset its disadvantages.

4.3 CONFIGURATION MANAGEMENT ON A NETWORK MANAGEMENT SYSTEM

As we have seen, configuration management tools can increase the network engineer's productivity by, in some cases, automatically gathering and updating data on network devices, providing for central storage of configura-

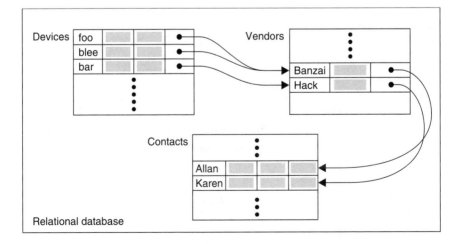

Figure 4.3 A DBMS allows the building of data relationships.

tion data, enabling modification of network data, and facilitating the production of network inventory and other reports. Which of these facilities a tool can provide will depend on its complexity.

A Simple Tool

A simple configuration management tool should, at the very least, provide for central storage of all data network information, such as network address assignments, serial numbers, physical locations, and other pertinent device data. An autodiscovery mechanism should exist for finding all of the devices on the data network; the tool should then query the devices for the relevant information to fill in the needed information automatically, if possible.

Accomplishing this task would require the tool to perform autodiscovery to find the devices on the data network. For each device found, the tool would then have to attempt to communicate with the device by using a network management protocol.

Automatic data acquisition is particularly important because it ensures that the information obtained is current. Thus the network engineer would probably feel more confident about polling devices only when necessary or during periods of low network usage. (The frequency of updates would be a configurable parameter.) Ideally, the tool would use a network management protocol to canvass the devices and get their configuration data.

Although the simple tool performs autodiscovery, it does not necessarily have to perform automapping. If the device supports a network management protocol, the tool could then query the device to determine the vendor and then extract any relevant vendor-specific information.

In many cases the simple tool may discover a device but be unable to extract information from it because the device does not support a network management protocol or because of security restrictions. In these cases you still would have to undertake the laborious and time-consuming task of manually entering all the required data into the tool. To facilitate this process, the tool could prompt you for the information it needs. A simple tool could also provide another important facility, a search function, which would enable you to locate information about devices easily.

The simple tool does exist in a rudimentary form on network management platforms today; they do have the ability to discover the devices on the data network and then gather information about them. Yet in practice the platforms gather only the most essential information about each device (name, network address, number of interfaces). Although that information is useful, this lack of functionality often means that you have to query each device manually to gather additional information necessary for configuration management.

A More Complex Tool

A more complex tool could be developed by adding a feature to automatically compare a device's current configuration with that stored in the system. The tool further could enable you to view a device's running configuration graphically and make configuration changes. And finally, as with a simple tool, the more complex version should provide for centralized storage and easy retrieval of data.

As illustrated in Fig. 4.4, the tool should enable you to compare a device's running configuration against its stored configuration. Further, it should either initiate a process that would enable you to change the configuration or perform the change itself automatically. In a common scenario the tool would probe the device for its current setup and then compare it against the stored configuration. If any discrepancies were found, the tool would ask you whether it should change the device configuration to match the stored version. Perhaps this feature could run automatically (without making changes)

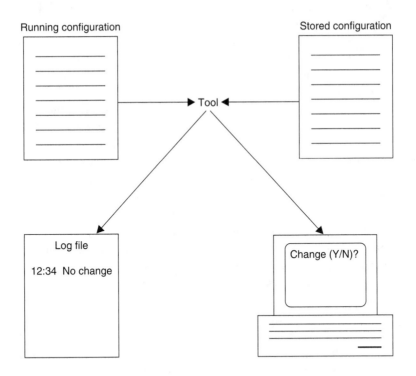

Figure 4.4 A configuration management tool can compare a device's running configuration with a stored configuration, note differences between them, and prompt the network engineer for input.

on a periodic basis and send the network engineer electronic mail about any differences found.

Note that not all configuration details will always be equally important. To work well in various data network environments, the tool should therefore include the means for specifying which configuration errors generate warning messages and which prompt an alarm. For example, an option on a terminal server could configure the bit rate for an incoming connection, which would be useful for simultaneously communicating with many devices at different bit rates. Suppose that stored configuration information indicated that each asynchronous line out of the terminal server should be set at 9600 bits per second (bps). However, when the tool queried the device, one line was found to be set at 2400 bps. In this instance the tool may not care about the configuration but would simply issue a warning message to a log file. In contrast, if the tool found a secure line on the terminal server without a password, it would alert you of the situation by immediately setting off an alarm.

Flowchart 4.1 shows how a tool could check the current operating system, IP address, and subnet mask of each device on the network against the stored configuration. In this case if the version of the operating system for the device does not match the stored configuration, the tool would simply report the difference. However, if the tool found a different IP address or subnet mask, it would report the discrepancy and reset the configuration to match the stored values.

The more complex tool should present a graphical view of a device's configuration with its current network connections. The information about the physical characteristics of the device can be found by using a network management protocol. Although the graphical view does not have to present a picture of how the device physically looks, this view is often helpful to network engineers. In some cases a physical view of the device will take up a lot of screen space on the network management system, and if there is not relevant information taking up this space, many engineers prefer a concise, logical view of the device. Both the logical and physical views of the device should depict the current configuration of the device and its associated network interfaces.

The tool should allow users to select parameters on the physical or logical view and to find their current status (often a fault management feature) or make configuration changes. The configuration changes may include the operational status, the network addresses, encapsulation methods, and device-specific parameters. For example, on a device with network interfaces, it may be possible to select the graphical representation of the interface on the screen and find out the current status of the selected port. The user may then be able to change the administrative status of the port, either enabling or disabling it.

A new local area network technology, called a *virtual LAN*, will offer new challenges for the more complex tool. A virtual LAN logically connects local

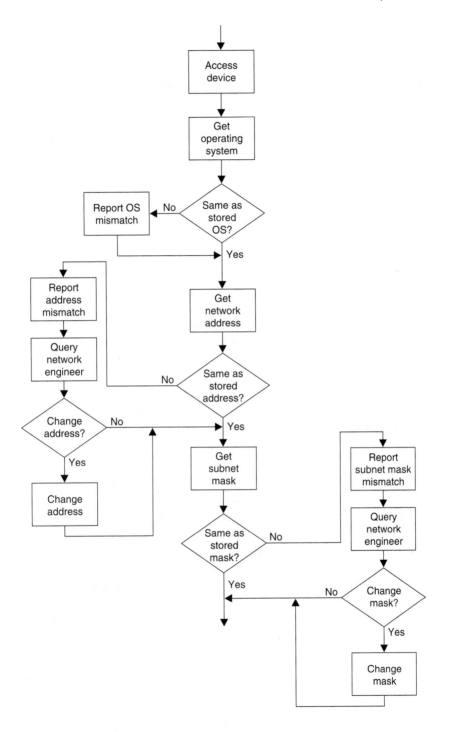

Flowchart 4.1 Functionality in the more complex tool.

area network devices at different physical locations to form one logical local area network, allowing the virtual LAN to span multiple locations. The connection between these locations may be a high-speed technology, such as asynchronous transfer mode (ATM) or fiber distributed data interface (FDDI).

The concept of virtual LANs may change how the graphical configuration of a device and its network connections are depicted by the more complex tool. In a typical LAN environment today a single port on a device may connect to a physical segment (such as the port on a router or a bridge). All devices connected to that segment are, in turn, understood to belong to the same network segment. A typical situation may have a router connecting to an Ethernet hub and then the hub connecting to all the hosts on the segment.

With the virtual LAN, the router could connect to an ATM switch, which could be emulating many unique LAN segments through a single interface. The graphical configuration tool will have to depict this information to the network engineer, perhaps by drawing separate logical interface ports for each virtual LAN and then physically grouping them under a single label. Color-coding the different ports in the same virtual LAN is another way to graphically depict the current configuration of the switch.

The inital setup or changing the configuration of the virtual LAN may require the complex tool to configure multiple devices at the same time. Some devices on the virtual LAN may be attached to a hub in one building, whereas other devices you want on the same virtual LAN may be attached to another hub in a different building. The more complex tool allows you to start to configure a virtual LAN by first selecting the relevant ports on the logical or physical views of all of the affected devices. Then you tell the complex tool to make each of these ports belong to the same virtual LAN (perhaps by dropping the graphical representation of the ports onto a virtual LAN icon). The complex tool could then configure each of the affected devices and ports.

Some network management applications on the market provide most of the functionality described for the more complex tool. Some vendors have a tool that checks the current configuration of a device and compares it to a configuration stored in a database. Also, vendors have applications that graphically show the configurations of their devices. These features are often vendor specific and have different user interfaces for each vendor device. This means that the network engineer needs to learn how to perform these functions on a vendor-by-vendor basis, using the appropriate network management application.

An Advanced Tool

Whereas the more complex tool would allow for changing the running configuration of a device, an advanced configuration management tool would be even more effective if it used a database management system to store, relate, query, and inventory network information. To be optimally functional, the tool also would be capable of evaluating device configurations.

A tool's ability to relate one set of data to another is important for configuration management. For example, if one engineer is responsible for 100 devices, relating the engineer's name to all the devices would be easier than entering and storing the same name once for each device.

A DBMS not only allows for complex manipulation of data but also permits complex queries. These queries usually are written in the *Structured Query Language (SQL)*. Using SQL, you can find specific information stored within the database. Suppose, for example, that you discover that version A of a software program on an Ethernet bridge is causing network errors. To correct this situation, you first would need to find all bridges running that software version. Let's say that all the possible devices on the network are stored in a table named *devices*. Therefore to find all affected Ethernet bridges, you could issue the following SQL command:

```
SELECT * FROM devices WHERE type = bridge AND software = A
```

The output resulting from this command would show you all bridge devices in the table *devices* that are running software version A (see Fig. 4.5).

SQL queries also can produce output such as *inventory reports*. For a network device, the inventory should include the device:

- Serial number

- Make and model

- Operating system

Device name	Vendor	Serial #	Type	Software	Location	Contact
ENGRBR1	RouteMe	0180106	bridge	A	ENGR	Allan
ADMINBR	Bridgelt	AB62	bridge	A	Admin	Boss
MKTGBR23	Bridgelt	AB2301	bridge	A	Bldg10	Karen

Figure 4.5 The possible output from a sample SQL query.

- RAM capacity

- Network addresses

- Interface capacity

Let's say that you want to generate a report showing all devices and their serial numbers, made by a specific vendor, that were added to the network within the past year and therefore are still under warranty. You could use an SQL query such as the following:

```
SELECT device, sn FROM devices, vendors WHERE vendors.name
= Banzai AND devices.months <<= 12
```

The resulting report would show all the devices and their serial numbers on the network from the Banzai Company that are still under warranty (see Fig. 4.6).

You could also use a DBMS to generate other reports, such as vendor contact inventories and leased-circuit inventories. For example, in an inventory of vendor information, you might want to include the vendor's:

- Name

- Address

- Maintenance contact/phone number

- Sales contact/phone number

- Main phone number

Device name	Serial #
Perfect	BB00888
Reno	BB1298
Pecos	BB11072
New Jersey	BB572
Blue Blazer	BB11

Figure 4.6 The listing of all Banzai Company devices on the network and still under their one-year warranty.

An inventory of leased circuits might include:

- circuit ID

- speed

- vendor

- end points on network

- known down times

Although you could compose SQL queries to explore specific parts of the database, it really shouldn't be necessary for you to learn SQL. Rather, ideally, the tool should provide an interface to help you locate critical data stored within the database without your having to use SQL. The tool should ask you for the data to search for, then follow all pertinent relationships, and finally present the information in a form you can understand. For example, finding a device at address P.Q should not require you to know that the address resides in the database table called *addresses*. Instead, you should be able to tell the tool to find P.Q and then be shown all known information about the device, including the device's physical location, its administrator, its hardware description, and so forth.

So far, our advanced tool can store the necessary information, compare it to current configurations, modify them, and handle queries. Now let's consider an additional feature: evaluation. Periodically the tool should evaluate the configuration of all network devices and show you where duplicate network addresses, names, or functions are employed. Suppose, for example, that a LAN has grown without management. Many PC file servers exist on this LAN. The configuration management tool could tell you that two of these servers provide the same functions and applications to the users. This may be intentional redundancy, or it could be a configuration management issue in need of resolution.

In another example the tool could evaluate the communication capabilities of the network configuration. WAN devices, such as cluster controllers and front-end processors, require configuration of their interfaces in order to communicate at the proper speed. In a typical setup (see Fig. 4.7) many cluster controllers exist at a single site with WAN links back to the central site, which houses a mainframe computer. Suppose that on one controller the response time from each terminal was slower than that from terminals on the other controllers. In evaluating this setup, the configuration management tool would recognize that the speed setting on that cluster controller was set to transmit at 4800 bps and that the front-end processor at the other side of the link was set to receive at a maximum of 9600 bps, resulting in a maximum speed of 4800

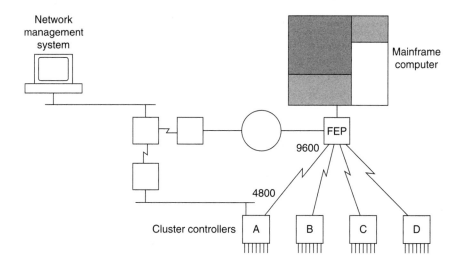

Figure 4.7 The setup with a configuration error brought to the attention of the network engineer by the configuration management tool.

bps. In contrast, all the other cluster controllers at the same site and talking to the same front-end processor were set up for 9600 bps communications on both sides. The tool would conclude that the discrepancy in bit rate of the controller caused its slower response time. As a final step in the evaluation, the tool would use the relational database to determine the speed of the wide area link. Thus the tool would have found a problem in the network configuration automatically by evaluating the configuration management information.

The advanced tool brings together many configuration management concepts that require using a DBMS. Tools on the market store information in a DBMS and help you build queries (SQL or otherwise) for the stored information. These tools typically come from the manufacturer of the database software. Some products also help the network engineer by producing inventory reports. Yet in many environments inventory reports contain organizational-specific information, so you may have to customize them. The main piece of the advanced tool that will require the most work in the future is the evaluation of network configurations. Not many products today perform this function, because every vendor has a unique way of describing the configuration of its device. Some vendors accomplish this through written commands; some do it through an encoded file. Building a tool that understands each of these methods would be complex and time consuming. Each vendor could produce its own tools for this task, but ideally you would want a tool to evaluate the configuration of the entire network as one entity.

4.4 GENERATING CONFIGURATION REPORTS

In the preceding discussion we emphasized that a configuration management tool must generate reports that enable the engineer to keep abreast of the overall network configuration. Although this type of tool generally is not required to relay information as quickly as is a fault management tool, sometimes prompt reporting is necessary, as when the tool finds duplicate network addresses or names. Also in contrast to fault management, a configuration management tool does not depend on the use of color or a graphical interface to be totally functional. If the engineer has access to the data on an ASCII terminal, the full range of configuration management facilities is potentially still available. Of course, the easier the tool makes it for the engineer to generate the necessary reports, the more likely the tool will be used.

One type of report details the overall configuration of each network device, including, as applicable, its name, network addresses, serial number, manufacturer, operating system, and the local person responsible for it. If the device is attached to serial links, the report also could list circuit numbers, useful for reporting link failures to circuit vendors. Other optional data that could be included are the vendor contact name and the device's physical location. This information represents the minimum you would probably want for each network device. The frequency with which this report is generated would vary for each network, ranging, for example, from weekly on a rapidly changing network to monthly on a stable network.

Armed with this report on the current network setup, you next would need a summary of all the recent network modifications. This report should list all the changes to the network by category, the names of those who made the changes, and when the changes took place. Categories could include all new devices and changes in hardware, software, and administration. By subcategorizing this report, you can quickly access important information. As with the network configuration report, the frequency with which you have this report generated will vary, depending on how often the network changed.

Finally, the configuration management tool should create a summary report on the total network inventory. This report, crucial for the bookkeeping effort necessary on any data network, would most likely need to focus only on devices. For each piece of equipment purchased, the report should show its serial number, physical location, date put in service, length and type of warranty, and complete upgrade history. Depending on the network environment, additional information on each device may be required. Because it usually is necessary only for bookkeeping purposes, this report could be produced as infrequently as monthly.

SUMMARY

Managing the configuration of a host of network devices in various physical locations is a demanding but necessary task for the network engineer. Its challenge is to provide the engineer with the means to handle the various aspects of this task most efficiently.

Configuration management offers the following benefits:

- In some cases it automatically gathers and updates data on network devices.

- It provides a central storage location for configuration data. This location could be as simple as a notebook or as complex as a relational database system.

- It enables the network engineer to modify network configuration on line.

- It facilitates the production of network inventory and other reports.

The configuration management process involves three steps: (1) obtaining information from the data network, (2) modifying the configuration of the network devices, and (3) storing the information for future use. These steps may be accomplished in methods ranging from manual data entry and retrieval to automated data entry and retrieval into a sophisticated relational database system.

On a network management system a configuration management tool can enable the network engineer to accomplish these tasks easily and efficiently. A simple tool can give the engineer a central location for storing information. A more complex tool can also provide a way to automatically obtain information from the network, to compare a device's running configuration against its stored configuration, and to change the configuration automatically. An advanced tool can go a step further by using a relational database to relate one set of data to another, permit queries to the DBMS, and evaluate the configuration of the entire network.

A final aspect of configuration management involves producing reports pertaining to specific device setups, recent network modifications, and inventory. These reports can be generated automatically or on demand.

FOR FURTHER STUDY

Madron T., *Enterprise-Wide Computing*, New Work: Wiley, 1991.

Rhodes, P., *LAN Operations*, Reading, MA: Addison-Wesley, 1991.

Chapter 5

Security Management

In This Chapter:

Chris spent the morning working out the technical details of the remote-access project. Many MegaNet *users want to be able to gain access to the network and its resources from their homes. Setting up the remote-access systems had been somewhat of a technical challenge but nothing that could not be handled with a bit of persistence and a grudging look at a technical manual. The problem now was how to permit this remote access while still maintaining the security of the network. If someone accesses resources on* MegaNet *while in a building, then presumably a card reader somewhere has a record of entry. But with a remote-access network, Chris needed to think about the security of the network—where to place security restrictions and how to keep track of access.*

Security management involves protecting sensitive information on devices attached to a data network by controlling access points to that information. Sensitive information is any data an organization wants to secure, such as payroll data, customer accounts, and research and development schedules.

Security management enables network engineers to protect sensitive information by limiting the access to hosts and network devices by users (both inside and outside of the organization) and by notifying the engineer of attempted or actual breaches of security. It consists of the following aspects:

- Identifying the sensitive information to be protected

- Finding the access points

- Securing the access points

- Maintaining the secure access points

Security management should not be confused with application security, operating system security or physical security. Security management is achieved through specific configuration of network hosts and devices to control access points within the data network. Access points may include software services, hardware components, and network media. Network media, in particular, is an area of vulnerability. If a person has access to the media that carry sensitive information, measures taken to secure the sensitive information on hosts or network devices are not useful.

Operating system security involves setting up file, directory, and program protection; physical security involves locking computer room doors, installing card access systems, and providing for locks on keyboards. However, although these types of security systems are not a part of security management on a data network, without them security management would be useless. Properly set up and administered, security management can prevent an unauthorized person from accessing hosts on a data network; however, if the same person can walk up to the computer and remove the disk drive containing the sensitive information, data security is lacking.

In this chapter we present the benefits of security management and discuss the four steps required to accomplish it. Then we describe three security management tools. Last, we discuss the advantages of an audit trail, which can be obtained from reports of security events. We strongly urge you to read this chapter and then research this topic further in relation to the specific needs of your data network.

5.1 BENEFITS OF THE SECURITY MANAGEMENT PROCESS

The primary concern many users have about attaching hosts to a data network is the potential lack of security for sensitive information located on the host. To avoid this problem, a host possessing sensitive information could eliminate network access altogether and transfer information on movable media, such as magnetic tape and optical discs. In this way only those people with the physical access to the host could reach the sensitive information. However, this method, although secure, is not particularly efficient and effectively removes the need for a data network.

Properly set up and maintained security management can offer a more practical alternative while assuaging users' security concerns and increasing their confidence in the network's effectiveness and security. This building of confidence and the securing of sensitive information are the main benefits of security management.

The drawbacks of not having security management on a network are easy to envision. Suppose that an organization's private data network connects to a public data network and that a computer within the company network that contains payroll information also provides a service that gives any user any information requested. As you can see, the consequences of such unrestricted access could be catastrophic for the organization.

The disastrous results a lack of security management can produce were dramatically demonstrated in November 1988, when the *Internet worm* was let loose. The worm used a common service on many hosts to gain access to information throughout the Internet and was able to propagate itself throughout hundreds of computer networks. One method the worm used was a UNIX service called *sendmail* to connect to a computer, spawn a shell, and then execute itself. Some versions of *sendmail* allowed the worm access to one of the program's debugging modes without imposing any security. The worm also used another UNIX service, called *finger*, to gain privileges on hosts.

The *sendmail* and *finger* attacks are examples of how a worm exploited security weaknesses in a network access point. Interestingly, the most successful method the worm used to log in to hosts was to try common passwords, a host security weakness. The worm could have destroyed file systems, corrupted data, or performed many other malicious actions. Fortunately it was not written with that intent; however, because it reproduced itself many times, the worm brought numerous computers to a halt because of excessive processor load.

Another vivid example of how inadequate security management can hurt an organization is given in the book *The Cuckoo's Egg*, by Clifford Stoll. The book relates how the author watched as a devious user walked easily through some well-known unsecured access points on a data network.

5.2 ACCOMPLISHING SECURITY MANAGEMENT

Effecting security management requires the network engineer to balance the need to secure sensitive information with the needs of users to access information pertinent to performing their jobs. This form of network management involves the following four steps:

1. Identify the sensitive information.

2. Find the access points.

3. Secure the access points.

4. Maintain the secure access points.

These points are illustrated in Fig. 5.1.

First, let's view these steps in a common everyday example. Suppose that you have decided to secure the contents of your new house. Instead of putting locks on each item, you might instead *find the access points* by determining that the windows and exterior doors of the house require securing. Accordingly you would then *secure the access points* by installing locks on those doors and windows. Further, you would have only one copy of the keys made for your own use. At this point, you feel confident that the access points—the windows and exterior doors—are secure.

However, locking all the windows and exterior doors does not fully secure your possessions. Someone could easily enter the house either through an unlocked door or by breaking and climbing in a window. Therefore you would

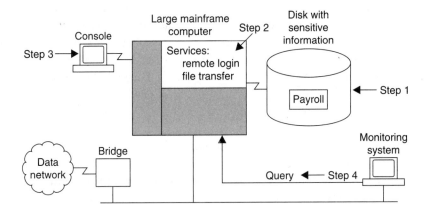

Figure 5.1 Security management involves four steps. Here the payroll data on the large mainframe is sensitive information. The access points are remote login and file transfer. The engineer secures the access points by configuring the system on the console to permit only authorized users. The monitoring system ensures the maintenance of the security by logging unauthorized login attempts.

want to *maintain* the house's access points by checking periodically for unlocked doors and broken windows.

Next, let's consider an example related to data networks. A computer that stores a company's payroll data, which has been defined by the organization as sensitive information, has only one access point: through the data network, using a remote login program. You therefore would need to control this remote login program. To do this, you first could ensure that only people possessing proper authorization to see the payroll information would have user accounts. Next, you could ensure that the login program required passwords for each user account. To enhance security further, you also could have the password program give out randomly generated passwords that require periodic renewal. Thus having installed these security measures, you might feel confident that you have secured the sensitive information.

Yet this single perimeter of defense may not be enough. In addition to requiring passwords for each account, you might want to provide that remote login requests to the payroll host come only from *authorized remote hosts*. To gain access to the payroll data, a user would therefore have to first log on to an authorized remote host and authenticate that access with a password. Then the user could proceed to log on to the payroll machine, again going through a user and password authentication sequence.

Note that in these two examples we did not attempt to secure the sensitive information itself. Although the sensitive information is secure on the computer where it resides, we will see that it is often necessary to secure it in transit between secure locations. Also, be aware that in some cases not every point of access will require securing. For example, suppose that a payroll computer accessible by remote login also provides a service to tell network users the time, which usually is not sensitive information. In this case you would want to allow free access to the time service but to limit access to the payroll information (see Fig. 5.2).

Identifying Sensitive Information

Your first step in accomplishing security management is to determine which hosts on the network have sensitive information. Most organizations have well-defined policies regarding what information qualifies as sensitive; often it includes accounting, financial, customer, market, engineering, and employee information. So at first glance this process may seem straightforward. However, what is defined as sensitive can differ, depending on the environment, for each such environment potentially can have sensitive information unique to it. Further, the most difficult part of identifying sensitive information can be finding on which hosts the data reside.

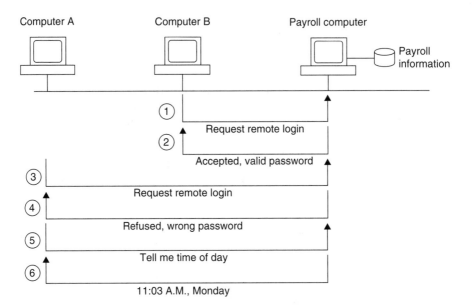

Figure 5.2   A user on Computer B makes a remote login request to the payroll computer (1) and is accepted with a valid password (2). A user on Computer A tries to login remotely to the payroll computer (3) and is denied because the password was wrong (4). Yet that user can ask the payroll computer for the time of day (5) and get a response (6). Payroll information is sensitive, but the time of day is not.

Finding the Access Points

Once you know what information is sensitive and where it is located, you next would want to find out how network users can access it. Keep in mind that the first access points to any data network are its physical wires. Finding other access points on the data network is often a tedious task that will usually require you to examine each piece of software offering a service on the network, and many computers have dozens of such programs. The access these programs have to the data network constitutes the access points to the sensitive information on the computer, as illustrated in Fig. 5.3. Fortunately on some computers you can simplify the task of locating access points by isolating how the computer provides for remote login and file transfer.

Most computers on a data network provide for remote login by users. If this login facility doesn't identify users uniquely and limit their movements within the system to authorized areas, you would want to examine this access point as possibly needing to be secured.

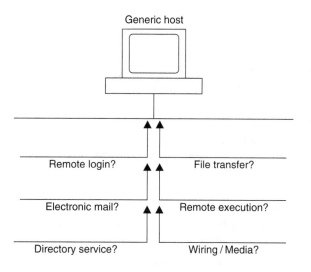

Figure 5.3 Identify the access points for each computer.

Also, many computers can perform file transfers across the data network. Like the remote login facility, if this service cannot uniquely identify users, its use should be limited. An example of a file transfer service that would require security management scrutiny is the "anonymous" login in FTP. FTP is the file transfer protocol used by many TCP/IP hosts, and many versions of it allow users to log in with the user name "anonymous." The password for this account is not used, so users can type any string for the password and be logged in to a special account in the remote system. The saving grace of this "anonymous" login is that the files the user can retrieve from this account usually are limited to a small subset of directories. This configuration of FTP often is used to distribute public software and documents. This application also can be used when the computer administrator doesn't care who can access the files in the limited directory structure. Thus if a computer offers the "anonymous" login to the FTP service, network engineers for that computer must carefully regulate what information is contained in the accessible directories.

Remote login and file transfer are probably the most popular types of software that provide access points into a computer. However, other programs, such as electronic mail, remote process execution, file and directory servers, and name servers, also may give access points into a computer that need to be secured using security management. For example, on a computer running UNIX the services offered by the computer can be seen by executing the *process status* (ps) command, which can show all processes that are running on the computer. The Network File System (NFS), found on many different types of computers, allows one computer to access another file system as if it were on the local computer using the data network. NFS, although useful for resource sharing, can often open up access points to sensitive information.

Similarly, many personal computers may have a file or application that lists the services the computer can offer. This file may be the common NET.CFG file or something a bit more complex hidden in an .INI file. Finding the applications on a personal computer that may use the network can be difficult. You may need to use a network protocol analyzer to make the final determination as to which network protocols a personal computer is using.

As an example, in the personal computer environment Microsoft's Lan Manager uses the NetBIOS protocol to communicate between clients and servers. This environment has a concept of domains, a region of the network where a server resides. A server broadcasts on a periodic interval its own name and the domain in which it resides. Clients must be listening to updates from a particular domain name before they can see the servers in the domain (and then potentially connect to them). Although a domain in this context is meant to be an administrative way to segmenting traffic, it is also often used as a security measure. Yet a sophisticated Lan Manager user can alter the domain names its client listens to and then potentially connect to any server in the known domains. Of course, the user needs a login on the server before being able to access data, but the finding of other domains in the network may lead to a security breach. Nevertheless, the server broadcasts are an example of an access point that announces the presence of a network service and may need to be carefully administered. In this example security management is accomplished by hiding information from client systems. Security by hiding information is generally not a sound practice but often works. Packet filters, which deny server broadcasts from the client segments, would provide more effective security management in this setup. The best approach, although configuration intensive, may be packet filters that allow only an authorized set of clients to send packets to their respective servers.

The concept of a network region that contains certain services offered to users exists in many network protocols other than NetBIOS. For example, in Appletalk the regions of the network are called Zones. An Appletalk client discovers the Zones in the network by sending out a ZIP (Zone Information Protocol) request. Once the Zones are found, the user can select which Zone to access and the type of service to find within the Zone (using an application called the Chooser). If a network cracker finds the existence of a Zone, it may be possible to find the hosts within the Zone with sensitive information.

Facilities that allow users to monitor packets as they traverse network media are another access point to sensitive information. Sometimes the need to gather packets is required to examine why the network is functioning in a certain manner. This is often done with a protocol analyzer or host. The need for this functionality often outweighs any security concerns, because if the network does not function properly, no sensitive data will traverse it. However, network engineers should be aware that users do have this ability and can gather packets and potentially discover passwords or other sensitive information. As we will discuss in the next section, encryption of the data in packets may help eliminate the gathering of sensitive information by network analyzers.

Because the network analyzer can monitor all of the packets on the network, it is an excellent tool for finding exactly which hosts on the network use which types of protocols to communicate. Often users do not know the network protocol their applications use, and the network analyzer can eliminate any doubt for the network engineer. Many companies, such as Hewlett-Packard, Network General, and Bytex, make network analyzers that can help you determine which protocols a given host uses to communicate.

Many computers offer seemingly nonsensitive information through network management protocols. However, on closer examination of the information you may discover that restricted access should be enforced. For example, nearly every network management protocol has the ability to ask a computer for basic information, such as network addresses, names, operating system versions, and length of time in operation—generally innocuous information. Suppose, however, that the computer running the network management protocol is testing a new version of the operating system for the vendor. When queried by a competitor, the operating system version returned is one not yet publicly known. This leak of information, although small, may affect the marketing of competitors' products.

Another, often overlooked location that contains sensitive information on the data network is the network management system itself. The network management system gives the users many methods for discovering sensitive information, both on the network and from within the relational database. When determining the access points to a data network, you should consider the network management system as a host that needs special security considerations.

Many organizations commit substantial resources to standardize security points for all their network devices and hosts. These network security standards serve as a rule for dealing with the many ways to access sensitive information. You can establish these standards along any number of parameters; for example, you could define access points by host manufacturer or type of operating system. In these cases the organization could decide that all hosts from a certain manufacturer with sensitive information cannot have an "anonymous" login for FTP, or it could determine that a network software package for personal computers does not provide enough security and so prohibit its use. The key here is for you to set standards for the manufacturer of hosts that can hold sensitive information and the applications that can run on these hosts without compromising security.

Securing the Access Points

The next step in security management is to apply the necessary security techniques. Security can be used at multiple layers on the data network:

- On the data link level you could use encryption.

- On the network level devices may secure traffic flow based on packet filters.

- On every host each access point to information could have an associated service, and each of those services that gives access to sensitive information could provide one or more of three types of security: host authentication, user authentication, and key authentication.

Encryption

Encryption of data as it traverses a LAN or WAN can prevent unauthorized access to sensitive information. *Encryption* means to encode, and in this case an encryption device uses an algorithm to scramble, or encipher, the plaintext information to be sent. Once the plaintext has been run through the encryption algorithm, it is known as ciphertext. After the ciphertext is relayed, it is unscrambled at the receiving end by performing the reverse of the algorithm to get back to the original text. An encryption key is either a software- or hardware-defined stream of bits that controls the encryption algorithm. Each unique sequence of bits in the encryption key generates different ciphertext from the original text. The encryption algorithm must generate ciphertext that is extremely difficult to decipher without the knowledge of the encryption key. A user must not be able to decipher the ciphertext without knowing both the encryption algorithm and the encryption key.

Encryption is very useful when sending data over satellite and microwave links, which involves transmitting information through the air, where it is susceptible to being received by anyone, authorized or not, who can receive the signal. Some organizations use encryption for local area network segments to ensure that the physical wiring of the LAN is not an access point. Unfortunately this is often costly, because it requires encryption hardware or software for every LAN device. Also, LAN encryption can make troubleshooting of network problems difficult.

Two types of encryption techniques are commonly used today: private key and public key. The private key encryption technique relies on the fact that both the source and the destination are using the same encryption keys for enciphering and deciphering the text information, making the algorithm straightforward once the encryption key is known. Because the key may be broken, however, you would want to change keys on both the source and the destination on a regular basis by physically transferring a new key (either software or hardware) to each device performing encryption. The physical transfer of keys can consume both time and resources, but it is the safest method for transferring keys (if the key were sent electronically and the old key had been broken, the new key would be compromised). Although private key encryption devices can be difficult to maintain, many organizations prefer to use this method for securing sensitive information.

A commonly used private encryption scheme is the data encryption standard (DES), which was adopted for use within the United States by the National Bureau of Standards in 1977. Using DES, plaintext is encrypted in 64-bit segments. At the source system each plaintext segment is encrypted using a 56-bit encryption key. A small deviation in the makeup of the 56-bit key results in vastly different ciphertext. A complicated algorithm takes as input 64 bits of plaintext and encrypts it into 64 bits of ciphertext. At the destination system the reverse process transforms ciphertext back to plaintext.

The public key encryption technique does not rely on the source and destination system sharing the same encryption key. This method removes the problem of keeping the encryption keys synchronized. In fact, some systems use the straightforward private encryption key technique for data and a public encryption key technique for exchanging the value of the private key.

Public key encryption uses an algorithm that has one key split into two pieces. One piece is kept private, and the other is made publicly available. By knowing only the public piece of the key, one can encipher a message that can be deciphered with the private piece. Simply knowing the public piece will not allow you to decipher an encrypted message from ciphertext to plaintext. Deciphering requires knowing the private piece of the encryption key.

Using public key encryption, if a source system wants to send an encrypted message to a destination system, it needs to know both the encryption algorithm both systems use and the destination system's public piece of the encryption key. The source enciphers the message with the public piece of the destination's encryption key (assuming that the source knows the public piece of the destination's encryption key; otherwise a query is made). The destination deciphers the message using its private piece of the encryption key.

As you can see, if a system wants to change its encryption key at any time, it changes both the public and the private pieces. The private key encryption need to distribute the same encryption keys simultaneously to both the source and destination is eliminated. Public key encryption does have the drawback that every system that wants to send ciphertext to a destination must first query the destination for its public piece of the encryption key. Also, for two-way encrypted transmission, each system needs to know the other system's public piece of the encryption key. As we will see in Chapter 8, SNMPv2 uses the public key encryption technique.

Packet Filtering

Many network devices, such as bridges, switches, and routers, can perform packet filtering based on network or MAC (medium access control) addresses. *Packet filtering* stops packets to or from unsecured hosts before they reach an access point that may yield sensitive information. However, although this approach may help provide security, it does present problems.

First, the packet filters must be configured within each network device. Thus for each new or changed address, you would need to change the filters. Second, using a filter doesn't work if the unsecured host changes addresses without telling you. For example, consider an Ethernet bridge that filters packets between segments based on a MAC address. Since MAC addresses typically are burned into a read-only memory (ROM) chip on the Ethernet interface, if the interface board on the unsecured host were to be changed, the new board will not contain the same MAC address, and the packet filters would no longer stop information to and from the unsecured host. This problem could be caused not only by devious users but also by a network engineer who changes the interface because it is defective or needs upgrading, without realizing that the new board has a new MAC address. Some hosts provide software configuration parameters that allow you to set up their MAC addresses, potentially avoiding this problem or making it easier to circumvent the filter.

Host Authentication

The *host authentication* method allows access to a service based on a source host identifier, which is commonly a network address such as that used by IP, DECnet, X.25, or even MAC addresses. Figure 5.4 shows a common setup.

Many computer services use host authentication schemes. In a common example a computer that communicates by X.25 through a serial connection may decide to accept or reject calls based on the source X.121 address. Or, one computer may not allow every computer to access a service, just a subset of all the possible source network addresses.

Because host authentication is based on network addresses, many network devices also can help accomplish this task. A Token Ring bridge can do so by

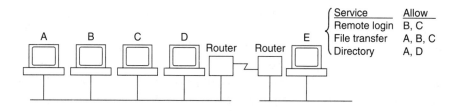

Figure 5.4 Computer E uses host authentication to decide the services allowed.

setting up access restrictions to allow only certain source systems to send data to computers on the other side of the bridge. Packet filters, too, can help accomplish host authentication, although you should not rely on this as the sole method for securing the host.

In another example, a central network management system has a large color display for the network operators to use. Although the many tasks on the network management system may run on multiple computers on the data network, each network management process can display its results on the central system's display. The central system could use host authentication to verify that the computer requesting use of the display is an authorized host. The popular X11 window system uses this strategy. In this case X servers use host names, which are translated into network addresses, to authorize computers to access the local display.

On many systems you can specify which hosts can use your local display by using the command

```
xhost [+|-] <hostname>
```

To permit host "allan-hp" to use your display, you would issue the command

```
xhost +allan-hp
```

The name "allan-hp" would be resolved to an IP address, and then all X11 packets from this network address would be accepted and processed by your system.

Personal computer file servers often use host authentication to decide which computers will be allowed access to file systems. For example, if a personal computer without a disk is turned on, it may request a file system from any file server available. If a particular file server contained sensitive information, you might not want all personal computers using this file system. You could accomplish this by having the file server allow file system access only from authorized personal computers identified by network address.

Host authentication is useful for providing security for some access points, but it is not perfect. If a service on a computer provides access to sensitive information, simply knowing the source host's identity may not be enough qualification for giving out the information. Consider also the following example. Suppose that a host named *Trust* offers a service that allows employees to copy programs for company use only. To protect these programs, *Trust* uses host authentication to allow only the host *Innocent* to access the programs. But then suppose that a user decides to copy, for personal use, the programs on *Trust*. To do this, the user could turn off *Innocent* and reconfigure the computer *Devious* to have the same network address as *Innocent*. Then, when *Devious* accessed the programs on *Trust*, it would be allowed access because to *Trust*, *Devious* is *Innocent*.

In another example, suppose that a host named *Master* offers a service that allows users to remotely execute software that is under development. As the software on *Master* is not to be shared with every user in the organization, you could use the host authentication method to permit only users on the host *Servant* to execute the program. Let's say that the system administrator of *Servant* assures you that only authorized personnel who can access the new software have accounts on *Servant*. But you are not convinced. You know that relying on the host authentication method means that any person who has a valid login on *Servant* can execute the software on *Master*. Thus you decide to boost security for the software on *Master* by going a step further: You employ the user authentication method.

User Authentication

User authentication enables the service to identify each user before allowing that user access. User authentication provides a finer degree of control on a given service than does host authentication, because it allows each service to identify the exact user.

A common method used to distinguish users is the password. However, although effective, passwords are not perfect; they are not always as secure as one could hope. One problem with using passwords is that some network services use *cleartext* to transfer the password from the source host to the destination host; using *cleartext* makes it easy for anyone to discover the passwords by simply capturing packets. A common solution to this problem is to send encrypted passwords, but this method breaks down if the encryption key is broken.

Another problem is that users tend to make passwords easy to remember, which means that they can be easy to discover. Often the passwords selected are common words that can be discovered through repeated attempts. The alternative is to provide passwords that are not common words either by randomly generating the passwords or by including in them special characters or digits. Doing this, however, can render them difficult to remember, resulting in users writing them down—usually near the host! Despite their drawbacks, passwords still are used frequently to identify users. Engineers simply need to realize their weaknesses and protect against them.

Yet another derivation of using passwords involves a password server and a one-time password generator, such as those manufactured by Enigma Logic and Security Dynamics. The password server is a system that can authenticate a user based on a database of user names and a password. The user's password comes from the one-time password generator, typically a small device with a keypad kept by the user. On the password server there are many ways to know which password is valid for a given user, some based on a sequence of valid passwords, others based on time synchronization between the one-time password generator and password server. A user who wants to get a one-time password follows these steps:

1. Initiates a session to the destination system

2. Enters a unique key into the password generator, which runs the key through an algorithm to produce the password

3. Types in the one-time password

The one-time password is then sent with the user name to the password server for authentication. TACACS (Terminal Access Controller Access Control System) is an example of a standard protocol that defines a mechanism for communicating between the destination system and the password server that many vendors implement.

This method of using one-time passwords has the advantage that if a cracker captures the one-time password while it traverses the network, subsequent uses of this password will not provide proper user authentication. This method also has the advantage that the user will probably not write down the password, since it is useful for only a single authentication. The obvious disadvantage of this system is that it requires the user to carry the password generator and enter the key into it each time authentication is necessary.

Let's return to our example using *Master* and *Servant* and consider how we could install more effective security management. Instead of allowing every user who has an account on *Servant* to access the software on *Master*, you could use a service that gives access only to those with a valid account on *Master*. Under this arrangement, to run the software from *Master*, a user first would have to start on an authorized host and second would have to enter a unique password.

In another example, a computer named *Snoopy* provides a service that allows users to access a database consisting of an organization's customer information (see Fig. 5.5). Only employees working in the organization's customer service department are authorized to access this sensitive information. Accordingly, when customer service agents need information about customers, they use a program on their personal computers to connect to *Snoopy*. However, before *Snoopy* gives out information to an agent, the database program asks the agent for a password that identifies that user as authorized to use the database. Thus not every user who walks up to a computer at the desk of a customer service agent can acquire information about customers.

Although user authentication is generally more effective than host authentication used alone, it does have one distinct disadvantage. Nearly all user authentication methods rely on the correct configuration of the computer. Obviously, if the computer provides user authentication for a service but makes the password the same for every user, the desired security will not be realized.

The combination of host authentication and user authentication provides a more effective means for securing access points than either method used alone. To demonstrate, let's return to our example of *Snoopy*. We had planned to have each user authorized by a password. But will this provide all the security we need? Any user with a personal computer and a password for an account with database access can access the sensitive information from *Snoopy*. To enhance security, we would want to apply both host authentication and user authentication to this service. This two-layered approach will ensure both that users requesting the service come from only authorized hosts and that they are authorized users.

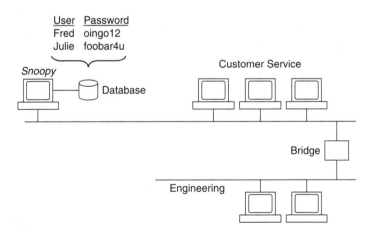

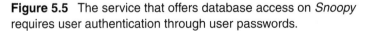

Figure 5.5 The service that offers database access on *Snoopy* requires user authentication through user passwords.

Key Authentication

A *key authentication* system provides a means to accomplish both host authentication and user authentication with the added advantage of not having to rely solely on the destination host. Key authentication works by assigning a host on the network called a key server.

The key server is responsible for issuing keys to authorized users. When a service is requested, the source computer asks the key server for a key. The server then might have the user type in a password for authentication. Now the key server can identify both the source computer and the user requesting the service. Based on this data and on the security rules resident within the key server, the server may issue a valid key. This system works because the destination computer will allow the service only if the request for access is accompanied by a valid key. On some key authentication servers valid keys eventually time out. This can have the effect of stopping the user's session, but it also ensures that a single valid key does not allow indefinite access. As you can see, because the key server authenticates users and grants access to services, it would need to be under stringent physical security.

A sample request for remote login using key authentication would work as follows (see Fig. 5.6):

1. The source computer (called "source" for short) requests remote login service to the destination computer (called "destination" for short).

2. The remote login process requests from the key server a key that allows the user to log in to destination.

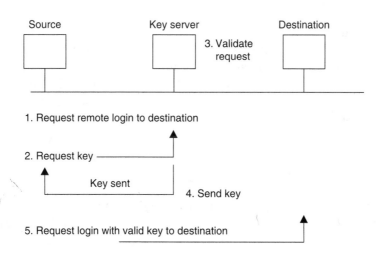

Figure 5.6 A sample service request with key authentication.

3. The key server validates source and ensures that the user is authorized to use the remote login service on destination.

4. If all checks out, the key server issues source a valid key for remote login on to destination.

5. The valid key is sent to source.

6. Source requests the remote login service from destination with the valid key.

In the key authentication method, the key server is critical for maintaining security on access points to data network services. It is also vitally important that the key server be correctly configured and administered. Note, however, that for key authentication to work, each service on the source computer must request a key from the key server before beginning the transaction. Further, the services on the destination computer must accept requests for services only when such requests are accompanied by a valid key. This means that you cannot simply install a key server and start using key authentication. All of your applications and services must also be changed to accommodate using the key server.

Key authentication has become popular in recent years on UNIX computers with the *Kerberos* suite of services from the Massachusetts Institute of Technology. Today many computer vendors offer some form of key authentication system.

Maintaining the Secure Access Points

The last step in effectively securing network access points is maintenance. As we have already seen, keeping the security measures on a data network up-to-date and secure is a difficult task requiring an organizational commitment in both time and resources. But just as the engineer must maintain a network no matter how well planned and well built it is, once the huge task of establishing a security system is complete, maintenance and modification of it will be required.

The key to maintenance is locating potential or actual security breaches. In some cases this may be done by engineers responsible for auditing network security. They may use as the basis for the audits, for example, the network engineer's documentation of potential network access points and their required security. Unfortunately, keeping such a document current with the wealth of networking software on the market today is another huge task, so in these cases sometimes the best the auditors can hope for is understanding the issues in security management and the organization's guidelines regarding it.

In other situations network engineers may deploy programs on hosts to check for commonly known security problems. Simple programs could attempt security breaches by trying passwords and encryption keys at random. More sophisticated programs could launch attacks on the network and computers in a variety of ways. In either case each program would inform the network engineer of its success or failure in breaching security. The logic behind this is that if one program can break a security measure, another must be able to perform the same feat. The advantage of this approach is that a problem located by a program enables the engineer to close the affected access point, preferably before it is found and exploited by an unauthorized user. There are many examples of these programs on the market today. You should ask your computer system vendor about which programs to deploy.

A more unusual approach has been attempted by some more daring organizations: offering on the public networks cash prizes if people can prove that they have broken into the organization's network and shown how. Although perhaps a bit drastic, this approach does seem to help guarantee security by assisting engineers in locating security breaches.

Unfortunately, no methods suggested here guarantee that security will be maintained properly. Audits cannot be performed every day. Programs that test security cannot check for every possible hole. Network engineers need to understand the security measures in place and make an effort to convey to the organization the necessity of having help in maintaining them.

5.3 ATTACHING TO A PUBLIC NETWORK

Section 5.2 described the steps involved in accomplishing security management for services on a host. An organization having a data network that does not connect to a public network could find that those steps will provide the necessary security. However, for an organization with a data network connected to a public data network, accomplishing security management requires a different approach.

Three types of access are possible from a public data network to an organization's data network:

- No access

- Full access

- Limited access

A private data network that allows no remote login access from a public data network may simply use its connection to a public network as a means of sending and receiving electronic mail. For example, the connection may be established every few hours through a modem for the sole purpose of placing mail onto and receiving mail from the public data network. All transactions with the public data network would be initiated from within the organization's data network. With this method the organization does not need to find the access points to the public data network, because they do not exist.

In contrast, if an organization places no restrictions on transactions between their computers and a public data network, all security management must reside on each individual computer within the organization. In this setup the organization may allow any data to enter its network and rely on the computers to provide host authentication or user authentication before releasing sensitive information.

However, suppose that an organization wants to access some services from a public network or offer some to a public network but has no host or user authentication on most of its computers. Obviously, opening itself up to a public network would pose a security risk. The limited-access method can help assuage security concerns in this case.

Allowing limited access involves authorizing only a small subset of hosts to provide service between the organization's network and the public network. A set of computer systems or network devices are put between the organization's network and the public network to enforce security management. This popular scenario, sometimes called building a *firewall*, enables the network engineer to control every computer that offers service to the public data network, thus limiting services available to the public network and better securing access points on the organization's network.

A firewall is a combination of security management features on a series of network devices designed to let only certain information pass from one side to another. In this case a firewall would let only certain data from a public network pass through into the private network. A firewall is often built by using routers to provide network layer packet filtering and by using computers as gateways to control the flow of data between applications.

For example, let's say that the organization has on its data network a machine called *WideOpen*, which is an application gateway within a firewall. Your security setup provides that any data intended for the organization's internal data network must first be sent to *WideOpen* (see Fig. 5.7). You next would want to perform the steps outlined in this chapter to determine the allowable services for *WideOpen*. Often such services do not include enabling a public network user to use *WideOpen* as a stop-off point before entering the organization's data network. Also, you may want to allow *WideOpen* to act as an electronic mail relay between the public data network and the organization but not to allow any remote login or file transfer.

The connection between the network segment that *WideOpen* resides on and the public network will most often be through a network device such as a bridge

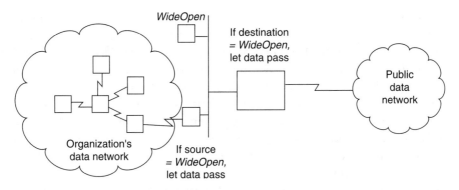

Figure 5.7 A setup allowing limited access from the organization's data network to the public data network.

or router. You should configure this device to allow traffic to and from *WideOpen* only with packet filters. The packet filters must be set up so that all packets entering from the public network have a destination address of *WideOpen* and all packets leaving to the public network have a source address of *WideOpen*.

Using these techniques, you can enable the organization to use the public network without fear of exposing sensitive information to unauthorized users on the public data network. (*Note*: The use of host authentication suggested in this example will work unless another computer is mistakenly assigned the same network address as *WideOpen*. However, you can avoid this by assigning to *WideOpen* a network number that is different from that used with the rest of the organization's computers.)

5.4 SECURITY MANAGEMENT ON A NETWORK MANAGEMENT SYSTEM

As we have seen, security management enables network engineers to protect sensitive information by limiting user access to hosts and network resources and by notifying the engineer of attempted or actual breaches of security. Security management on a network management system is accomplished through the use of software tools. How well this is done depends on the sophistication of the tool available to the engineer.

A Simple Tool

A simple tool for effecting security management on a network management system would need to show where security measures have been set up. Relying on input from the graphical network map, this tool could produce a screen showing all security measures applicable to any device or host a user selected.

Additionally, to enable you to locate all places in the network that restrict a certain user or network address, the tool should be able to query the configuration database and produce a screen of the necessary information. This security management tool, using the configuration management information already present in the network management system, can be very useful in solving complex connectivity or reachability problems on the network.

The simple tool queries the network management system's relational database for the configuration of the device selected on the map. A problem in today's environment is that many network management applications do not have a method for storing the configuration of a device in a database. Or, if they do store that configuration, it is not broken up into logical pieces to help the tool determine which parts of the configuration are relevant to network security. Thus the tool needs to be able to parse configuration information for a variety of devices. The only solution today for network engineers is to have a tool that can view the portions of the device's configuration and make a manual inspection of the security features that are enabled.

A More Complex Tool

A more advanced tool could be designed by including a real-time application that monitors the access points to sensitive information. After spotting a potential security problem, this application could change the colors of affected hosts or network devices on the graphical network map. Or, if having too many colors for different events becomes confusing, the tool could report its findings in some other method, such as ringing the system bell and logging its findings in a window that pops up on the network management system automatically (see Fig. 5.8).

Using a network management protocol, you can query devices for the number of security events recorded. The more complex tool can poll for this information periodically (once an hour should be more than sufficient in most environments) and look for a large delta in security-related events.

For example, such an application could report when a single user has made numerous unsuccessful remote login attempts on a computer. This report could be accomplished in two ways, depending on the computer's intelligence regarding reporting events. If it can send events to the network management system concerning unsuccessful login attempts, this would be ideal. Otherwise, the security management application would need to have the intelligence to check a computer's log files concerning failed remote login at-

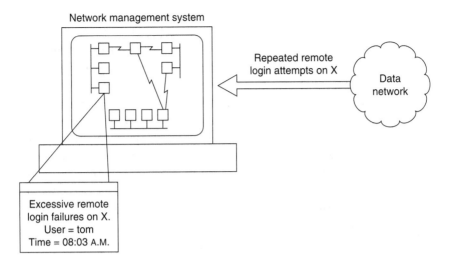

Network management system

Repeated remote
login attempts on X

Data
network

Excessive remote
login failures on X.
User = tom
Time = 08:03 A.M.

Figure 5.8 A real-time security management application reporting
many unsuccessful attempts to gain access to the remote login
service on computer X.

tempts. (Many computers will log failed login attempts in a file, or *audit trail*,
for later examination.) Unfortunately, this method requires that the security
management application be written to examine specific file formats.

This application could be further developed to produce more useful information, such as reporting repeated denials of user attempts to access a particular service or to access a file containing sensitive information. This
reporting would be generated in a manner similar to that described previously. One common trick to find a file that has been accessed is to have the
tool look at the time stamps on the file. On many operating systems the time
stamps will show when the file was created and when it was last modified.

The tool also could be designed to notify you when an unauthorized user
or host attempts to access a service that has an access point to sensitive information. By doing this, the tool could guide you to a needed reconfiguration of a host. For example, suppose that a user at a personal computer is
requesting file service from an accounting server that holds sensitive information. The user does not intend to gain file service on the accounting server
but rather on a local server, and perhaps the user doesn't know the necessary
configuration to stop the computer from requesting all services available on
the network. This tool, monitoring the service access points to the accounting server, could not only advise you of the misguided attempt to gain access
but in the process also alert you to the misconfiguration.

This tool already would bring possible security concerns to your attention.
However, it could also help build security restrictions at points within the

network. To do this, you would first select a point on the data network and then supply the tool with input about the users or network addresses allowed and denied through the point. Next, the tool would build the correct filters or other measures necessary to produce the desired action. And finally, the tool could confirm the entire process with you.

Although the tasks required of this tool are not complex, a certain amount of sophistication is involved in producing such an application, because nearly every network device or host has a unique method for applying security measures. The tool would first need to query the host or device where security is to be applied and then query the user for the appropriate information. For example, applying security to limit network address traffic is vastly different when performed on a repeater, bridge, front-end processor, or router. Further, for each device manufacturer, the application of security can take a completely different form.

An Advanced Tool

The advanced security management tool would go even further than the complex tool and use data gathered about traffic patterns to guide you on the implications of imposing security. More complete security management requires this functionality, as well as the features mentioned for the simple and more complex tools.

The advanced tool would examine the type of security you intend to install on a computer or device and alert you to possible repercussions of such installations. This tool would use input from you in conjunction with historical data to do a full analysis of how a particular security measure would affect the traffic on the network. For example, let's say that you plan to install a packet-filtering scheme that should stop all traffic between two areas on the data network, *Chaos* and *Ordered* (see Fig. 5.9). This tool would analyze the pattern of traffic between the two areas of the network and then inform you that the planned security would stop 85 percent of the traffic between the two areas. This percentage effective rate may be the effect you intended; on the other hand, it could be the result of some error in the system or in the design of the scheme. Regardless, the advanced tool would have either reinforced your efforts or warned you about a possible misconfiguration.

Few, if any, tools on the market can perform the function of the advanced tool. The advanced tool would need to work very closely with the performance management information stored within the database on the network management system to find the total traffic traversing the network between *Chaos* and *Ordered*. The tool would have to evaluate the data in terms of traffic patterns and then perform the necessary analysis on the proposed security.

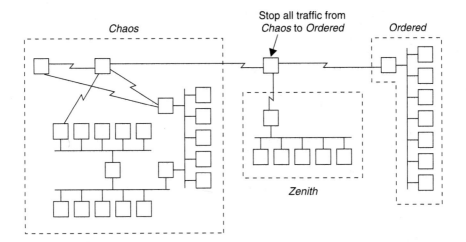

Figure 5.9   A security management application could inform the network engineer of the implication of setting up security to stop all traffic between *Chaos* and *Ordered*.

The first hurdle for this application on today's internetworks is finding the traffic pattern data on network devices. Some products, such as RMON probes, can gather information about a matrix of traffic between source and destination MAC addresses. If you are setting up security on MAC addresses, this information could easily be analyzed to do the function of the advanced tool. Yet if you wish to set up a complex packet filter on network-layer addresses and application types, RMON information may not do the job.

Some vendor proprietary techniques exist for accounting for traffic patterns across a network. These techniques typically permit a network device to count the number of packets and bytes sent between two systems on a per network layer protocol basis (such as IP and Novell IPX). If the advanced tool could determine that the device on which you are applying security measures had this feature, it could then query for this information from the network management system database.

The second implementation problem with the advanced tool would be the analysis of the proposed packet filters for the associated network devices. As we saw in Chapter 4, nearly every type of device has its own method for configuration. This means that every vendor will have a unique method for configuring packet filters, making a tool to analyze these packet filters an enormous task. Some network management applications have features to analyze packet filters, but this analysis is not commonly tied to traffic pattern data, which is necessary to produce even a limited version of the advanced tool.

5.5 REPORTING SECURITY EVENTS

Like real-time applications, audit trails that summarize and report security information are critical to accomplishing security management. With the help of applications that make entries into an audit trail, you can determine patterns of when access points are threatened and hence stop unauthorized access. Also, as with real-time applications, such data can help you find unauthorized requests that result from misconfiguration.

For example, suppose that the network engineer responsible for managing and configuring your data network is planning to leave the organization for a competitor. The first step in dealing with this situation would be to immediately remove that person's physical access to your organization's buildings, wiring closets, or any place where physical access to sensitive information is possible. This step may involve changing key codes, deactivating card keys, and so on. The second task is to remove the person's accounts on all computer systems. Depending on the former employee's access, this step should also involve changing all privileged passwords (such as root, supervisor, and system manager) on all computer systems and network devices. In conjunction with these first two steps, you should also change the passwords and encryption keys on all network devices that connect the organization to a public network (or those that could be accessed by the outside world), such as all modems, network devices, and hosts in the firewall. As a final step, you would want to set up, or confirm the existence of, audit trails on these devices and tell the security management tool to watch all devices on the data network where the former employee could access. This security management tool could have the functionality of the more complex tool. An additional step would be to run a program designed to look for files or applications the former employee may have altered to produce a security hole in the future. Looking for new executable files or files that have recently been altered is a task many programs can perform as part of a systems management function (although not in a completely foolproof way in all cases).

The key to ensuring that your data network is still secure is a comprehensive audit trail and a process put in place to monitor it. In this situation the security of the audit trail (presumably on the network management system) is also important. Producing an application that produces an audit trail is not particularly difficult, provided each security management application that finds potential violations enters its findings in the database on the network management system. For example, an application that discovers numerous unsuccessful remote login attempts also could add an entry into the database when it alerted the network engineer of a problem. The database then could be used to generate the summary reports.

Although these applications are relatively simple to accomplish with the correct network management system architecture, their usefulness should not be underestimated. Consider the sample daily report shown in Table 5.1, which shows how a security management application can present useful data to network engineers. It identifies two major access points, the invalid attempts found for the day, the source computer, the user name given when the attempt failed (if available), and the time the event occurred. Similar applications that produce relevant data for longer periods, such as a week or month, also are critical to security management on a network management system. Reviewed regularly, these reports can help the engineer keep the network secure and be aware of potential or actual security breaches.

SUMMARY

Security management enables the network engineer to control access points to a data network for the purpose of protecting sensitive information from unauthorized access. Protection through security management tools is achieved through specific configuration of network hosts and devices to control access points within the data network but usually does not deal with securing the sensitive information. Security management should not be

Table 5.1 April 1—Security Summary—Allan's Network

Invalid File Transfer Attempts:			
Reported By:	*Source*:	*User*:	*Time of Day*:
Manet	Picasso	Steve	08:03
Manet	Picasso	Steve	08:05
Cezanne	Manet	Julie	08:26
Monet	Rembrandt	James	17:21
Invalid Remote Login Attempts:			
Reported By:	*Source*:	*User*:	*Time of Day*:
Renoir	Goya	Carol	08:03
Pissarro	Goya	Jim	12:10
Cezanne	Dali	Alex	12:45
Renoir	Pissarro	Carol	13:26
Pissarro	Monet	????	15:01
Pissarro	Monet	????	15:02
Pissarro	Monet	????	15:03
Cezanne	Manet	guest	15:23
Manet	VanGogh	Steve	18:23

confused with the different concepts of physical security and operating system security. Its primary benefit is securing sensitive information and calming the security concerns of users about attaching hosts to a data network.

Using security management, network engineers can protect sensitive information by limiting the access to hosts and network resources by users and by obtaining reports of attempted or actual breaches of security. It consists of the following four steps:

1. Identifying the sensitive information to be protected

2. Finding the access points

3. Securing the access points through encryption, packet filters, host authentication, user authentication, and key authentication

4. Maintaining the secure access points

Connecting to a public data network provides many opportunities for security breaches against computers attached to a data network. Accordingly, an organization may elect to control public access to its information by allowing no access, full access, or limited access to the data.

The engineer can use a variety of tools for accomplishing security management. A simple tool can summarize the security barriers set up throughout the data network; a more complex tool can go further and notify the engineer when a user has attempted access through locked access points. This same tool also could help put the proper mechanisms in place to stop unauthorized access to sensitive information. An advanced tool goes even further and evaluates the implications of putting restrictions on sensitive information, based on historical network traffic information.

FOR FURTHER STUDY

Cheswick, W., and Bellovin, S., *Firewalls and Internet Security*, Reading, MA: Addison-Wesley, 1994.

Curry, D., *UNIX System Security*, Reading, MA: Addison-Wesley, 1992.

Stoll, C., *The Cuckoo's Egg*, New York: Doubleday, 1989.

Chapter 6

Performance Management

In This Chapter:

Chris had MegaNet *running like a smooth oiled machine, or so it was presumed. No complaints from users, so no worries. Yet somewhere a little voice told Chris that it might be beneficial to monitor the performance of the network just to see how things were and to help predict if there would be a problem in the future. Of course, the one thing Chris wanted to avoid was a day when that little voice became the booming voice of the department manager saying that access to another network location was too slow—and demanding to know why. Reflecting on this potentially awkward situation, Chris decided to examine ways to analyze the current performance of* MegaNet.

A data network is like a highway on which information travels throughout the organization. And just as a highway can become chronically congested, the capacity of a network highway can become overtaxed from the increasing demands of users. Network devices become overloaded, LAN and WAN links become saturated, and consequently, performance suffers.

Performance management involves ensuring that this network highway remains accessible and uncrowded. This is done by

- Monitoring network devices and their associated links to determine utilization and error rates

- Helping the network provide a consistent level of service to the users by ensuring that the capacity of devices and links is not overtaxed to the extent of adversely impacting performance

Performance management entails the following steps:

1. Collecting data on current utilization of network devices and links

2. Analyzing relevant data to discern high utilization trends

3. Setting utilization thresholds

4. Using simulation to determine how the network can be altered to maximize performance

In this chapter we present the benefits of performance management, followed by a discussion of the four steps involved in accomplishing it. We then describe three performance management tools, from simple to advanced, for your consideration. Last, we discuss the methods for reporting performance management information.

6.1 BENEFITS OF THE PERFORMANCE MANAGEMENT PROCESS

The primary benefit of performance management is that it helps the network engineer to reduce network overcrowding and inaccessibility to provide a consistent level of service to users. Using performance management, the engineer can monitor the utilization of network devices and links. Such data can also help the engineer to determine utilization trends, isolate performance problems, and possibly even solve them before they adversely impact network performance. In this way performance management also can aid in capacity planning.

Monitoring the current utilization of network devices and links is critical for performance management. The data obtained not only can help you immediately isolate components of the data network that are heavily utilized but also, perhaps more importantly, can help you find answers to other potential problems. For example, users' complaints about slow remote access to a database server could have many probable causes. The problem could lie on any link or device from the source to the destination. Performance management could help you determine quickly that a link between the remote site and the database server is over 80 percent utilized and therefore the likely cause of the slow access (see Fig. 6.1).

Performance management techniques also can assist you in examining network trends. You can use trend data to predict peak network utilization and consequently to avoid the poor performance that can result from a saturated network. For example, if you know the average response time between a user's terminal and a mainframe computer, you can set up procedures to let you know when the response time is too long. As we will see throughout this chapter, network devices and network management applications can be set up to send alerts when a potential performance problem is found or when a user-defined threshold is crossed.

An RMON (Remote Network Monitoring) device, discussed in Chapter 11, can gather real-time information about a network segment, sample the data at scheduled intervals (perhaps every five minutes), and store the historical data for later retrieval by a network management system. This capability of RMON is one example of using real-time network data for long-term trend analysis.

You also could plot utilization of the network against time to determine times of high usage. Knowing this can help you schedule large data transfers for nonpeak times. On many data networks users schedule large transfers for times when network usage is presumably low, such as 12:00 A.M. Although few users may notice a performance problem at that time, network usage can, in fact, reach a fairly high utilization then. Let's say that on such a network a group plans to transfer each night large graphic images of a circuit board design under development. The people working on this project ask you when the optimum time is to deliver these images. Because you have been monitoring network utilization, you instruct them to transfer at 3:00 A.M. daily, a time that trend analysis indicated has an average of only 5 percent utilization.

Capacity planning benefits both the users and the network engineers. Using performance management information, network engineers can determine the current capacity of the network by using a network management

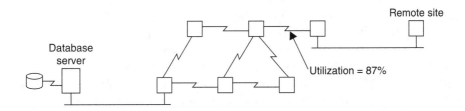

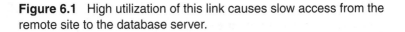

Figure 6.1 High utilization of this link causes slow access from the remote site to the database server.

protocol to gather information about all of the bytes sent and received on network interfaces. The total of these numbers gives the network volume. Keep in mind that in many data networks you need to be careful where you gather the information about the bytes sent and received, to avoid counting the same data twice. In this situation you would want to count the number of bytes at places where traffic is headed for a unique destination (or set of destinations). Once you know the current capacity of the network, you can make determinations about how additional traffic will affect the overall network.

6.2 ACCOMPLISHING PERFORMANCE MANAGEMENT

Performance management involves the following four steps:

1. Collect data on current utilization of network devices and links.

2. Analyze relevant data.

3. Set utilization thresholds.

4. Simulate the network.

Collecting Utilization Data

Determining the utilization of a device is usually not a straightforward task. Each type of device may have different characteristics denoting utilization. Although we provide some common utilization measurements here, you should generally work with your device vendor.

For example, the utilization on a file server may best be measured by processor load, disk access rate, and network interface card utilization. A busy processor may perform user tasks slowly, a disk continually being accessed may read and write new files more slowly than desired, and a busy network interface card may slow access to the network.

On a bridge or router device, utilization can be measured by packet forwarding rate, the processor load, percentage of dropped frames on each interface, and number of packets being held in a queue. These devices are best measured by examining their forwarding rate versus their forwarding capability in a given network scenario, because they typically can process frames more quickly than their associated links can deliver them. A high processor load tells you that the device has little idle time. Keeping the processor on a device busy is usually not a problem, unless the device becomes busy 100 percent of the time and cannot continue to process network traffic. In this case the high utilization of the device may result in packets being discarded, forcing the source system to retransmit them (and potentially make the performance problem worse). If the device can process the packets but needs to queue them, this can also affect overall network performance. The device may be waiting on a heavily utilized network link, a link with many errors, or another network device that may be experiencing performance problems.

The utilization of a link on the network is a much easier number to determine. Keep in mind that although a link may not be 100 percent utilized, a lower percentage of link utilization may still cause performance problems. For example, an Ethernet can accommodate bursts of traffic to a very high utilization, but if normal traffic load exceeds 40 percent, the segment may provide bad performance.

Link utilization is the amount of bits sent per second and bits received per second divided by the total available bandwidth (also measured in bits per second):

$$util\% = (total\ bits\ sent + total\ bits\ received)/bandwidth$$

Note that this formula does not work on full-duplex serial links, which can send and receive at the full bandwidth rate in both directions simultaneously. This means that the utilization percentage could calculate to 200 percent! So you should use the following formula instead, which takes the maximum of sent bits per second and received bits per second and uses that number to compute utilization:

$$util\% = MAX(total\ bits\ sent,\ total\ bits\ received)/bandwidth$$

Because computing link utilization is critical to performance management, we discuss this topic further in Section 6.3 and again in Chapter 9.

A significant manifestation of overutilization on network devices and links is a noticeable decrease in the level of service to users. To measure the level of service, you would want to determine the following:

- Total response time

- Rejection rate

- Availability

Total response time is the amount of time it takes a datum to enter the network and be processed and for a response to leave the network. For example, the total response time for a remote login session can be measured from the time when the user first types a character on the keyboard to the time it takes that information to travel through the network to the destination machine and back again to be displayed back on the local terminal.

Many transport-level protocols, such as the internetwork standard Transmission Control Protocol (TCP), measure the round-trip time in milliseconds for every datum sent from source to destination for flow control purposes. You could use this number to get a good approximation of total response time. The value of the round-trip time will not be identical to the total response time, because the transport layer receives the datum before the application processes it, and the application processing will add some time. Regardless, the round-trip time should be a significant portion of the total response time.

Rejection rate is the percentage of time the network cannot transfer information because of a lack of resources and performance. To measure rejection rate, many devices record the number of attempts to initiate a connection and the number of total connections made. Dividing the number of connections made by the total number of attempts gives a rejection rate percentage. In many situations a rejection rate greater than 2 percent is significant.

Availability is the percentage of time the network is accessible for use and operational and is often measured as mean time between failure, or *MTBF*. Availability can be measured on a theoretical level, and most device vendors can provide those numbers. On a more practical level most devices and links can tell you how long they have been operational. This number, compared to the total time elapsed since the device or link has been in service, can give you availability.

You could use a network management protocol to collect this data from the network. You will find that this information can be important both for real-time network troubleshooting and for trend analysis.

Analyzing the Data

Your analysis could result in a graphical representation of the utilization of a network device or link either in real time or from a historical perspective. For example, you could use line or bar graphs, which are most useful for performance analysis.

Real-time graphical analysis can show current network usage or errors, as seen in Fig. 6.2. For example, a real-time plot showing you the number of packets transmitted versus the number of errors seen at the same time can give you direct clues as to network performance problems. Although many real-time graphs can help diagnose network performance problems, the most common ones that will be useful concern the resources of the devices on the network and their associated links:

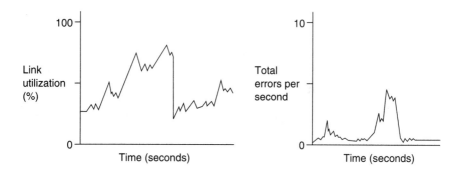

Figure 6.2 Real-time graphs of network link utilization and total errors are useful for troubleshooting performance problems.

- Device information: memory usage, processor(s) utilization, disk access rate, number of sessions, and so on

- Link information: utilization, error rates, error percentages, and so on

Graphs that plot historical data for the network won't show you the current status of the network but are useful for illustrating trends. Trend data can help you predict when the user demand for the network will exceed the capacity of a device or a link. This can help you plan to increase the network capacity or redesign the network to account for the user demand. Often you use historical plots to look at weekly, monthly, quarterly, and yearly trends.

A graph can show not only the increase or decrease of utilization on a network link but also other useful statistics, such as error rates on a link and processor usage for a device for a given time period. If you notice a trend for the amount of errors a device experiences, you may be able to diagnose the problem before it affects performance. For example, if you notice that a network device is slowly increasing the amount of processing power it uses over time, you may decide to alleviate the traffic flow through the device before the processing power reaches a critical level. Another alternative may be to upgrade the device to a more powerful processor.

Setting Thresholds

Another step in the performance management process is setting utilization thresholds. You can set threshold on a variety of items that can affect network performance. For a network device or host these may include processor utilization and alarm durations. On a link you may choose to set thresholds on such items as error rate, average utilization, and overall throughput.

Once thresholds are set, performance management tools can report to the engineer when the performance of the network reaches a certain error rate or utilization. Determining the value to set as a threshold may be difficult; however, most often you will find that trial and error will produce a reasonable value. Thresholds can enable you to locate and fix a problem before it affects network performance. Combining the graphical presentation of the utilization data with utilization thresholds is a powerful tool for accomplishing performance management.

Using Network Simulation

Network simulation is yet another performance management tool you can use. With this tool you can be better assured that the network you build will perform to users' expectations.

Note: Building the model for network simulation is a difficult task. (Few software companies can simulate even fairly simple network configurations.) Therefore this text does not cover that topic but instead addresses how to use network simulation to accomplish performance management.

You can use simulation to determine how to alter a network for more efficient use and higher performance. For example, consider a network's remote site, where users are experiencing poor response time using a new application that communicates across a wide area network to a central data center. Often this poor response time results from a heavily congested link. After investigating the usage of the link to the remote site, you find that it averages over 80 percent utilization. Consequently you decide to upgrade the bandwidth of the link. Yet after the upgrade, users at the remote site are still experiencing poor response time with their new application.

Searching further, you find that the transport-layer protocol used by the new application uses a stop-and-wait protocol (window size of one packet). This transport-layer protocol uses a flow control mechanism that sends a single packet at a time for each session, waiting for the packet to be acknowledged before transmitting the next packet to be sent. More bandwidth on the link to the remote site will allow more packets to be sent at a given time, but this will not help the overall delay seen by the network users.

Thus upgrading the link did not solve the poor response problem. Using a sophisticated simulation application of the network and the transport-layer protocol before upgrading the link probably would have helped you detect this deficiency with the transport-layer protocol. The appropriate solution to the problem would be to have the application use a protocol stack (and associated transport-layer protocol) that uses a flow control mechanism with a window size greater than one designed for wide area data networks.

6.3 PERFORMANCE MANAGEMENT ON A NETWORK MANAGEMENT SYSTEM

Performance management on a network management system involves using intelligent tools that can examine the state of the network in both real-time and historical perspectives. As with the other types of network management we have discussed, the effectiveness of performance management depends on the level of tool available to the engineer.

A Simple Tool

A simple tool for performance management should provide real-time information about network devices and links, preferably in graphical form, such as a line or bar graph. This tool can help you find network bottlenecks and isolate performance problems.

You will be able to graph any statistic available from the network by using a network management protocol. This gives you the greatest flexibility when trying to analyze the network's performance. The simple tool will also provide a way for you to find out that basic information about a device or link without having to know the details of the network management information. In many situations you do not want to know the details of all of the network management information on the device (it can be thousands of pieces of information); you just want to know how the device is performing.

For network devices the simple tool should provide an easy way, such as a button click or a menu item, to gather data about processor and memory utilization. High processor utilization may mean that a device cannot handle the network traffic, whereas excessive memory utilization may mean that a device is buffering vast amounts of data. A real-time graph of these values can alert you to a potential performance problem with the device, as seen in Fig. 6.3.

On network links the simple tool also should be able to show you current utilization and error rates. For example, a graph of packets per second and bits per second for the link is useful for showing overall link performance. Another useful value to graph is the current utilization of the network link, found by dividing the rate of bits per second on the link by the maximum bits per second. In a troubleshooting situation you may want to examine the number of errors on a link versus the amount of good data sent. The simple tool could overlay these two graphs and produce the necessary result.

Many tools on the market have the functionality of the simple tool. Most major network management platforms allow you to produce real-time graphs of any piece of information available from a network device. Further, many

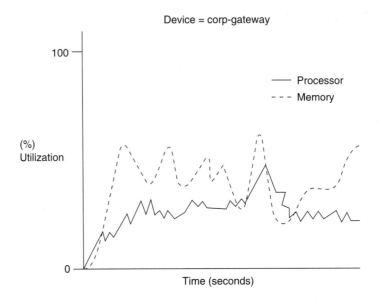

Figure 6.3 Functionality of the simple tool.

network management applications are designed by vendors to give you a graphical representation of the health of a device.

A More Complex Tool

A complex tool would go a step further by allowing you to set thresholds for utilization and error rates. If the network exceeded those thresholds, the tool could perform a prescribed action. This tool also could gather real-time information and store it in a database management system, which can be used to do historical studies and produce graphs to view the past performance of the network.

Thresholds

Setting thresholds that can trigger a subsequent action gives the engineer considerable functionality. The tool should enable you to specify the action; the one you select could be simple, such as ringing a bell or flashing a light, or more advanced, such as enabling a backup circuit, calling a pocket paging system, or sending electronic mail. For example, in many parts of the world Switched 56 or ISDN services offer high bandwidth circuits on demand, using a special modem or adapter. The billing of these dialed circuits is based on time, thus making the circuits cost-effective for periods of high use on network resources. The tool could use this technology to dial a new circuit, based on utilization, error rates, or any threshold set by the network engineer.

A threshold is vital to the functionality of the complex tool; however, you can go further to optimize this facility. The complex tool could warn you about not only an incident that crosses a threshold but also a situation that nears the threshold. For example, the tool may be set up to monitor the utilization of a processor on a network device. Suppose that on a certain device the point where the processor utilization affects network performance is 90 percent of total capacity. The tool could be set up to notify you when the processor utilization reached 80 percent of this threshold, thus allowing you to examine the network as a performance problem is occurring.

Thresholds should also have a notification priority. There should be at least three levels of notification priority (low, medium, high). A high-priority threshold overrides a medium priority, which in turn overrides a low priority. Each priority may have a different color on the network map or event log on the network management system.

Sometimes, however, different situations may cause the same priority threshold. For example, imagine that you have set up a threshold to monitor the utilization of a link. If the link exceeds 40 percent utilized, the tool crosses a low-priority threshold; 65 percent utilization crosses a medium-priority threshold; and 75 percent crosses a high-priority threshold. Later you set up another threshold that watches memory utilization on the device. If the device has less than 100 Kb (kilobytes) of memory left, the complex tool issues a high-priority threshold. Within seconds of the medium-priority threshold for link utilization being crossed, the high-priority threshold for memory is crossed. The complex tool now needs to keep a list of all thresholds exceeded for the device and present them to the network engineer in priority. If the complex tool uses the network map to present the current thresholds exceeded for the device, one color for the device will not work.

Further, the tool should be able to rearm the threshold in a reasonable manner. Suppose that an alarm rings when utilization reaches the threshold of 60 percent, then stops an instant later when the utilization drops to 58 percent, and rings again a few seconds later, when the utilization reaches 61 percent. To prevent this redundant and annoying progression of multiple alarms, the tool should be set up so that when the threshold is reached the first time, the tool sets off an alarm. Subsequently the tool would rearm the threshold only if the utilization dropped below another defined value, such as 40 percent (see Fig. 6.4). With this arrangement the tool would sound an alarm when the threshold is exceeded; another alarm would sound only if the utilization dropped below 40 percent and then again exceeded 60 percent. Flowchart 6.1

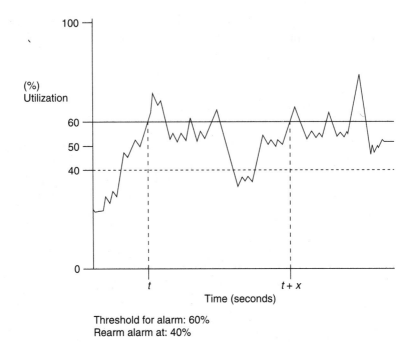

Figure 6.4 In this example of a complex tool, an alarm rings twice
for the utilization graphed, at time *t* and time *t* + *x*.

demonstrates this example. The tool could be set up to use this same concept
for checking error rates on network links as well.

   Most major network management platforms deal with thresholds. Using a
network management platform, you should be able to set a threshold, specify
an action if a threshold is crossed, specify the priority of the threshold, and automatically rearm the threshold. Some network management applications automatically set up thresholds to watch critical criteria for their specific devices.

Graphing the Network's Historical Data

The more complex tool also should be able to graph the historical performance management data put into the database management system. When
a data network experiences a performance problem, often the engineer can't
simultaneously examine all relevant aspects. Further, in many cases the user
may complain about the problem after its occurrence. In these situations the
real-time graphing ability of the simple tool can't help you. However, being
able to retrieve the necessary information and then examine it in graphical
format can significantly help in resolving this type of problem.

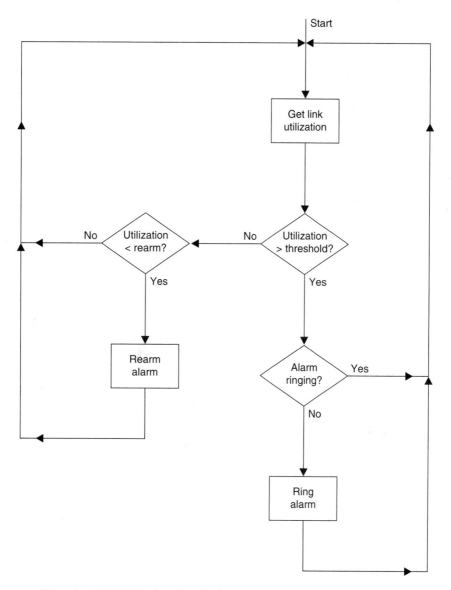

Flowchart 6.1 This flowchart is for a tool that checks link utilization and rings an alarm based on threshold and rearm values.

The tool should produce line, bar, and pie graphs. Line graphs are useful for examining trends in data, such as utilization. Bar graphs are effective for comparing values such as memory consumed on a network device versus the number of packets handled. Pie graphs are valuable for demonstrating the percentage of values, such as the types of traffic passing through a network device during periods of slow performance. An example of each graph format is shown in Fig. 6.5.

Let's examine further how graphs can help you in performance management. Suppose that two users are logged in to two personal computers on a token ring network: *Gatsby* and *Daisy*. Both use the token ring to share an application that clerks need in order to enter sales and order processing information prior to a nightly download to the company's mainframe. At seemingly random times the users experience a brief period of interrupted service when no data seem to pass on the token ring network.

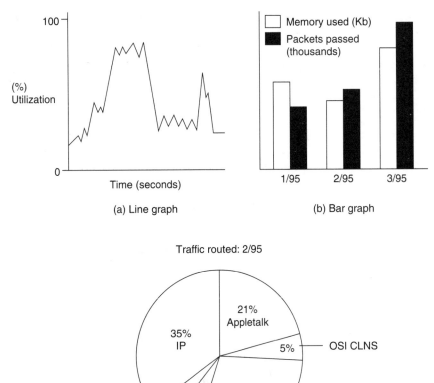

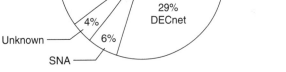

Figure 6.5 Types of graphs produced by the complex tool.

To help isolate this common problem, you first could have the performance management tool graph the error rate on the token ring network segment for the previous two days. Let's say that a line graph shows a very small number of errors occurring within normal operating specifications. Because the error rate on the ring is apparently not the problem, you then could have the tool produce a line graph of the utilization of the ring for the same period. This graph shows peak utilization just before 12:00 P.M., at 3:00 P.M., and at 12:00 A.M., all times when the network is busiest and system backups are most likely to occur. However, the users report that they are experiencing performance problems at other times.

Accordingly you could rightly conclude that this problem doesn't lie within the token ring network. Next, you could graph the processor utilization of both *Gatsby* and *Daisy*. If the graph shows many times during the past two days when the utilization peaked at 100 percent, you could ask the users on the hosts if they were doing any processor-intensive operations during these periods of inadequate performance. Both users state that at those times, they were simply typing in information that feeds the order processing application.

Because the application running on the personal computers most likely is not causing the processor load to skyrocket, you realize that some other outside influence must be the cause of the problem. You know that most manufacturers can potentially speak a different network protocol, so examining the types of traffic on the token ring that the personal computers see may shed some light on the problem. Therefore you next could have the tool make pie charts showing the percentage of different types of traffic on the token ring. To accomplish this, you have the tool query *Daisy* and *Gatsby* at five-minute intervals and make a chart for the types of traffic observed.

After a few hours, you examine the charts. Some show a wide distribution of different network protocols on the token ring; however, others show that a protocol not understood by either *Gatsby* or *Daisy* dominates the token ring. Further analysis reveals that the times when the processor load hit 100 percent on *Gatsby* and *Daisy* correlate exactly to when the network protocol they don't understand contributed a major portion of traffic to the token ring. Your final step, then, would be to determine why the two personal computers react poorly to the foreign network protocol. You find that the protocol uses specific token ring packets to locate network services (printers, file servers, routers, and so on) and so conclude that for some reason, *Gatsby* and *Daisy* react poorly to these packets. As a possible temporary solution, you finally could move these computers to another token ring segment until the true cause of the problem can be uncovered.

The ability to graph historical data is not very common in the marketplace today. This functionality requires that the network management platform and all of the applications running on it use the same database system. Given the number of different database systems available, the chances of an application requiring a different database than the platform is common.

A solution to this problem is to have each vendor write applications to use the database provided with the network management platform. This makes it difficult for the vendor to move applications between platforms, resulting in the end user having fewer platform choices. Another solution would be to have all network management platforms use the same database system (not likely) or at least have the same application programmers interface (API) for each database system.

An Advanced Tool

The advanced tool would offer additional functionality. It would explore the past state of the network, perform network simulation, and predict response time, rejection rate, and availability.

Examining the Network's Historical Data

The advanced tool should be able to use information found in the relational database to examine the state of the network at any point in the past to look for probable performance problems and aid in capacity planning. To accomplish this task, the tool would need to be able to:

- Receive user input about the state of the network and performance problems

- Retrieve information from the database

- Analyze the state of the network

The first step of this process requires that you tell the tool at what time in the past it should examine the data on the network. You also would need to tell the tool which hosts, devices, or links it should look at. For example, you could instruct the tool to review the performance between two hosts on the network for the previous month.

Next, the tool would need to retrieve information on the network management system from the relational database. For each element it is to examine, the tool would need to know what information to extract. For example, on a network device the tool could gather processor, buffer, and memory utilization; for a network link the tool could fetch data about error rates and bandwidth utilization.

Note: You should be able to specify any additional information the tool is to obtain from the database.

The tool then would analyze the data to determine the source of a particular performance problem. It would examine predefined events, such as high error rates, an incident of a threshold being exceeded, or an overall increase in traffic. Using the Structured Query Language (SQL), you could add rules to the analysis; for example, the following statement adds the rule to look for a host with more than ten users:

```
SELECT * FROM hosts WHERE users > 10
```

In another example the advanced tool could help you to perform capacity planning for network links with information from the relational database. When network links are used above a certain percentage, they can affect network performance. This percentage can differ dramatically, depending on the intended use of the link and the response time the users require. A common problem is that once you discover that a link has reached its critical utilization percentage, it often takes a long time (around forty-five days in the United States) to order and receive a link upgrade to one with more bandwidth.

The advanced tool can use information from the relational database to help you predict when a link will surpass the critical utilization threshold in advance. Thus you can start to upgrade the link and have it installed before the users see a performance problem. First, you must provide input about how long it typically takes to upgrade a link and at what percentage utilization the users begin to see a performance problem. For example, you may tell the tool that it takes forty-five days to install a new link and that users begin to see a performance problem at 60 percent utilization.

The relational database should have information that allows the tool to compute the average utilization of a link for each hour since it became operational. To gather this information, the tool would have to poll the interface on a network device that connects to the link at least once an hour and note the link's current utilization.

Once this information was in the relational database, the advanced tool could internally compute the trend of the actual utilization and project when the utilization will surpass your set threshold, as seen in Fig. 6.6. If this projected time is less than or equal to the time it takes to upgrade a link, the tool should warn you that it is time to start the upgrade. For instance, if the tool measures the utilization of a link at 23 percent and notices that if the utilization continues to increase at its current rate, it will surpass the 60 percent threshold in forty-five days, it should warn you. It may do this by sending an electronic mail message or bringing up a message on the network management system.

The advanced tool could save you significant amounts of time while assisting you in drawing conclusions about areas on the network that could experience unacceptable performance. (Note that this tool potentially can

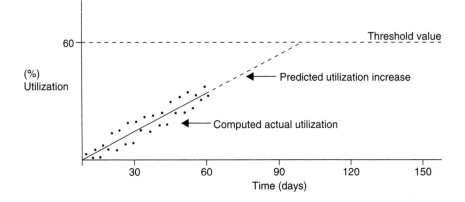

Figure 6.6 The current actual utilization trend shows that the link utilization will surpass the 60 percent threshold. The tool should warn the network engineer in enough time to allow the upgrade of the link to be performed before users see a performance problem.

consume large quantities of storage. You would want to decide how much historical information to save and provide the necessary space for it.)

In another example, suppose that you receive input that users transferring data from the computer *Mars* to the computer *Venus* have been encountering slow performance over the past week. Figure 6.7 shows the applicable network configuration. You could have the tool analyze the portion of the network that interconnects *Mars* and *Venus*. Let's say that the analysis reveals that the error rate on a link connecting two remote bridges on the path between the two computers has been steadily increasing. This rate has increased enough to warrant examination but not enough to trigger a threshold alarm. The advanced tool could produce a line graph to show this error rate progression, thus enabling you to call the circuit vendor and report the problem with less time wasted than if you had not had the tool.

The analysis done by the advanced tool is not typical of network management applications available today. The ability to gather the data does exist, but automatic analysis of the data as described here will often require the network engineer to develop network management applications or database queries.

Simulating the Network

The advanced tool should also help you analyze future performance and determine what configuration can produce the greatest performance. This could be done through network simulation, with the tool taking input data from

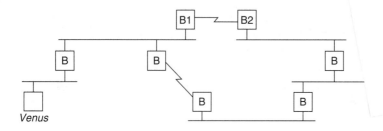

Figure 6.7 The advanced tool quickly analyzes the problem: an increasing error rate on the link between B1 and B2.

the running network or simulation and making predictions about users' perceptions of the network's performance.

The most difficult part of producing an adequate network simulation is building the network model. The model defines how the simulation should calculate each component of the network and how it should react to the simulation criteria. Essentially, the model is a set of rules the simulation needs to follow.

A few companies produce network simulation tools for complex data networks. The piece that every tool needs is the ability to generate a proper model. The information the advanced tool has in the database management system could help build the simulation model, which in turn would produce a more accurate network simulation. However, using the products available today, the network engineer would use the more complex tool to gather information and then manually feed the result of this analysis to the simulation piece of the advanced tool.

Predicting Response Time, Rejection Rates, and Availability

Given sufficient input, the tool should also be able to simulate traffic and show probable response times, rejection rates, and availability, thus helping you to purchase the proper network devices and allocate the correct bandwidth. This feature can be particularly useful when you are building a data network; it can help you ensure that the network performs optimally and possibly avoid future problems.

For example, suppose that a new site wishes to connect to a network. The users expect a response time of less than half a second, nearly zero rejection rate, and 100 percent availability for the connection between their site and a remote sales office. Using the advanced tool, you could model various links from the new site, using different speed links, and then prepare the model with the appropriate number of network devices and hosts.

This part of the advanced tool uses network simulation. Given a good network simulation model, predicting response time, rejection rates, and availability could be accomplished. Of course, this functionality has the same number of caveats as the network simulation component. Today network engineers have to produce such a tool themselves, as not many network management applications of this nature exist.

6.4 REPORTING PERFORMANCE INFORMATION

Many methods are available for reporting performance data. The most common format is a text report, which can be displayed on nearly any computer and can be easily printed, typically showing the utilization and error rates for network devices, as shown in Table 6.1. Although such a report is useful for obtaining performance management information for network devices, generating a similar report for network links is also worthwhile, as shown in Table 6.2.

A text report can contain valuable information. But since it can also be beneficial to represent performance management information in a graph, ideally the software would be able to turn text reports into graphs.

The bitmapped display found on network management systems provides another method for graphical representation of the data. Many imaginative methods exist for reporting performance management information in such a display. For example, you could set up the display so that as the utilization of a link increases, its picture appears thicker or changes color on the network map when crossing a threshold. The picture for a network link experiencing errors could flash; that for a network link experiencing a large error rate could be represented by a broken line.

The bitmapped display offers the same advantages for network devices. For example, as devices increase in utilization, their picture on the network map could grow larger; that for a device with excessive utilization could ap-

Table 6.1 Report for May 1994

	% Utilization		% Errors	
Network device	*Average*	*Peak*	*Average*	*Peak*
Dallas-GW	6	23	1	1
Phoenix-Bridge	12	13	4	5
New York-GW	23	56	8	12
Houston-GW	42	78	12	22
New Jersey-Bridge	3	10	0	0
Corp-HUB	12	54	1	3

Table 6.2 Report for May 1994

Network link	% Utilization		% Errors	
	Average	Peak	Average	Peak
Dallas-Houston	4	8	0	1
New York-New Jersey	22	64	3	14
Corp-Seattle	56	69	12	62
Corp-Houston	56	83	2	5
Phoenix-Houston	12	21	0	0

pear to perspire; and that representing a network device that has seen an increase in error rate could develop a crack. By taking advantage of the bitmapped display, you could tell at a glance the general performance of the network links and devices.

SUMMARY

Performance management involves ensuring that the data network remains accessible so users can utilize it efficiently. Performance management accomplishes this by monitoring the utilization of network devices and their associated links and ensuring that the capacity of devices and links is not overtaxed to the extent of adversely impacting performance.

This form of network management consists of the following four steps: (1) collecting data on current utilization of network devices and links, (2) analyzing relevant data to discern high utilization trends, (3) setting utilization thresholds, and (4) using network simulation to determine how the network can be altered to maximize performance. Performance management is beneficial in that it helps prevent network overcrowding and inaccessibility and thus aids in providing a consistent level of service to users. For the engineer, it provides the means to collect and analyze data on performance, to set utilization thresholds, and to arrange for warning messages when thresholds are near or at capacity. It also assists the engineer in planning for future capacity.

The engineer can use a number of tools for accomplishing performance management on a network management system. A simple tool can monitor the real-time performance of network devices and produce graphs for engineer review. A more complex tool can capture performance management data in a database and present it in the form of graphs for later review. It also provides the means of setting thresholds to help monitor the network and allows the setting of alarms based on those thresholds. An advanced tool for performance management would, in addition, offer the advantage of allowing historical analysis and the means to perform network simulation.

Various methods for reporting performance information are available. Although text reports are the most common way to format these reports, representing the data in either a graphical format or on a bitmapped display also can be of great help to the network engineer.

FOR FURTHER STUDY

Daigle, A., *Queuing Theory for Telecommunications*, Reading, MA: Addison-Wesley, 1990.

Fortier, P., and Desrochers, G., *Modeling and Analysis of Local Area Networks*, Boca Raton, CRC Press, FL: 1990.

Greiner, R., and Metes, G., *Enterprise Networking*, Maynard, MA: Digital Press, 1992.

Stevens, R., *TCP/IP Illustrated*, Volume 1, Reading, MA: Addison-Wesley, 1994.

Chapter 7

Accounting Management

In This Chapter:

Chris knew that this day would come. Since Chris has helped make MegaNet *a valuable resource for the company, the company now wants to institute network billing to account for the usage of the network by the various departments. The money being billed would just be internal "funny money," a transfer of funds from one department to Chris's department. The idea was that the other departments would offset the money Chris's department was spending on the implementation and support of* MegaNet. *To Chris, this meant bribes, blood feuds, and conspiracies—obviously, something far more political than technical. But in fact the technical aspects of doing network billing are not trivial. A small smile crept across Chris's face—maybe escaping into the technical side of this argument could mean avoiding the politics. . . .*

Accounting management involves measuring the usage of network resources by users in order to establish metrics, check quotas, determine costs, and bill users. Accounting management involves the following process:

- Gathering data about the utilization of network resources

- Setting usage quotas using metrics

- Billing users for their use of the network

Accounting management is the process of gathering network statistics to help the network engineer make decisions about the allocation of network resources. These numbers are useful in managing system resources, such as disk space, processing power, and doing backup storage, even though these are not necessarily a part of network management.

In this chapter we first examine the benefits of accounting management and next the steps involved in achieving it. We include a detailed discussion of network billing and then describe three accounting management tools. Last, we examine methods for reporting accounting information.

7.1 BENEFITS OF THE ACCOUNTING MANAGEMENT PROCESS

Accounting management enables the engineer to measure and report accounting information based on individual and group users and then use the data to bill those users, allocate resources, and compute the cost, by user group, of transmitting data across the network. Accounting management also increases the engineer's understanding of user utilization of network resources, which can help in the creation of a more productive network.

Billing users is essential for recovering expenses involved in building and maintaining the data network. Most organizations need to set up some form of chargeback accounting to help recover the cost of installing, operating, and maintaining the data network. Accounting management can provide for this chargeback and, coupled with billing policy, help provide for fair distribution of these costs. It can also assist in budget and personnel planning. Often an organization views these vital aspects of accounting management as the most important, since they allow for cost recovery of the network infrastructure.

By examining metrics and quotas, you can ensure that each user has sufficient resources to accomplish required tasks. You also could use these statistics to track the usage of various networked resources, such as application servers, compute servers, file servers, and print servers. For example, a documentation group may use the network to access a desktop publishing system on an application server at a remote site. Using accounting management information, you find that the majority of the network traffic is the documentation group accessing this application server. This may or may not be a resource issue for the network, but accounting management provides the information that allows you to make an informed decision about whether the documentation group warrants its own application server.

In a traditional network environment that relies on modem connections to a central host, accounting management can help you allocate time in a time-share situation for a group of terminals, as illustrated in Figure 7.1. Certain users might have priority use on the terminals. Accounting management can assist in your determination of whether these users use the terminals a large percentage of the time or whether the priority scheme needs modification.

The use of accounting management is helpful for understanding the behavior of users on the data network and may allow a network engineer to influence their behavior to make more optimal use of network resources. For example, a network site may consist of many distributed personal computer file servers, which contribute multiple functions on the network, ranging from print spoolers to database servers. On *MegaNet* a file server called *Hercules* contains important stock market information in a database. Suppose that a user of this file server decides to back up his or her entire personal computer 40-megabyte disk onto *Hercules*. The user starts the backup and then leaves the office for the night. After the backup procedure finishes, only one megabyte of storage remains on *Hercules*. Early the next morning, *Hercules* executes a program that gathers important stock information from another server; however, while downloading this data, *Hercules'* disk becomes full and the transfer halts.

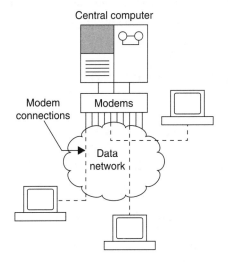

Figure 7.1 Accounting management helps keep track of which users and groups access the terminals with modem connections to the central computer. This information can help the network engineer make decisions about the allocation of network resources.

A few hours later when people attempt to retrieve the stock information, they receive an error message. In investigating the problem, you examine the accounting management statistics for *Hercules* and notice that a user downloaded a number of files that took a long period during the night. You now have some options, depending on your own network operational procedures. You may elect to contact the user or forward your information to the system administrator of *Hercules* for appropriate action.

Because networking technology is changing rapidly, accounting management techniques are also used to determine where network resources are allocated and the cost-effectiveness of different technologies. Consider an organization that knows the operating cost of its wide area data network, which uses dedicated data circuits leased on a monthly basis from a circuit provider. Since these recurring lease costs represent a large portion of the organization's monthly budget for the wide area network, the use of the most cost-effective technology is always an issue.

Using these recurring costs only as a base, and given the amount of data the network transports in a month, the organization can calculate the amount of money it costs to transport a byte of data over the wide area network. Since the organization wants to transport the most data possible for each dollar it spends in recurring costs, the network engineers may decide to use a new wide area technology, such as Frame Relay, or ATM. After installation of the new wide area network, the organization can recompute the cost-effectiveness of the network. Accounting management has thus helped the organization make a decision on a technology option.

7.2 ACCOMPLISHING ACCOUNTING MANAGEMENT

Accounting management consists of the following steps:

1. Gathering data about the utilization of network resources

2. Using metrics to help set usage quotas

3. Billing users for their network use

Gathering Data About Network Utilization

To obtain information about metrics and quotas, you might find that you need to gather accounting management data infrequently, such as once or twice daily. You might determine that you need to retrieve billing data more often, but if network devices can store a sufficient amount of activity data, periodic retrieval of data might suffice. If a device supports a common network management protocol, such as SNMPv1, the counters can hold values up to $2^{32} - 1$ (4,294,967,296).

As we will see later in this chapter, the information you will want to gather from network devices could include the number of total transactions or the total number of bytes or packets sent and received. You can often gather this information by querying activity logs on individual hosts or gathering traffic counters off network devices, such as bridges, switches, or routers.

Using Metrics and Setting Quotas

Metrics can assist you in learning to what extent users employ network resources. For example, a metric can reveal the number of connections made to a terminal server, the number of transactions made across the data network with a particular database, or the total login time by a user to a supercomputer. As part of utilizing accounting management, you would want to decide which network resources to measure and then begin collecting metrics about their use.

Some work on using metrics and setting quotas has been done. Request for Comments (RFC)[1] 1272, titled "Internet Accounting: Background," focuses on the background information required for defining services to be metered and usage reporting. This document also presents the dominant factors for and against the accounting process. The general accounting model presented in RFC 1272 defines the types of information necessary at various layers of a protocol stack for usage accounting.

Metrics work with quotas to help ensure that each user gets a "fair share" of network resources. You might elect to set up quotas and then penalize users for exceeding those quotas, for instance, by denying them use of the network resource in question. Another common penalty is to increase the bill of a user or group exceeding its quota.

Commonly users access a large computer with a database of information through a data network. The company that has the database might then charge the user for this access. In one section of *MegaNet* a group maintains a large online law library; the network setup for this example is shown in Figure 7.2. Users pay an access fee and for dialup connections to the library. Each participant on the network is allowed to use the library for ten hours a week. Although this might seem like a short amount of time, users log in, search the library for data, download pages of information and then log out. The connection time is used searching for data and transferring information, and casual perusal of the information is done off line.

---

[1] RFCs are a numbered progression of papers that contain many ideas and concepts initiated by the networking community. Many RFCs have gone on to become network protocol standards.

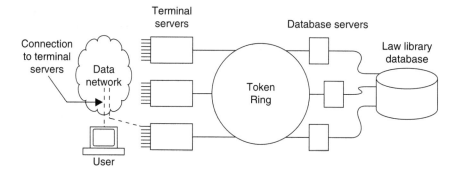

Figure 7.2 Users access the law library database through modem connections to terminal servers.

The organization offering the service has determined that the metric of ten hours is reasonable for most users. A user exceeding this quota will pay a larger monthly fee, based on how much additional time is used.

If you are the network engineer who helps run this service for *MegaNet*, you would want to monitor the users who connect to the modems. Terminal servers would then connect the modems to the main network, where the database machines reside. You could query the terminal servers on an hourly basis to learn who has connected and for what duration. You could then determine the large users of the database and compute the average connection time per user and the time period during which the highest volume of calls is received. If the terminal servers who connected to them logged on to a file on the network management system, you may only need to write a program to parse the log and extract those users. Perhaps an optimal way to do this would be to write a program to extract information from the activity log and put it into the network management system database. Then you could use SQL to check quotas and generate activity reports.

Billing Users

Usually you will want to collect billing data regularly. Most network devices have statistical counters that enable you to poll the device for information relatively infrequently and then note the changes since the last poll. To help you accomplish this, a network device could keep an accounting table that records source/destination address pairs in conjunction with the number of transactions, packets, or bytes sent between them.

Users often are billed based on one of the following scenarios: one-time installation fee and monthly fees or fee based on amount of network resources consumed.

One-Time Installation Fee and Monthly Fees

Under this scenario the user is billed for the installation of the network connection and then a standard fee for each month of use. Accounting management is not necessary for billing, because no information from the network is required. Although this is the easiest system to implement, it can become difficult to justify why one user who continually utilizes the network is billed the same amount as the casual user.

Fee Based on Amount of Network Resources Consumed

Some organizations use this technique in conjunction with charging small installation and monthly fees. Implementing this technique requires statistics on user network utilization. The following criteria, used individually or in combination, could be measured to determine network resource usage: total number of transactions, total packets, and total bytes. Measurement of total packets or total bytes could be based on either user input to the network or user output from the network.

By counting the total number of transactions per user, an organization can measure several criteria, including the number logins to a compute server, connections made from a terminal cluster controller, electronic mail messages sent, remote login sessions established, and so forth. An example of this billing design is shown in Figure 7.3.

Although this design is relatively easy to implement, each transaction results in the same amount charged, regardless of the time or network resources used. Thus if one user makes a single transaction that sends 500 megabytes of information, that user is billed the same as one who sends a 100-byte mail message. Many users probably would object to such a billing strategy.

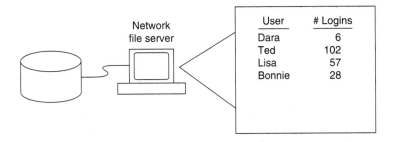

Figure 7.3 This billing model charges users based on the number of logins to a compute server. Each login denotes a use of network resources.

Another method is to count the total number of packets, thus reflecting network usage. Every time a user sends or receives a packet, the bill increases. The drawback of this method is that the bill for a given number of packets is the same, regardless of the amount of information sent or received.

For example, one user might send small packets for interactive traffic that do not burden the network devices or links. But another user might initiate a file transfer that relies on large packets. If both the interactive traffic and the file transfer need 1000 packets to complete, their bills would match. However, that's not the way it works: The file transfer with its larger packets will use more network resources and yet be billed the same as the interactive traffic, which uses fewer resources.

The disadvantages of the first two methods can be avoided by billing total bytes used; the consumer is billed according to the amount of network resources used. Keep in mind that network resources, such as bandwidth, are consumed byte by byte (or bit by bit), not necessarily on a per packet basis. The next decision to make is whether to bill total bytes sent or received.

For network applications that use a reliable transport-layer protocol, such as the TCP (Transmission Control Protocol) or Novell's SPX (Stream Packet eXchange), the receipt of data packets is confirmed by the destination with acknowledgment packets. For these applications, counting only the bytes in the data packets makes sense, since they are typically the larger packets that consume more network resources. Applications that do not use a reliable transport layer require you to count only the bytes in a single direction across the network.

Many environments have a combination of applications that use a reliable transport layer and those that do not. Most organizations choose to bill on bytes received from the network, bytes sent to the network, or some combination of both schemes. There are clear advantages to each of these policies, along with their associated flaws.

Billing on bytes sent to the data network intuitively makes sense. When a user sends something across the network, the bill should increase. Unfortunately, in the client/server model of networking prevalent today, this billing structure has some serious flaws. Billing on output tends to discourage users from offering services from their own servers. To illustrate, suppose that one user on the network has a file server that contains important data for a research project. Many users connect to the file server and download vast amounts of information daily. Those who gather information send small packets to the servers, requesting information. The file server then transfers large amounts of data back to the user, as illustrated in Figure 7.4. If billing is based on output bytes, the user offering the information will receive a large bill, which in turn causes the user who runs the file server to bill its users in an effort to recover expenses.

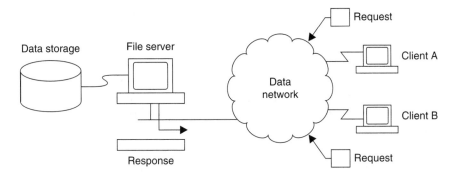

Figure 7.4 The file server receives small requests from the clients and returns large responses. If bytes sent to the network are billed, the group that runs the file service gets a large bill.

Billing on the basis of bytes received from the data network eliminates this problem. There is no bill for sending large amounts of data to the network, only for receiving it.

In a classic network setup in which billing on bytes received is appropriate, consider a the main data center on *Meganet*. At this site is an IBM mainframe computer named *Hulk*. Users connect to *Hulk* through a front-end processor (such as an IBM 3745 front-end processor), which connects to a series of cluster controllers with terminals, such as IBM 3174-type controllers, scattered throughout various token rings on *Meganet*. In this particular setup smaller packets are sent from the terminals to *Hulk*; larger dumps of information are received back from *Hulk* to the terminal.

Users in many network environments can configure a host to allow access to certain files without explicit permission being required. On IP (Internet Protocol) networks one method to accomplish this is through anonymous FTP (File Transfer Protocol). For Appletalk networks the same effect is achieved through sharing of folders. On a Novell file server a directory can be left unsecured for clients to deposit or retrieve data. Most of these services are designed to establish a central location for users to pick up documents and applications. By billing bytes received from the network, a company can help ensure that a user offering a service does not automatically receive a large bill.

Billing bytes received does have some flaws. First, many network protocols send acknowledgments from the destination to the source, resulting in users who offer services to the network receiving unrequested bytes of data from the network. Fortunately, acknowledgment packets are usually quite small. These bytes could be ignored, however, by using statistics on network devices that can compute the total number of acknowledgments seen. Also, the organization that computes the bills can recognize the users who offer services to the network and possibly offer them a discount on their bills.

Another problem with billing based on bytes received is that unsolicited network data, such as electronic mail, adds to the user's bill. This flaw can perhaps be overlooked because many users send and receive mail on the same order of magnitude. This might not be the case, however, when a user is on a mailing list and receives many mail messages. Since the user is on the mailing list for a reason, the bill should reflect the receipt of this data as a result of this network service. Unfortunately, the growth of the Internet has led to a proportional growth in the incidence of unsolicited "Junk e-mail," which could penalize users on a bytes-received billing scheme.

Still another possible imperfection in this billing method arises from each user receiving data from the network as the organization monitors it for management reasons, as illustrated in Figure 7.5. However, much of this data will be sent to the user regularly, in a pattern, and for a given time period—queries might come once a day or hour or every few minutes. It's possible to compute how many queries are sent typically in the billing period and how many bytes they comprise; if the organization bills monthly, you easily could compute the number of queries on average sent in a given month (for example, one 500-byte query sent every five minutes) and subtract these bytes from each bill. In theory, all other bytes sent for management reasons should occur while an engineer is troubleshooting network problems, which is a service to the user.

As we have seen, implementing a resource-based billing scheme requires the use of accounting management to gather the needed statistics. This then requires the organization to get the resource information, process it, and produce the bills based on the resources consumed. Although this process may

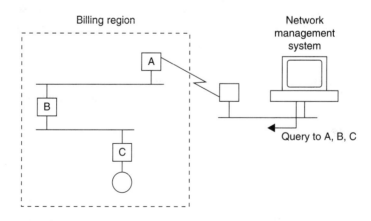

Figure 7.5 Queries from the network management system can increase the number of bytes a billing region receives, thereby adding to the total bill.

be complex on today's networks, it may be even more difficult on the virtual LANs of tomorrow.

As we have seen in previous chapters, a virtual LAN is a network technology that logically connects LAN devices at different physical locations to form one logical LAN, as shown in Figure 7.6. In reality the physical devices may be connected across a high-speed network (such as FDDI or ATM) or attached to the same network device. Today many vendors have virtual LAN software in their devices for forming multiple virtual LANs in a single network device.

The research and development group on *MegaNet* wants to use virtual LAN technology to connect various users across an ATM backbone. This setup will enable multiple users who are in distant locations to logically be connected to the same LAN segment. To help in accounting management, the ATM switch devices being deployed must be able to account for the traffic sent and received by each virtual LAN segment. Although this technology is still quite new and is in the process of being standardized, one method being discussed to set up virtual LANs involves using a centrally administered server to perform virtual LAN administration. If the research and development department of *MegaNet* deploys such a scheme, it may be necessary to gather the virtual LAN topology from the central server and then gather the traffic statistics from the associated ATM switches.

IPng (Internet Protocol next generation) is being developed by the internetwork community as a network-layer protocol to replace IP. Accounting management is being considered in the form of RFC 1672, "Accounting Requirements for IPng." This RFC recommends that each IPng packet contain an accounting tag, to identify the source party of the packet and potentially more information about the higher-level application data within the packet. As yet, few, if any, IPng protocol stack implementations are available in the marketplace.

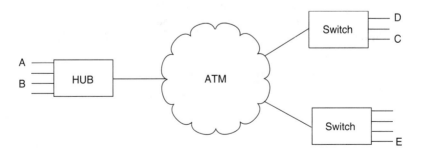

Figure 7.6 Virtual LAN technology makes it possible for Stations A, B, C, D, and E to belong to the same LAN even though they are at separate physical locations.

7.3 ACCOUNTING MANAGEMENT ON A NETWORK MANAGEMENT SYSTEM

How well accounting management accomplishes its three functions depends on the level of tool available to the engineer. We next examine three tools that can be used to achieve this facet of network management.

A Simple Tool

The simple tool should enable you to monitor for any metric that exceeds a quota. The metric data would be stored in the relational database that is part of the network management system architecture; the metric would be configurable by the engineer. To determine whether quotas have been passed, you would use an SQL query, and the tool would show the results of the query. Alternatively, you could use database technology to provide automatically generated reports when quotas are exceeded.

For example, if you need to monitor the number of users on an application server, you could instruct the simple tool to query the application server once every hour, determine the number of users, and then place the data into the relational database. Next, you could instruct the simple tool to look in the relational database by using the following SQL statement:

```
SELECT time, number-users FROM system-statistics
```

The simple tool then would show, hourly, the number of users using the application server. The results of this SQL query are shown in Table 7.1. Because the metric data would be stored in the relational database, these statistics could be displayed and used to establish metrics and quotas for the maximum number of users logged on to this application server.

Similarly, you might want to know when a user has been connected to the stock information file server, *Hercules,* for more than three hours. You could have the tool monitor this statistic by instructing it to query *Hercules* every fifteen min-

Table 7.1 Results from an SQL Query

Time	Number of Users
8:00 A.M.	6
9:00 A.M.	21
10:00 A.M.	22
11:00 A.M.	20
12:00 P.M.	8

utes for all users currently using the file server. The simple tool would then store this information in the relational database. The following SQL query would produce the necessary accounting information from the database user-logins table:

```
SELECT user, hours-connected FROM user-logins WHERE hours-
connected > 3
```

Accordingly, the tool would give you the user's name and the number of hours connected, if more than three, as illustrated in Table 7.2.

One drawback of the simple tool is that you must initiate the SQL queries. There are tools to set up queries to occur at regular intervals by the database, but it would be beneficial to have a method whereby the database generates a report only when a quota is exceeded. This may be useful for both security management (such as finding unsuccessful login attempts) and accounting management (finding when a quota has been surpassed). Therefore many databases can set up triggers that can invoke an action based on the result of an SQL query. The simple tool will have the ability to set up triggers in the database if you specify that you wish to know when a quota is exceeded.

The simple tool relies on database technology. The database must allow for ad-hoc SQL queries, formatting of results, and triggers. These pieces of functionality exist in popular database products from Oracle, Sybase, and Ingres, for example. If the network management system uses such a database, producing the simple tool should be relatively straightforward.

A More Complex Tool

A more complex tool should enable you to perform network billing. Implementing a billing process on a data network can be extremely difficult and time consuming. The complex tool should take as input the topology of the data network and the billing domains and then compute the necessary bills for users.

Table 7.2 Accounting Information Produced from the Database User-logins Table

Remote User	Hours Connected
Norm	3.25
Cliff	4.50
Frazier	3.25
Woody	5.30
Paul	4.75

The complex tool would need data from both the network management system and the engineer to perform its functions. It should be able to obtain the network topology from the network management system relational database. Further, because the hierarchical map of the network management system is in the database, this information also would be available to the tool. Next, the tool must be able to understand how the logical topology of the network is broken up into billing domains, a step that would require engineer input.

One way to accomplish this task is for you to use the mouse on the network management system to denote a billing region on the network map. To do this, you would place the mouse on the map and size a rectangle to surround a group of network devices, hosts, and links. For example, a group to be billed has hosts that reside behind a single network device. The tool would compute this fact and poll the single network device for the necessary statistics.

Going a step further, the tool would be able to determine where to poll for billing information. Consider a network that consists of many hosts on a LAN, as in Figure 7.7. Each of these hosts is connected to the LAN by a twisted-pair (10baseT) concentrator. Using the network map, you would select a region that denotes a single floor of an office building, where all the hosts happen to connect to one of two concentrators. Because all the hosts connect to the concentrators, the tool could easily deduce that polling the concentrators is the correct behavior.

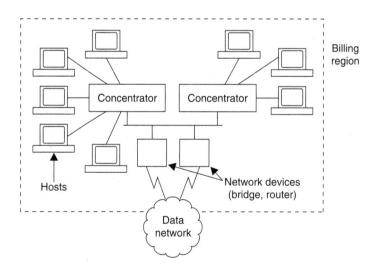

Figure 7.7 All the hosts in this billing region connect to one of two 10baseT concentrators. The more complex tool discovers this and polls the concentrators for billing information.

However, suppose that you instructed the tool to produce billing information for a region that has three hosts: two on a single concentrator and the third on another. Now the tool should be able to figure out that the correct approach is to query each host individually for the necessary information.

Note that many networks contain redundant links, loops, and devices that operate only when another device has a fault. These redundancies can make it difficult for the tool to isolate which devices to query. If the tool encounters any such difficulty, it should query you.

To determine where to poll for accounting management data, the tool needs to produce a tree of network connectivity. By doing a breadth-first search of this connectivity tree (from the leaves upward), the tool can find the optimal place to send queries. If there is no intersection between the different devices to query, the tool can conclude to poll each individually. The tool can compute the tree of network connectivity by receiving input from many locations: the network management system topology information, the routing tables on a network device, or the spanning tree found in bridges. Each of these pieces of information is available to network engineers today. For example, in HP OpenView you can examine the topology database with the "ovtopodump" command. SunNet Manager provides a similar ability through its map files. Routing tables for the IP and other protocol are available in standard network management protocols, as are the spanning-tree components in a transparent bridge environment. Although this information is available, it would be up to the tool to process the data into a connectivity tree.

Once you have denoted a region of the network, the tool should ask for the following types of information:

1. Billing method

2. Pricing for the region

3. Polling frequency

At this point the billing process for the region would begin; that is, the billing data would be gathered and placed into the relational database, as shown in Flowchart 7.1.

An Advanced Tool

The advanced tool should further enhance the accounting management capabilities by forecasting the need for network resources. This forecasting ability can help you establish reasonable metrics and quotas. Another feature of the advanced tool would help users predict their network billing costs.

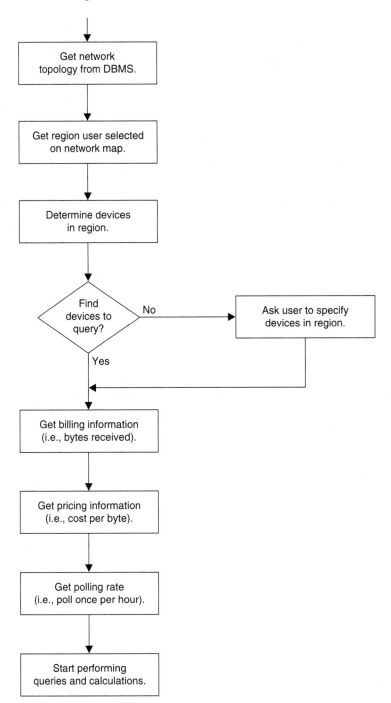

Flowchart 7.1   Flowchart for billing with the more complex tool.

Metric data and quotas can help you determine whether network resources are sufficient. Using the relational database allows the advanced tool to produce statistics about how often users have exceeded quotas over a specific time period. In addition, the advanced tool should be able to determine whether a trend on the network is going to cause a quota to be reached and thus alert you to upgrade the resource, add more equipment to the resource, change the quota, or whatever other action you determine might be required.

For example, users on a private LAN segment within *MegaNet* employ a pool of modems to dial public machines to retrieve information. It would be reasonable for these users to have limits on the length of time they can use a modem. Let's say that when you first set up the modem pool, you had established an arbitrary time limit of five hours for a single call, after which the modems disconnect the call. For many years this time limit has been adequate.

But recently this part of *MegaNet* entered into a joint development agreement with another organization. As part of this agreement, megabytes of information have had to be transferred between the two companies each night. At first, the transfers took only three hours, but with expansion of the development effort, the transaction will now exceed the time limit for use of a single modem. However, because you had installed the advanced tool, the transfers can continue without disruption—the tool had noted that connection time was approaching the quota and informed you so you could change the quota. In this scenario accounting management information led to a capacity redistribution decision.

The advanced tool also should be able to predict a network bill for users. To do this, the tool must be able to perform two steps: examine the relational database to determine any trend in bills for a particular user for past billing cycles and then take all data available for the current billing cycle and extrapolate it to the end of a particular billing cycle.

For example, if the manager of a user group asks you to predict the group's next network bill, you could input the data on the group into the tool, which would then search the billing information in the network management database and find all past records for the group. Suppose that these records show an increase of 5 percent for each of the last ten billing cycles. The tool next would check the information in the database for the current billing cycle. Extrapolating this information to the end of this cycle, the tool finds a 6 percent increase probable since the last billing cycle. This correlates closely to the 5 percent increases in the past. As output, the tool then would produce a bill for the requested billing cycle that includes a 6 percent increase over the last billing cycle.

However, suppose that the extrapolation of information did not correlate closely to the past billing fees. This could happen if the current billing cycle has just begun and the data sample does not reflect a full billing cycle or if the group has had an increase or decrease in network activity. In these cases the tool would need to output a prediction based on the historical data and then one derived from the current billing cycle.

The technology to produce the advanced tool exists. This tool uses data from a database and then extrapolates the information to help predict network quotas and network bills.

7.4 REPORTING ACCOUNTING INFORMATION

Accounting management information reports can be in the form of real-time messages and text reports. Real-time messages can inform you of the value of a certain metric; text reports can provide historical accounting and billing information.

For example, you could request the network management system to bring up a real-time message window showing a metric for a device, as seen in Figure 7.8. This message could show you the number of sessions being handled by the network device. This metric is important because the device performs protocol translation and can optimally support only a certain number of sessions.

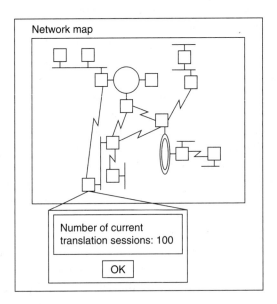

Figure 7.8 The screen of the network management system with a real-time accounting management message.

The system also must generate text reports of accounting management statistics. These reports, similar to the output of the simple tool, can be historical summaries of metrics or trend predictions of the future usage of a network resource. You can use this information to plan realistic quotas for the network resources.

Also important are reports to give to users about their network bills. These reports show the information used to derive the current bill and also predict the price of the next bill. Such a report might be similar to Table 7.3.

SUMMARY

Accounting management enables the network engineer to measure the usage of network resources. Data obtained from these efforts can be used to establish metrics, check and enforce quotas, determine costs, and bill users.

This form of network management offers several benefits. By using the data obtained, the engineer can accurately bill each user to recover developmental and maintenance costs associated with the network.

Accomplishing accounting management involves three steps: (1) gathering data about how users employ network resources, (2) using the data gathered to set and enforce usage quotas, and (3) billing users for their use of network resources.

As with the other forms of management, how well the engineer can achieve accounting management depends on the level of tool available. A simple tool should be able to monitor for metrics that exceed quotas and to report that data. The tool also should be able to store the metric data in the network management system relational database and calculate quotas, using a formula based on data from the database.

Table 7.3 Network Usage Bill: Marketing Group

Billing period: November 1992–December 1992
Number of total bytes received from network: 123 megabytes
Devices polled to determine above amount: MtkgHub1, MktgBridge

Price per megabyte:	$30.00
Current bill:	$3690.00
Bill last period:	$3240.00
Percent change:	14% INCREASE
Prediction for bill next period:	$4200.00
Prediction for percent change:	10% INCREASE

A more complex tool should enable the engineer to perform network billing and determine where to poll for billing information. An advanced tool should be able to forecast the need for network resources, which can help the engineer establish reasonable metrics and quotas, and to help users predict their network billing costs.

Methods for reporting accounting information include real-time status display and text reports. Real-time messages keep the engineer informed about the current value of a metric; text reports provide valuable historical accounting and billing information.

FOR FURTHER STUDY

Brownlee, N., RFC 1672, "Accounting Requirements for IPng," August 1994.

Jones, P., RFC 1346, "Resource Allocation, Control, and Accounting for the Use of Network Resources," June 1992.

Mills, C., Hirsh, D., and Ruth, G., RFC 1272, "Internet Accounting: Background," November 1991.

Rhodes, P., *Lan Operations*, Reading, MA: Addison-Wesley, 1991.

Terplan, K., *Communications Network Management*, 2nd ed., Englewood Cliffs, NJ: Prentice-Hall, 1992.

PART 2

Network Management
Protocols

Chapter 8

SNMP/SNMPv2: Network Management Protocols (I)

In This Chapter:

Chris had spent a good deal of time thinking about the functionality needed to manage **MegaNet**. *The applications necessary to provide for all areas of network management were either in place or at least being thought about. Progress, at last. One thing missing from the puzzle was exactly how to acquire the information from the varieties of network devices. It is definitely possible to write a program to grab the needed information from every device, but that program would have to be modified if the device interface changed. Also, the program would have to support each type of device on all of* **MegaNet**. *Reeling at this possibility and at the same time realizing that job security is nice to have, Chris decided to explore the use of a network management protocol to monitor and configure network devices.*

As we saw in previous chapters, effective network management depends on the network engineer's being able to monitor and control the data network. Without this information, the engineer would be forced to make network management decisions without the benefit of adequate qualitative or quantitative measurements.

In this chapter we introduce two network management protocols and review the development of this type of protocol. We also discuss the methods available for getting and setting information on a data network, without which accomplishing the goals of network management would be impossible. The material presented in this chapter should help network engineers to rate the various methods and to determine which is most suitable for their own data network.

8.1 HISTORY OF NETWORK MANAGEMENT PROTOCOLS

Until recently, engineers needed to learn a variety of methods in order to gather information from network devices. As new networking products were developed, their manufacturers installed proprietary methods for enabling data collection from their products; the result was that two devices having the same functionality but coming from different manufacturers could provide vastly different methods for data collection.

For example, suppose that *MegaNet* uses two types of DECnet routers to connect Digital minicomputers. The first type is produced by a company called *RouteMe*; the second by a company named *FastRoute*. Both types of routers allow access through a remote login facility. However, the method used to access the data differs significantly. To ask a *RouteMe* router about the number of interfaces and operating parameters, you would use a menu-driven system; to ask the *FastRoute* router, you would use three commands from a command line interface. Figure 8.1 shows examples of these two user interfaces.

In a heterogeneous network environment it can be slow and cumbersome to use such diverse query methods. Needing a consistent method to gather information about all the components on the data network, network engineers turned to generic but standard tools. However, although these tools were simpler to use than the many methods provided by the manufacturers, they were not designed specifically for network management and so had their drawbacks.

On Internet Protocol (IP) data networks, network engineers can use the Internet Control Message Protocol (ICMP) Echo and Echo Reply messages to gather limited information useful for network management. Originally intended for sending control message information between two network

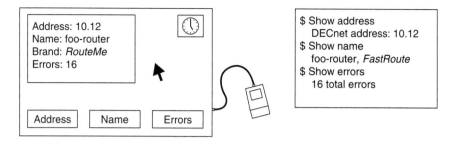

Figure 8.1 The same statistics displayed using a menu-driven interface and a command line interface.

devices, most ICMP messages are difficult for humans to interpret. However, the combination of ICMP Echo and Echo Reply messages, which exists on any device with the complete IP protocol suite, provides a quick method of checking the network connectivity to a remote device.

Using these messages, a host device on a network that receives an ICMP Echo must return an ICMP Echo Reply to the source host. A reply not received by the sending host can, but not always does, indicate a lack of network connectivity between the two hosts. An application called *ping* (Packet InterNet Groper) tests network connectivity to a remote device by sending an ICMP Echo to the device and then waiting for the ICMP Echo Reply. Figure 8.2 shows the messages sent and received by a host using the ping application.

Most implementations of ping also can tell the overall turnaround time (usually in milliseconds) between the Echo message sent and the Echo Reply received, as well as the percentage of lost ICMP Reply messages between the source and the destination. TCP/IP is not the only protocol suite with a tool like ping. The Echo/Echo Reply paradigm exists in several other protocols, such as Appletalk, Novell/IPX, Xerox XNS, and Banyan Vines.

This model has some drawbacks, however: unreliable delivery, need for polling, and limited information provided. Most Echo/Echo Reply packets directly use the network layer and are not guaranteed to be delivered by the transport layer. Thus the failure of an Echo to travel between two locations does not always mean a lack of connectivity. It might indicate that a network device dropped the Echo or Echo Reply because of a temporary lack of buffer space. Or the packet might have failed because of congestion on a data circuit at the time of transmission.

To find out current information using Echo/Echo Reply, you must continuously poll network devices. Performing this polling is a popular method of fault isolation, as it can be done quickly and easily and does not require any special privileges or additional hardware. A large percentage of lost Echo Replies could indicate a connectivity problem. However, this is the extent of

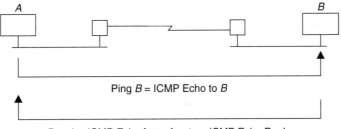

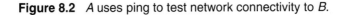

Receive ICMP Echo from *A*, return ICMP Echo Reply

Figure 8.2   *A* uses ping to test network connectivity to *B*.

the troubleshooting capability provided. The network engineer needs to rely on other methods to isolate and fix the problem. A protocol for network management should offer the ability to have devices send unsolicited messages to a management system. This may occur in addition to polling, but it is a more efficient method for gathering important network management information.

A primary reason for this deficiency is that Echo and Echo Reply messages were not written to provide much information. Hence the information yielded often is not enough on which to base firm network management decisions. For this purpose, you would be better off using a protocol written specifically for managing data networks, one that would provide more of the necessary information. To be most useful to the engineer, this protocol also should work across a wide spectrum of network devices.

Because of these drawbacks, it became apparent within the industry that a standard system was urgently needed. Consequently the networking community has been developing two divergent technologies designed specifically for network management. The first, the *Simple Network Management Protocol (SNMP)*, so far has proved to be quite successful. A second version of this protocol, *Simple Network Management Protocol version 2 (SNMPv2)*, is also beginning to impact the networking community. Both SNMP and SNMPv2 provide a means of obtaining information from or giving instructions to network devices, although neither offers direction in the use of the information gathered. Additionally, both conform to the OSI Reference Model. The OSI[1] (Open Systems Interconnection) Reference Model is a seven-layer network architectural model developed by the ISO and CCITT[2] (International Telephone and Telegraph Consultative Committee).

---

[1] OSI is a protocol suite for use on data networks.

[2] The CCITT is an international organization that defines standards and recommendations for the connection of telephone equipment.

8.2 DEVELOPMENT OF STANDARD PROTOCOLS

The examples and problems discussed in Section 8.1 don't do justice to the issues involved in managing a complex data network. It is unlikely that any data network would be built entirely from products provided by a single company. Eventually the need could arise for networking products, such as hubs, bridges, routers, and hosts, from many companies. Network engineers must plan for the change and growth of the network.

Network management protocols recently have emerged to provide a uniform way of accessing any network device made by any manufacturer for a standard set of values. Queries for network devices may include the following:

- Device name

- Software version in the device

- Number of interfaces in the device

- Number of packets per second on an interface of the device

Settable parameters for network devices may include the following:

- Device name

- A network interface address

- Operational status of a network interface

- Operational status of the device

Standardized network management protocols carry the additional benefit of providing a uniform appearance of the data sent and returned by a device.

Before going into any more detail about SNMP and SNMPv2, we have to take a quick detour into the background of how they developed and the players involved. The Internet Activities Board (IAB), which oversees the work in networking technology and protocols for the TCP/IP internetworking community, took on the task of coordinating work in selecting a standard network management protocol. The IAB comprises two subgroups: the Internet Engineering Task Force (IETF) and the Internet Research Task Force (IRTF). The IETF is chartered to identify problems and coordinate problem solving in the areas of Internet management, engineering, and operations. The IRTF is responsible for researching problems concerning the TCP/IP network community and the Internet.

Around 1988 development of three network management protocols was being pursued:

- High-level Entity Management System (HEMS)

- Simple Gateway Monitoring Protocol (SGMP)

- Common Management Information Protocol (CMIP) over TCP

A small war ensued over which one the IAB would recommend. RFC 1052 states the conclusions of the IAB about the future use of each protocol.

As a short-term solution, the IAB recommended the immediate implementation of SNMP, which was based on SGMP, for use as a common network management protocol with TCP/IP-based networks. The IETF was responsible for the implementation of SNMP. The IAB emphasized that further development of SNMP should be aimed at keeping the protocol simple and focused on the areas of fault management and configuration management. Today, however, many organizations use SNMP in all areas of network management.

For the long term, the IAB recommended that the Internet research community explore CMIS/CMIP as the basis for a network management protocol to satisfy future requirements. CMIS/CMIP was developed by the ISO with different goals from those of SNMP. SNMP was originally intended for use by IP devices only, whereas CMIS/CMIP was intended to be nonprotocol specific and for use in the management of all network devices.

When the IAB evaluated CMIS/CMIP, it considered an implementation of the protocol that uses TCP (Transmission Control Protocol) for transport. This combination of CMIS/CMIP over TCP became known as CMOT. Today CMOT is no longer being considered as a protocol for wide use.

The IAB and ISO are not the only organizations involved with the development of standard protocols. The CCITT and the IEEE[3] (Institute of Electrical and Electronic Engineers) also have worked toward the development of standard network management protocols. CMIS/CMIP, CMOT, and other network management protocols are discussed in detail in Chapter 9.

SNMPv2 was developed by members of the networking community in 1992 to help solve some of the deficiencies with SNMP. Some of the deficiencies with SNMP, as we will see later in this chapter, are that it was standardized only for IP networks and is relatively unsecured.

8.3 THE MANAGEMENT INFORMATION BASE

The *Management Information Base (MIB)* is a precise definition of the information accessible through a network management protocol. In RFC 1052, the IAB recommended that high priority be placed on defining an extended MIB

---

[3] The IEEE is a professional organization that defines network standards.

for use with SNMP and CMIS/CMIP, although this effort to make one MIB for both protocols is no longer realistic, because of the semantic differences between the two protocols.

Using a hierarchical, structured format, the MIB defines the network management information available from a device. Each device, to comply with the standard network management protocol, must use the format for displaying information that is defined by the MIB.

RFC 1065 describes the syntax and type of information available in the MIB for the management of TCP/IP networks. Entitled "Structure and Identification of Management Information for TCP/IP-based Internets (SMI)," this RFC defines simple rules for naming and creating types of information. Some of the types of information allowed by the SMI include a Gauge, an integer that may increase or decrease, and TimeTicks, which counts time in hundredths of seconds (see Table 8.1). RFC 1065 later was adopted by the IAB as a full standard in RFC 1155.

Using the rules of the SMI, RFC 1066 presented the first version of the MIB for use with the TCP/IP protocol suite. This standard, now known as MIB-I, explains and defines the exact information base needed for monitoring and controlling TCP/IP-based internets. RFC 1066 was accepted by the IAB as a full standard in RFC 1156.

RFC 1158 proposed a second MIB, MIB-II, for use with the TCP/IP protocol suite. This proposal, formalized as a standard and approved by the IAB in RFC 1213, extends the information base defined in MIB-I by expanding the set of objects defined in the MIB.

To facilitate the migration of vendor-specific protocols to a standard management protocol, RFC 1156 allows for expansion of the MIB for vendor-specific

Table 8.1   The Data Types Defined by RFC 1155 (SMI)

Defined Type	*Meaning*
NetworkAddress	An address from one of possibly several protocol families. Currently only IP is present.
IpAddress	32-bit IP address
Counter	Nonnegative integer which increases monotomically from 0 to a maximum value of $2^{32} - 1$.
Gauge	Nonnegative integer which may increase or decrease and has a maximum value of $2^{32} - 1$.
TimeTicks	Nonnegative integer which counts time in hundreths of a second since some point in time.
Opaque	Arbitrary syntax; used for text data.

enhancements. For example, suppose that a company wants to make the CPU utilization of its Ethernet bridge available through a network management protocol. MIB-II does not contain an object that corresponds to CPU utilization. However, since vendor-specific enhancements within the MIB are allowed, the Ethernet bridge vendor can define a new object for CPU utilization. This ability to create new objects using the same standard SMI makes available information other than that in MIB-II. Several companies have extended MIB-II and developed vendor-specific MIBs that contain more objects than in MIB-II. Many vendor-specific MIBs exist today, as most network devices have software agents that support MIB-II and their own private extensions.

An effort is under way within the networking community to produce MIBs that do not directly relate to TCP/IP environments. Each MIB would focus on a specific technology, such as FDDI, Token Ring, Ethernet, or bridging. This significant development would move the MIB from being a general source of data to defining information specific to a media type or device. Some of the proposed MIBs under development and their corresponding RFC numbers are summarized in Table 8.2.

ASN.1 Syntax

A subset of the ISO Abstract Syntax Notation One (ISO ASN.1) defines the syntax for the MIB. Each MIB uses the tree architecture defined in ASN.1 to organize all available information. Each piece of information in the tree is a *labeled node*. Each labeled node contains an object identifier and a short text description. The *object identifier* (OID) is a series of integers, separated by periods, to name the node and denote the exact traversal of the ASN.1 tree. The *short text description* describes the labeled node.

A labeled node can have subtrees containing other labeled nodes. Each labeled node in a subtree is numbered in ascending order. This *lexigraphical ordering* provides a scheme for numbering all of the objects in the MIB tree.

If the labeled node has no subtrees, or *leaf nodes*, it contains a value and is known as an *object*. Leaf nodes are also numbered in ascending order.

Table 8.2   Some Proposed MIBs

MIB Name	Proposed Standard
IEEE 802.5 Token Ring Interface Type MIB	RFC 1743
Remote Network Monitoring MIB (RMON)	RFC 1757
FDDI Interface Type MIB	RFC 1512
Bridge MIB	RFC 1493

Figure 8.3 shows a sample MIB tree with the corresponding ASN.1 numbers; the lexigraphical order of the sample MIB tree is: 1, 1.1, 1.1.1, 1.2, 1.2.1, 1.2.1.1, 1.2.2, 2. The lexigraphical ordering of the MIB tree allows you to discover, without prior knowledge of its structure, all of the object identifiers that a given network device can support.

Traversal of the MIB Tree

The root node of the MIB tree doesn't have a name or number but does have three subtrees, as follows:

- ccitt (0), administered by the CCITT

- iso (1), administered by the ISO

- joint-iso-ccitt (2), jointly administered by ISO and CCITT

The syntax, such as *ccitt (0)*, denotes that a labeled node named ccitt has object identifier number 0 at this level of the MIB tree.

In addition, several other subtrees exist under the iso(1) node, including the ISO-defined subtree for other organizations, org(3). Under the org(3) subtree, a particular node of interest is the one used by the U.S. Department of

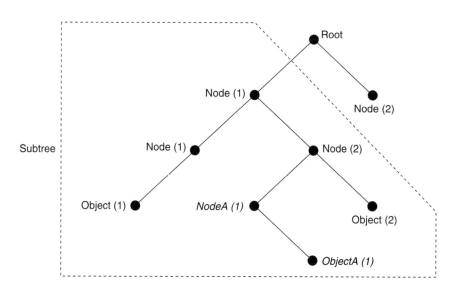

Figure 8.3 In this sample ASN.1 tree, *objectA* can be referenced by the OID as 1.2.1.1 or {*nodeA 1*}.

Defense (DOD): dod(6). All the information gathered from devices communicating by means of the DOD protocols, such as TCP/IP, resides in the subtree that has the complete object identifier of 1.3.6.1. This object identifier is known as internet. The text description for this identifier is {iso org(3) dod(6), 1}. Figure 8.4 shows the structure of the top of the MIB tree.

Four defined subtrees are under the internet object identifier, as follows:

- directory (1)

- mgmt (2)

- experimental (3)

- private (4)

In keeping with the accepted syntax, the text description for the directory node is {internet 1}, the mgmt node is {internet 2}, the experimental node is {internet 3}, and the private node is {internet 4}.

Directory (1) Subtree

The directory (1) subtree is reserved for future use. This subtree will contain information about the OSI directory service (X.500).

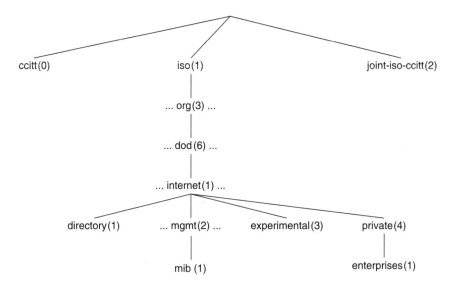

Figure 8.4 The structure of the top of the MIB tree.

Mgmt (2) Subtree

Figure 8.5 shows the structure of the mgmt (2) subtree and includes some of the objects within each category. The mgmt (2) subtree is intended for the assignment of management information for DOD protocols. Today the objects in this subtree are the most widely implemented. MIB-I (RFC 1156), originally assigned the object identifier 1.3.6.1.2.1, or {mib 1}, has been superseded by MIB-II (RFC 1213). MIB-II has retained the same object identifier.

Beneath the mgmt (2) subtree are the objects used to obtain specific information from the network devices. These objects are broken down into the eleven categories shown in Table 8.3.

The address translation (3) category maps IP addresses to Ethernet addresses. However, the MIB is intended to specify management information for protocols other than IP (such as the OSI network protocols). RFC 1213 removed this category in favor of letting the translation occur in each protocol-specific subtree. The cmot (9) category, discussed in Section 8.6, exists only for historical reasons.

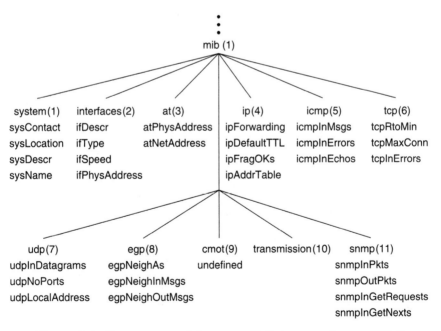

Figure 8.5 The structure of the mgmt (2) Subtree and some MIB-II objects.

Table 8.3 Categories of Mgmt (2) Subtree

Category	Information
system (1)	Network device operating system
interfaces (2)	Network interface specific
address translation (3)	Address mappings
ip (4)	Internet Protocol specific
icmp (5)	ICMP specific
tcp (6)	Transmission Protocol specific
udp (7)	User Datagram Protocol specific
egp (8)	Exterior Gateway Protocol specific
cmot (9)	Common Management Information Services on TCP specific
transmission (10)	Transmission Media specific
snmp (11)	SNMP specific

Experimental (3) Subtree

Experimental protocols and MIB development intended to enter the standards track use the third subtree, experimental (3). All objects under this DOD subtree have object identifiers that begin with the integer 1.3.6.1.3. An experimental new MIB might be assigned the number 10, which correlates to the object identifier {experimental 10}.

Private (4) Subtree

The private (4) subtree is used to specify objects defined unilaterally. For many network management systems the most-accessed portion of this subtree is the enterprises (1), or {private 1} node. An enterprise is an organization that has registered its own specific extensions to the MIB. Each subtree under this node is assigned to a single enterprise. The enterprise then can create attributes under this subtree specific to its products. Vendor-specific MIBs are found at this location in the hierarchy.

For example, if a company named *Zeus* received the subtree designation of 22, its object identifier representation would be 1.3.6.1.4.22, or {enterprises 22}. A product of the *Zeus* company, such as its new multiport translational bridge, might have the object identifier 1.3.6.1.4.22.1.

Many vendor-specific MIBs are available on the market. If a device connects to a network and supports SNMP, it will most likely support a vendor-specific MIB in addition to the standard MIB. Vendor-specific MIBs are designed to complement the standard MIB and provide functionality necessary for network management of vendor-specific product features (or standard features on the product which the vendors feel requires more information than the standard MIB provides).

Vendor-specific MIBs exist for products that use many different networking and systems technologies. You can have a vendor-specific MIB for modems, ATM switches, hubs, bridges, switches, routers, servers, workstations, and so on. The most common objects found in these vendor-specific MIBs relate to information about the physical configuration (serial numbers, number of slots, number of ports, type of adapters, etc.) and software configuration (software version, features enabled, parameters set up, and so on) of the devices. Some vendors also provide objects that can be used in all areas of network management (such as technology-specific error counts, system memory usage, file system setup, and current system processes).

For example, U.S. Robotics has a MIB that contains information about its modems, modem configuration, and dialing strings. Cabletron Systems has a MIB with objects about the number of slots in a hub, bridging features enabled, and port configuration. The IBM ATM MIB has information about cell buffer sizes, maximum number of virtual circuits, and types of ATM connectors used. Looking at routers and switches, Cisco Systems has a MIB that contains chassis information, adapter card statistics, protocol per interface counters, and network accounting features. On a Hewlett-Packard UNIX workstation a MIB exists to examine the file system information, the processes currently running, and workstation cluster information. You should make sure that the products you want to manage on your network have the standard MIB and any vendor-specific MIBs you may need to perform all of the functional areas of network management.

8.4 SNMP

The network management protocol most in use for data networks is the Simple Network Management Protocol (SNMP). RFC 1067 first defined how information passed between network management systems and agents with SNMP. RFC 1098 later made RFC 1067 obsolete. Then, with RFC 1157, the IAB accepted the proposal of RFC 1098 and in doing so, recognized SNMP as a standard protocol. Table 8.4 summarizes the RFC numbers for the history of SNMP.

RFC 1157 describes the agent/station model used in SNMP. An *SNMP agent* is software capable of answering valid queries from an *SNMP station*, such as a network management system, about information defined in the MIB. A network device that provides information about the MIB to the station will have an SNMP agent. For the agent/station model to work, the agent and sta-

Table 8.4   RFC Numbers for the History of SNMP

Description	Proposal RFC	Standard RFC
IAB Recommendations	—	1052
SNMP	1067/1098	1157
SMI	1065	1155
MIB-I	1066	1156
MIB-II	1158	1213

tion must speak the same language. Figure 8.6 shows the relationship between an SNMP agent and a station.

Getting and Setting Information

The SNMP agents and stations communicate through standard messages. A message can be sent in a single packet between the station and the agent. Each packet, which contains all or part of a message exchange, is called a PDU (protocol data unit).

SNMP uses UDP (User Datagram Protocol) as the layer 4, or transport layer, protocol. UDP provides a connectionless service, so SNMP does not have to maintain a connection between an agent and a station to transmit a message. UDP provides fast transport-layer service with a minimum amount of resource allocation. However, UDP does not provide a reliable method for exchanging messages between an agent and a station. Figure 8.7 shows the ISO reference model for SNMP.

Message Types

SNMP has five types of messages:

- Get-Request
- Get-Response
- Get-Next-Request
- Set-Request
- Trap

The formats of these SNMP messages are shown in Fig. 8.8.

The SNMP station uses Get-Request to retrieve information from a network device that has an SNMP agent. The SNMP agent in turn responds to

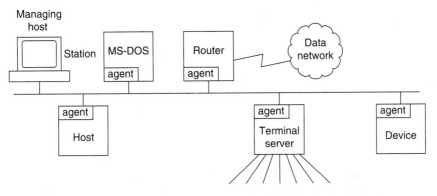

Figure 8.6 An SNMP station queries the SNMP agent present in network devices.

the Get-Request message with a Get-Response message. Information that might be returned includes the name of the system, how long the system has been running, and the number of network interfaces on the system.

A Get-Next-Request is used in conjunction with a Get-Request to obtain a table of objects. Get-Request retrieves one specific object; Get-Next-Request asks for the next specific object in a table in lexigraphical order. An agent responds to a Get-Next-Request with a Get-Response message.

You may want to use a network management system to query the IP routing table on a device. The IP routing table is dynamic, so you may not know exactly the number of rows in the table. To find the value of each column for every row in the table, the station sends a Get-Request message to the agent

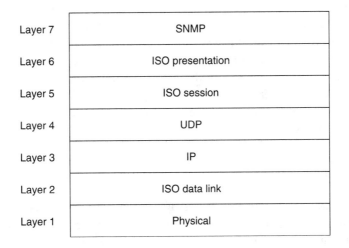

Figure 8.7 SNMP in the ISO reference model.

Version	Community	PDU type	Request ID	0	0	Name X	Value X	- - - -

(a) Get-Request, Get-Next-Request, Set-Request

Version	Community	PDU type	Request ID	Error status	Error index	Name X	Value X	- - - -

(b) Get-Response

Version	Community	PDU type	Enterprise	Agent Addr	Generic trap	Specific trap	Time	Name X	Value X

(c) Trap

Figure 8.8 The formats of SNMP messages.

on the device and asks for an object in the first row of the table. This message is followed by Get-Next-Request messages in lexigraphical order until the end of the table is found (when value in the next column in lexigraphical order is returned). One of the columns in the IP routing table is called the ipRouteDest. This is the destination host, subnet, or network number listed in the IP routing table. Figure 8.9 shows the sequence of queries to this object a station may send to an agent. Note that the syntax for the ipRouteDest object is not shown in its entirety here; we discuss this object further in Chapter 10.

Set-Request allows for the remote configuration of parameters on a device. Examples of Set-Request messages include setting the name of a device, shutting an interface administratively down, or clearing an address resolution table entry. In our example the network management system used Get-Request and Get-Next-Request to determine the number of interfaces on a particular device. Let's say that when the system examines the status of each interface, it discovers that one of the interfaces is not operational. By comparing the device parameters with an internal table, the system learns that the dysfunctional interface has the incorrect address. It then could use Set-Request to change the address of the interface in an attempt to bring it into an operational state.

SNMP Trap

An SNMP trap is an unsolicited message an SNMP agent sends to a station. These messages inform the server about the occurrence of a specific event. For example, SNMP trap messages can be used to inform the network management system that a circuit has just failed, the disk space of a device is near-

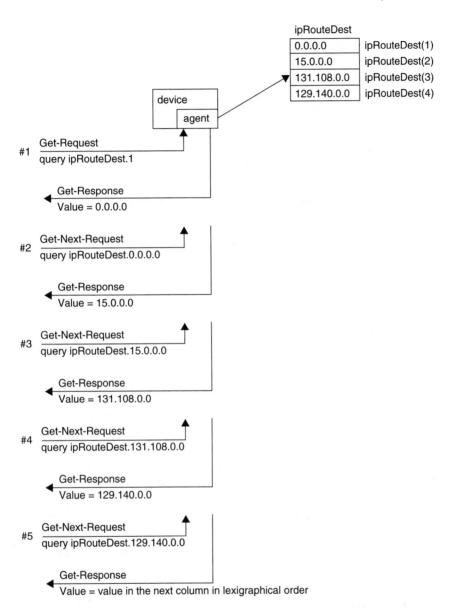

Figure 8.9 The use of the Get-Next-Request message to traverse a table in lexigraphical order.

ing capacity, or a user has just logged on to a host. The agent must be set up with the address of the station so it knows where to send the SNMP trap messages. Figure 8.10 shows the interaction between the SNMP station and an agent in a device sending an SNMP trap.

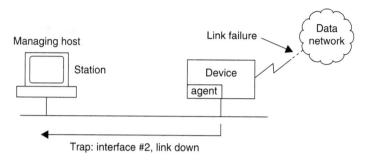

Trap: interface #2, link down

Figure 8.10 After receiving an SNMP trap, the management host can immediately inform the network engineer about a specific network event.

Seven types of SNMP traps are defined as part of MIB-II, as follows:

- Coldstart of a system

- Warmstart of a system

- Link down

- Link up

- Failure of authentication

- Exterior Gateway Protocol (EGP) neighbor loss

- Enterprise specific

The *coldstart* trap indicates that the agent sending the trap is reinitializing itself such that its configuration or protocol implementation has changed. A coldstart trap occurs when a device is powered on. The *warmstart* trap indicates that the device sending the trap is reinitializing itself such that its configuration or protocol implementation has not changed. If the SNMP agent in a device is reset, this action would invoke a warmstart trap. Typically this event occurs because of manual intervention.

A *link-down* trap means that a specific link on the source device has failed. A *link-up trap* signifies that a specific link from the source device has come up.

A *failure of authentication* trap message is sent to the network management system if an SNMP agent determines that a request does not provide proper authentication—for instance, if the agent gives the wrong SNMP community string. This information can lead to the implementation of security management.

An *Exterior Gateway Protocol (EGP) neighbor loss* trap is used by an SNMP agent to report the loss of an EGP neighbor. EGP is a reachability protocol used between data networks.

Like a vendor-specific MIB, an *enterprise-specific* trap is one implemented by a vendor to provide additional functionality that complements the generic traps. Enterprise-specific traps outnumber the generic traps by many orders of magnitude. Some companies have implemented traps based on disk usage on a workstation, maximum number of users, high processor load, and so on. Various network devices can send traps based on high utilization, error rates found on network links, or redundant power supply failure. Unlimited numbers of potential enterprise-specific SNMP traps can be implemented by vendors on their specific network devices.

Security

The SNMP protocol does not provide information or allow configuration changes of a network device without some form of security.

Community Strings

The SNMP agent in the network device can require that the SNMP station send a particular password with each message. The SNMP agent then would verify whether the station is authorized to access MIB information. This password is referred to as the SNMP *community string*. Figure 8.11 shows how an SNMP agent reacts to receiving valid and invalid community strings.

Some implementations of SNMP agents allow for different levels of security using the community string. For example, the agent could define a community string to allow Get-Request and Get-Next-Request messages from a set of stations having read-only access to the information in the MIB. Or the agent could allow Get-Request, Get-Next-Request, and Set-Request messages from another set of stations having full (read-write) access to the agent. Community strings are sent within SNMP packets in clear ASCII text. With little effort a network-literate person can learn the community string used by a given SNMP agent.

Problems

Although SNMP is a powerful protocol for network management, it has three drawbacks:

- It is officially standardized only for use on IP networks.
- It is inefficient for large table retrievals.
- It uses cleartext strings for security, leaving it relatively unsecure.

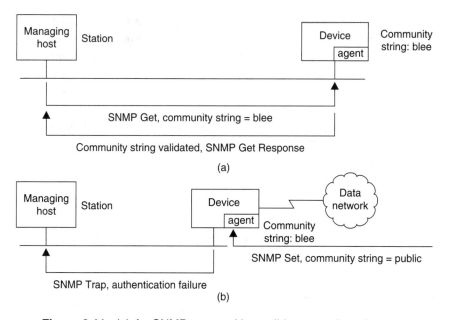

Figure 8.11   (a) An SNMP query with a valid community string; (b) an SNMP query with an invalid community string.

First, the RFC standard defines the implementation of SNMP only on IP networks. IP is a widespread datagram protocol and can be found on almost any computer today. However, not all networks rely on IP for delivery. Therefore some in the networking community recognize SNMP as a temporary solution to the need for a standard network management protocol.

A possible solution to this problem is the use of *SNMP proxy agents*, which can gather information from network devices that don't speak IP and convey this information to a management station with SNMP, allowing non-IP network devices to be managed with SNMP. However, specific software must be written for each network device using SNMP proxy agents.

Another problem with using SNMP is that it can be inefficient in retrieving large tables of data. As described earlier, retrieval of tables with SNMP is accomplished with Get-Next-Request messages. However, doing so can burden both the network and the destination SNMP agent. For example, suppose that you wanted to get a 2000-entry accounting table from a device. Each row in the accounting table has four entries: a source address, a destination address, a byte count, and a packet count. Using Get-Next-Request messages, in the best case (no retransmissions), you would end up with $2 \times 4 \times 2000$, or 16,000 packets. This product is derived by multiplying four requests per row by 2000 rows and multiplying that product by the number of associated Get-Request and Get-Response messages. If the station requested all four items for each row in a single packet, the total would be 2×2000, or 4000 packets on the data network. Even with this significant reduction of traffic, the SNMP agent on the destination device still must perform 16,000 lookups in the accounting table.

The final, and somewhat obvious, problem with SNMP is its use of clear-text community strings for security. Someone who can read a packet off a network segment can probably find the community string. If that happens, the person may be able to change the configuration of your network devices that use SNMP and allow SNMP Set-Request messages.

8.5 SNMPV2

The Simple Network Management Protocol version 2 (SNMPv2) has the same basic function as SNMP: to acquire and change MIB data on network devices. SNMPv2 was developed by members of the Internet community to overcome shortcomings in SNMP.

SNMPv2 was not the first proposed set of enhancements to SNMP. The first proposed enhancement added security to SNMP and was called *Secure SNMP*. Secure SNMP, which was defined in a set of RFCs (RFC1321 and RFC1351–RFC1353) in July 1992, did not solve the problems of inefficient table retrieval, IP as the only standard network layer, and other deficiencies. To work around these latter problems, a protocol called SMP (Simple Management Protocol) was developed and introduced in July 1992 in a set of eight papers (not as RFCs) submitted to the Internet community.

After this wealth of new proposals in July 1992, members of the Internet community began to realize that it would be beneficial to make a single transition from SNMP to a new protocol incorporating the properties of both Secure SNMP and SMP. Otherwise, it would be necessary for vendors to support SNMP, Secure SNMP, and SMP concurrently. Therefore vendors were encouraged not to support Secure SNMP and SMP as individual protocols; instead, the Internet community agreed to use these two protocols as a starting point for a new SNMP standard, now known as SNMPv2. The original SNMP is known as SNMPv1.

SNMPv2 has features that make up for the shortcomings of SNMPv1, including additions to the SMI, new message types, standardized multiprotocol support, significantly enhanced security, new MIB objects, and a way to coexist with SNMPv1. The RFCs that document SNMPv2 are listed in Table 8.5.

Structure of Management Information Enhancements

The SMI standardized for SNMPv1 had a few drawbacks. These included having a maximum unsigned integer value of $2^{32} - 1$, not differentiating between signed and unsigned integers, and having only IP network addresses represented.

Table 8.5 RFCs Documentary SNMPv2

Description	Standard RFC
SMI	RFC 1442
Textual conventions	RFC 1443
Administrative model	RFC 1445
Security protocols	RFC 1446
Party MIB	RFC 1447
Protocol operations	RFC 1448
SNMPv2 MIB	RFC 1450

SNMPv2 allows 64-bit integers, increasing the maximum unsigned integer value to $2^{64} - 1$, called a Counter64. The 32-bit unsigned numbers, called Counter and Gauge in the SMI for SNMPv1, were renamed to Counter32 and Gauge32. A Counter64 value is sufficiently large to handle count information that would otherwise cause a problem in 32-bit unsigned integer numbers. For example, if a MIB object had to count the number of bytes seen on a 100 Mbps FDDI (fiber distributed data interface) ring and the ring has an average of 30 percent utilization, a 32-bit unsigned integer would wrap in approximately 19 minutes:

$$30\% \text{ of } 100 \text{ Mbits/sec} = 30 \text{ Mbits/sec}$$

$$30 \text{ Mbits/sec} = 3,750,000 \text{ bytes/sec}$$

$$2^{32} - 1 \text{ (4,294,967,295) bytes}/3,750,000 \text{ bytes/sec} = 1145 \text{ seconds}$$

$$1145 \text{ seconds}/60 \text{ seconds/minute} = 19.09 \text{ minutes}$$

Using a 64-bit unsigned integer for a counter forces a wrap occurrence every 82,000,000,000 minutes:

$$30\% \text{ of } 100 \text{ Mbits/sec} = 30 \text{ Mbits/sec}$$

$$30 \text{ Mbits/sec} = 3,750,000 \text{ bytes/sec}$$

$$2^{64} - 1 \text{ (1.8446744E19) bytes}/3,750,000 \text{ bytes/sec} = 4.92 * 10^{12} \text{ seconds}$$

$$4.92 * 10^{12} \text{ seconds}/60 \text{ sec/min} = 8.20 * 10^{10} \text{ min}$$

One of the main problems with implementing 64-bit unsigned integers for all integer MIB objects is that the memory necessary to hold these values would be double that currently needed on a device. For some devices with limited memory (such as modems and interface boards), this could be an issue. Therefore many standard MIBs have only a limited number of objects represented as 64-bit unsigned integers.

The second issue in the SMI of SNMPv1 was the inability to represent both signed and unsigned numbers. The sign bit in binary numbers can be used to represent a positive or a negative number or may be used as an additional bit for holding values (thus increasing the maximum value for the number). As an example, if a 32-bit integer is unsigned, the maximum value it can represent is $2^{32} - 1$, or 4,294,967,295. If the same value is signed, the maximum value it can represent is $2^{31} - 1$, or 2,147,483,647. If a MIB object needs to be represented only by a positive integer value, the sign bit can be used to increase the number of bits used to represent the value.

The SMI for SNMPv2 also added a new datatype to represent OSI NSAP (network service access point) addresses, called NsapAddress. An NSAP is a hierarchical network address used by the OSI network layer.

Getting and Setting Information

The SNMPv1 set of message types (Get-Request, Get-Next-Request, Get-Response, Set-Request, and Trap) are all incorporated into SNMPv2. One main difference between the two protocols is that SNMP uses one message format for all messages except traps and Get-Response, whereas SNMPv2 uses a single message format for all messages except GetBulkRequest and Get-Response. Another main difference between the two protocols is how each handles the creating of tabular data and error messages. These two topics are beyond the scope of this discussion but can be explored further in many of the reference books cited at the end of the chapter.

Message Types

There are two new message types in SNMPv2: InformRequest and Get-BulkRequest. Each provides valuable functionality for both the SNMPv2 agent and manager (or station). Note that in SNMPv1 the names of the message types were hyphenated between words. In SNMPv2 the names of the message types now appear without hyphens. The formats of all SNMPv2 messages are shown in Fig. 8.12.

An SNMPv2 InformRequest is sent by a manager to another manager. This allows one management application to send information to another for manager-to-manager communication. This new message type can be used to provide a standard way for hierarchical or distributed network management

PDU type	Request ID	0	0	Name X	Value X	- - - -

(a) Get-Request, Get-Next-Request, Set-Request, Trap, InformRequest

PDU type	Request ID	Error status	Error index	Name X	Value X	- - - -

(b) Get-Response

PDU type	Request ID	Non-repeaters	Max repetitions	Name X	Value X	- - - -

(c) GetBulkRequest

Figure 8.12   Message formats for SNMPv2.

systems to communicate. As you recall from Chapter 2, an organization may choose to use a hierarchical or distributed management system for distributing network alarms and polling, dividing up management of different devices between systems, or allowing for multiple managers to simultaneously make configuration or network map changes. Before the SNMPv2 Inform-Request, most communication between network management system applications was done by means of proprietary methods.

The SNMPv2 GetBulkRequest message helps optimize the retrieval of large amounts of management information, one of the major problems with SNMPv1. An application using SNMPv1 retrieves large amounts of management information through the use of the Get-Next-Request message, potentially sending a request for each object. The GetBulkRequest works in essentially the same way as the Get-Next-Request message, retrieving the next value in the MIB (when traversing the MIB in order). Yet with Get-BulkRequest you can request multiple retrievals of the object with a single message. Each retrieval is the next value of the object as you traverse the MIB tree. So instead of asking for the value of the next object in a table, you can ask for the next X values in the table (where X can be any integer value). The GetBulkRequest message retrieves as much information as possible from the MIB for a given request. Additionally, you may request only a single value for some objects requested in a GetBulkRequest message.

To better understand the GetBulkRequest message, we define the following:

L = the total number of variable names (MIB object names) in the request

N = the number of variable names (starting from the beginning of the variable name list) that are nonrepeaters, for which you want only a single value

R = the number of variables following the first N that are repeaters, for which you want multiple retrievals

M = the number of times you want to traverse the MIB tree for each R variable

Using these definitions, you can see that $R = L - N$. The total number of variables requiring repetitive MIB queries is equal to the total number of variables in the request minus the variables that require only a single query. Also note that the total number of variable values requested in a GetBulkRequest message is $N + (M * R)$. This is the total number of single requests added to the total number of repetitive requests times the number of repetitions.

Upon receiving a GetBulkRequest, an agent must determine how many objects are being requested (L), find out how many objects only require a single query (N), find the number of objects that will require repetitive queries (R), and determine how many queries the message requests for each R object (M). The agent can then process the queries and attempt to return the values of the MIB objects efficiently.

For example, if an agent receives a GetBulkRequest with the values $L = 5$, $N = 2$, $R = 3$, and $M = 10$, there are five objects (L) being requested in the GetBulkRequest. The first two objects are nonrepeaters (N); the next three objects are repeaters (R). The agent will try to make ten (M) repetitive requests for each object specified in R.

Multiprotocol Support

SNMPv1 is standardized to work only in conjunction with IP networks. Thus on non-IP networks, such as an Apple Appletalk or Novell IPX network, you would have to set up IP to use SNMPv1. Since many devices do support IP, this is usually more of a configuration, maintenance, and monetary issue (you may have to buy software to run IP on your devices). SNMPv2, by contrast, is standardized on four major network protocol stacks: IP, Apple Appletalk, Novell IPX, and OSI Connectionless Network Service (CLNS). Therefore SNMPv2 messages should be able to run on nearly all of the networks in the world. IP is by far the most prevalent network protocol in the world today. Appletalk is used by organizations that use Apple devices, Novell IPX is the protocol that communicates between Novell file servers and clients, and OSI CLNS is compatible with Digital DECnet V.

Regardless of the protocol that carries SNMPv2 messages, the operation of the messages and the protocol remains the same. A GetBulkRequest sent by Novell IPX is interpreted by the agent exactly as if it were sent over IP. A SNMPv2 trap sent by Appletalk operates the same as one sent over OSI CLNS. These four network protocols reside at the network layer of the OSI Reference Model, whereas SNMPv2 sits on the application layer. Since SNMPv2 uses the network layer for delivery, it is possible to change network layers without changing the SNMPv2 protocol.

Security

The security mechanism in SNMPv1 is community strings. Although this mechanism does prevent indiscriminate access to monitoring and changing MIB objects, a knowledgeable network engineer can, given the proper equipment or software, determine the community strings in use on a network. Since using community strings for security does not provide a strong level of security, this is seen as a weakness in SNMPv1.

SNMPv2 has extensive security mechanisms that provide both authentication and encryption of SNMPv2 messages. The security information is found on the outside of the SNMPv2 messages, as shown in Fig. 8.13.

In the SNMPv2 message format, the srcParty field identifies the source manager or agent that is sending this message. The dstParty field identifies the destination manager or agent, which is repeated in the privDst field. This repetition is necessary because the SNMPv2 message may be encrypted in all fields following privDst, which remains in cleartext to allow the destination party to be easily identified. If a message requires authentication, it also contains a digest and a source (srcTime) and destination timestamp (dstTime).

This information is necessary so that the SNMPv2 agent can identify the proper party to deliver this message to and perform the proper security for the message when sent or received. An SNMPv2 party is a group (maybe only two) of entities that will communicate management information. Each party has a set of properties governing access and privileges to MIB information.

		Authentication fields					
privDst	digest	dstTimestamp	srcTimestamp	dstParty	srcParty	context	PDU

Figure 8.13 The general format of an SNMPv2 message, showing all fields needed for authentication. If a party chooses to not use authentication, the authentication fields are replaced by a zero-length string.

These properties include authentication, encryption, MIB views, and contexts. The flow of sending an SNMPv2 message is shown in Flowchart 8.1.

Authentication

SNMPv2 provides a secure method for authentication; this method is called the digest authentication protocol. The digest is a computation performed over the SNMPv2 message to make sure that the message received was the one sent and that the source of the message has been authenticated.

To accomplish these two tasks, the source calculates a message digest for the SNMPv2 message (using a protocol called MD5, or message digest 5), using an authentication key. The message digest is a 128-bit number specific to the message and its contents. The SNMPv2 message and the digest are sent on the network. Note that the authentication key is not sent in the message. When the destination receives the message, it recomputes the message digest, using its own local copy of the authentication key. If the newly calculated di-

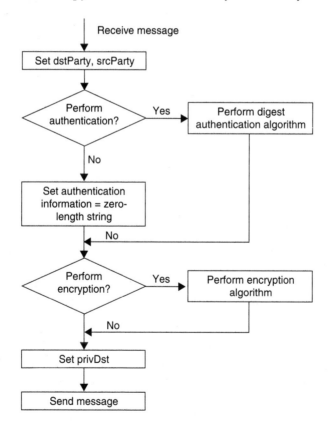

Flowchart 8.1 Sending an SNMPv2 message.

gest matches that found in the message, the message is authenticated. The use of the message digest confirms that the message received was the one sent, and the authentication key proves that the source is authenticated.

As an additional authentication feature, MD5 uses timestamps in the message to ensure that the message was not captured and replayed to gain unauthorized access. Each SNMPv2 party has a maximum age (called a lifetime) for each message, and the timestamps in the message ensure that the lifetime of the message has not been exceeded.

One of the issues with using the digest authentication protocol is distributing the authentication keys to the various systems within the SNMPv2 party. As we saw in Chapter 5, using public keys alleviates this issue. In fact, SNMPv2 does use a public key algorithm to distribute the authentication keys necessary to perform the message digest algorithm.

Encryption

If a party specifies that a message requires encryption, the Data Encryption Standard (DES) algorithm is used. Like all encryption algorithms, DES has a chance of being broken, in this case about 1×10^{72}. When encryption is specified for communication between members of a party, the entire SNMPv2 message, except for the privDst field, is encrypted before transmission. The destination party decrypts the message by using the same algorithm.

MIB Views

A party can have controlled access to portions of the MIB on the agent. The portion of the MIB that is accessible to the manager is called a MIB view. An agent may permit only certain managers to access certain parts of the local MIB database. For example, in many cases it may be desirable to have a few select managers access the portions of the MIB that configure a device (objects that require a Set-Request message) and permit other managers to access only informational objects. An operations center management system may need to view only the properties of a device, whereas a network engineering management system may need to be able to change the value of MIB objects. MIB views allow for this functionality. For each agent a manager communicates with, there needs to exist a party and an associated MIB view.

Contexts

An SNMPv2 context is a set of managed objects that a manager or agent can access. Locally, to a given SNMPv2 entity, a context is a MIB view. A local context defines which MIB objects the manager or agent can access. In a remote SNMPv2 context a manager and an agent communicate through a proxy agent. The proxy agent needs to understand the managed objects that are visible for an operation requested by the manager. In this manner a context is an abstraction that relates to the control of access of information and the MIB view through which the information is acquired. Each party needs a context to let the manager and the agent identify the operations that are allowed on a given set of managed objects.

Management Information Base

Three MIBs are defined to help with the management of SNMPv2: SNMPv2 MIB, manager-to-manager MIB, and party MIB. These MIBs provide vital information necessary for the administration, configuration, and monitoring of the SNMPv2 protocol.

SNMPv2 MIB

The SNMPv2 MIB, defined in RFC 1450, titled "Management Information Base for version 2 of the Simple Network Management Protocol (SNMPv2)," defines objects that describe the working of SNMPv2. The SNMPv2 MIB is divided into five groups: the SNMPv2 statistics group, the SNMPv1 statistics group, the object resource group, the traps group, and the set group.

The *SNMPv2 statistics* group provides objects that give statistics about this SNMPv2 manager or agent, in particular information about messages that could not be processed. This group is similar in function to, although more concise than, the SNMP group in MIB-II, which we explore in detail in Chapter 10. The SNMPv1 statistics group provides objects that give statistics about this SNMPv2 manager or agent that also communicates with SNMPv1. For example, an object in this MIB group counts the number of messages seen with the wrong community string.

The *object resource* group provides information that defines which objects an SNMPv2 agent is allowed to define dynamically. Each object resource has an object identifier (OID) and a description. By querying this table, a manager can determine which SNMPv2 parameters are allowed to be dynamically configured on an agent. One such object may be whether a party is performing authentication or encryption.

The *traps* group contains a table of information about each of the traps an agent can send. Each trap has an associated OID and a counter for the number of times the trap has been sent. This table may contain information saying that the agent can send a trap about when congestion occurs on a WAN switch port. The counter associated with this trap will tell you how many times the agent has sent the trap to a manager.

The *set* group provides a single object that allows multiple managers to send SNMP Set messages to a single agent without encountering coordination problems. This object, known as a set serial number, helps avoid conditions whereby two managers try to set the same MIB object simultaneously (or nearly simultaneously) by incrementing once for each Set Request processed.

Imagine if an agent receives an SNMP Set Request from manager *Alpha* to turn off an Ethernet interface. Before that operation completes, another SNMP Set Request arrives from manager *Beta* telling the agent to turn on the same Ethernet interface. When manager *Alpha* checks to see the status of the Ethernet interface, it finds it up, not down, and then thinks that the agent may be in error. To avoid this problem, manager *Alpha* needs to query for the set serial number before and after the processing of the Set Request. Since the set serial number increases for each Set Request the agent processes, manager *Alpha* can understand that another Set Request has been processed since, and that may be the reason the Ethernet interface is currently up.

Manager-to-Manager MIB

Defined in RFC 1451, "Manager-to-Manager Management Information Base," this set of objects provides information about how an SNMPv2 manager performs. The two groups in this MIB (the alarm group and the event group) are basically copies of the RMON alarm and event groups, which are discussed in Chapter 11.

Party MIB

This MIB, defined in RFC 1447, "Party MIB for version 2 of the Simple Network Management Protocol (SNMPv2)," contains objects that describe and configure the parties associated with an SNMPv2 entity. The four groups within this MIB are the party database group, the contexts database group, the access privileges database group, and the MIB view database group.

The party database group contains information which is stored on the device about all known local and remote parties. Some of the data in each party tells whether the party is local or remote, the authentication protocol being used, the party lifetime, and how the party information is stored (RAM, non-volatile RAM, or ROM).

The other three groups deal with privileges between a manager and agent. These groups allow for the control of the local and remote contexts on the SNMPv2 entity, the access control policies this agent or manager implements, and the currently defined MIB views and the parties that can access them.

Coexistence with SNMP

The SNMPv2 protocol was intended to be a follow-up to SNMPv1. Therefore the designers of the protocol wanted to be able to provide a smooth migration path from SNMPv1 to SNMPv2 so that vendors could quickly have their products support SNMPv2. To accomplish this transition, SNMPv1 managers and agents have had to confront issues dealing with SMI information and protocol message changes.

Changes in the SMI for SNMPv2 make it necessary for both agents and managers to be updated to understand the new constructs and data types. However, since the SMI for SNMPv2 is a superset of the SMI for SNMPv1, all SNMPv1 MIB definitions are compatible with SNMPv2 agents and managers. It is important for MIB definitions to conform to the SMI for SNMPv2 for standardization reasons but not strictly for operation reasons.

The protocol messages in SNMPv2 are also very similar to the messages in SNMPv1. Both protocols have Get-Request, Get-Next-Request, Set-Request, Get-Response, and Trap messages. Further, the SNMPv2 GetBulkRequest can be seen as a series of SNMPv1 Get-Next-Request messages. The easy translation between the two protocols' message types means that there are two strategies for communication between an SNMPv1 and SNMPv2 entity. The first strategy is to have a proxy agent perform the message translation. The second strategy is to have a manager that speaks both SNMPv1 and SNMPv2.

Today this second approach is more easily accepted because the manager can then make a dynamic decision about which protocol is needed to talk to each agent. The manager needs to query a new agent once with an SNMPv2 Get-Request (getting something every device has, like its name) and see whether the device responds. If it does not respond, the manager can send the device an SNMPv1 Get-Request asking for the same information. If the device responds, the manager can determine that this is an SNMPv1 device. If the device does not respond, no conclusions can be drawn about it yet (it may be off line). Using a bilingual manager also alleviates the need to set up proxy agents throughout the network as you transition from SNMPv1 to SNMPv2.

Problems

The SNMPv2 protocol is a well-defined and functionally complete network management protocol that makes up for the shortcomings of SNMPv1. The major challenge facing the protocol is lack of implementation. Because of the continued pervasive use of SNMPv1, it will take some time for SNMPv2 to have a major role in the world of network management.

SUMMARY

Before standard network management protocols existed, network engineers had to learn many methods for monitoring and controlling network devices. These methods could involve using a menu-driven system or memorizing specific commands for a network device. The networking community then turned to generic methods, such as ping on TCP/IP networks, to help gather information for network management. However, these solutions lacked functionality and the ability to get the needed data.

The need for a method that worked on many devices prompted the development of standard protocols. Three network management protocols were examined, each striving, in a generic manner, to solve the problems associated with network management. After investigating these protocols, the IAB set forth a plan for the development of network management. RFCs document this plan and the associated standards.

Specified in the RFCs, the SMI defines how the information is structured, and the MIB defines what information can be managed with the network management protocols. The MIB uses ASN.1 syntax.

SNMP was the first network management protocol in wide use. SNMP agents and stations communicate through a common protocol to get and send management information on data networks. However, SNMP by definition is to be implemented over TCP/IP-based internets, although there are proprietary protocol implementations as well.

However, SNMP had some shortcomings, which were addressed in SNMPv2. SNMPv2 defines additions to the SNMP SMI, has two new message types, allows for multiprotocol support, and has sophisticated security mechanisms. With the advent of SNMPv2, SNMP is now known as SNMPv1.

FOR FURTHER STUDY

Case, J., Fedor, M., Schoffstall, M., and Davin, C., RFC 1157, "Simple Network Management Protocol (SNMP)," May 1990.

Case, J., McCloghrie, K., Rose, M., and Waldbusser, S., RFC 1450, "Management Information Base for version 2 of the Simple Network Management Protocol (SNMPv2)," April 1993.

_____ . RFC 1451, "Manager-to-Manager Management Information Base," April 1993.

Comer, D., *Internetworking with TCP/IP*, Volume I (3d ed.), Englewood Cliffs, NJ: Prentice-Hall, 1995.

International Organization for Standardization, Open Systems Interconnection, "Specification of Basic Specification of Abstract Syntax Notation One (ASN.1)," International Standard Number 8824, ISO, Switzerland, May 1987.

McCloghrie, K., and Galvin, J., RFC 1447, "Party MIB for version 2 of the Simple Network Management Protocol (SNMPv2)," April 1993.

McCloghrie, K., and Rose, M., RFC 1156, "Management Information Base for Network Management Information of TCP/IP-based Internets," May 1990.

_____ . RFC 1213, "Management Information Base for Network Management Information of TCP/IP-based Internets: MIBII," March 1991.

Rose, M., *The Simple Book: An Introduction to Management of TCP/IP-based Internets* (2d ed.) Englewood Cliffs, NJ: Prentice-Hall, 1993.

Rose, M., and McCloghrie, K., RFC 1155, "Structure and Identification of Management Information for TCP/IP-based Internets," May 1990.

Stallings, W., *SNMP, SNMPv2, and CMIP: The Practical Guide to Network Management Standards*, Reading, MA: Addison-Wesley, 1993.

Chapter 9

CMIS/CMIP: Network Management Protocols (II)

In This Chapter:

> *"The FastRoute routers support the two industry standards for network management protocols: SNMP and CMIS/CMIP," Chris read. Well, Chris knew what SNMP was but was not familiar with CMIS/CMIP. The saying "The nice thing about standards is that there are so many of them to choose from" seemed to ring a little truer. . . .*

SNMPv1 has a large industry following and widespread deployment, and SNMPv2 has many features that network engineers desire. However, many people feel that the protocol suite that may be best able to satisfy network management needs is the OSI network management protocol Common Management Information Services/Common Management Information Protocol (CMIS/CMIP). CMIS/CMIP contains many features that make it useful for network management tasks.

CMIS defines the general services provided by each network component for network management; CMIP is the protocol that implements the CMIS services. A common structure for OSI protocol suites is a set of services defining operations available with the protocol, together with a definition of the protocol, which defines how the services are implemented. OSI network protocols are intended to provide a common network architecture for all devices on each layer of the OSI Reference Model. In the same manner CMIS/CMIP intends to provide a complete network management protocol suite for use with any network device.

To provide the needed network management protocol features over an array of network machines and computer architectures, the functionality and structure of CMIS/CMIP are significantly different from those of SNMPv1 or SNMPv2. The OSI network management protocols are not as spartan as SNMPv1 or SNMPv2, but they can provide the functionality needed to support a total network management solution.

A basic philosophical difference between CMIS/CMIP and either version of SNMP is that the CMIS/CMIP protocols ask a managed device to perform many more tasks. SNMP was designed to place the burden of management on the network management station, allowing the agent to remain simple. CMIS/CMIP distributes this burden more equally, asking for significant resource and capability requirements on each managed device.

To deal with CMIS/CMIP, you first need to understand the terminology of OSI as it relates to network management. A system—whether a network component, such as a source route bridge, or a workstation using the OSI protocol stack—is referred to as an *open system*. Two devices that communicate using the OSI protocols at the same OSI Reference Model layer are *peer open systems*.

9.1   OSI PROTOCOL STRUCTURE

The structure of the OSI network management protocols closely follows that of the OSI Reference Model. Network management application processes use the application layer of the OSI Reference Model. Also in this layer, the Common Management Information Service Element (CMISE)[1] provides the means for applications to use CMIP. CMISE, in turn, uses two more ISO application protocols: Association Control Service Element (ACSE)[2] and Remote Operations Service Element (ROSE).[3] Figure 9.1 shows these protocols in the OSI Reference Model. ACSE establishes and closes associations between applica-

---

[1] Specified in ISO 9595/9596.

[2] Specified in ISO 8649/8650.

[3] Specified in ISO 9072-1/2.

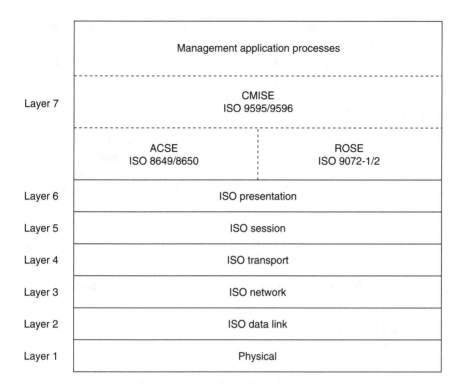

Figure 9.1 The CMIP protocols in the OSI Reference Model.

tions; ROSE handles request/reply interactions between applications. According to the OSI model, both ACSE and ROSE assume the use of the OSI presentation service and the remainder of the OSI Reference Model.

These protocols, and the applications that use them, comprise the framework for the OSI network management scheme. Other than those protocols defined on the application layer, OSI does not define protocols on the lower layers specifically for network management.

9.2 CMIS

CMIS services provide the basic building blocks and intrinsic functionality for a system as it works to solve the puzzle of systems management. Each CMIS service is a single operation that a network management application can perform. Any application that performs systems management is a *CMISE-service-user*. The existence of defined services for interaction between peer open systems is an important difference between CMIS and SNMP. CMIS has defined three classes of services for CMIS-service-users to use, as follows: management association, management notification, and management operation. Each association is designed for different aspects of network management. A peer open system may choose to implement one or all of these associations.

Management Association Services

The first class of service, *management association services*, controls the association between peer open systems. These services, used primarily to establish and release connections between systems, control the initialization, termination, and abnormal release of a connection of a management association with the following services:

- M-INITIALIZE: institutes an association with a peer CMISE-service-user for systems management

- M-TERMINATE: terminates a connection between peer CMISE-service-users

- M-ABORT: used when a connection between CMISE-service-users terminates abnormally

These management association services assume the use of services of ACSE for operation, since ACSE is used to establish and close connections between applications. Other CMIS services, which use an existing connection for management information, operate with ROSE.

Management Notification Services

Just as SNMP trap messages provide information about events on a network, *management notification services* provide similar functionality for CMIS. The M-EVENT-REPORT service tells a peer CMISE-service-user about an event that has occurred on another CMISE-service-user. If the CMISE-service-user on a system notes the change of a value (such as the state change of an interface), it can notify the managing system with the M-EVENT-REPORT service. Unlike with the standard SNMP traps, however, these events are not strictly defined. Rather, they are specific to the system that generated the notification, like enterprise-specific SNMP traps.

Devices that may choose to implement only management notification services are those having limited processing power or those simply needing to report a fault to a peer open system. An example of a CMISE-service-user that may require only notification services is a hierarchical network management system client reporting faults to the central system.

Management Operation Services

The *management operation services*, which comprise the third group of CMIS service, are as follows:

- M-GET
- M-CANCEL-GET
- M-SET
- M-ACTION
- M-CREATE
- M-DELETE

The M-GET service, used by a CMISE-service-user to retrieve management information from a peer CMISE-service user, is analogous to the SNMP Get-Request message. M-CANCEL-GET is used to cancel an M-GET request sent that is currently outstanding. So if a CMISE-service-user sends an M-GET request and decides, before receiving response, that it no longer needs the information, it can cancel this request with M-CANCEL-GET.

In a common example, suppose that you want to write a performance management application to watch the utilization of a token ring network. The CMISE-service-user would attempt to establish a management association with two machines *Daisy* and *Gatsby* (recall from Chapter 6), using the M-INITIALIZE service. Then, to get the necessary management information, the application would use the management operation service M-GET. After receiving the information, the application could then produce a graph of the data, showing the utilization of the token ring.

The CMIS M-SET service allows a CMISE-service-user to modify the management information of a peer CMISE-service-user. This service is similar to the SNMP Set-Request message, which allows modification of information on a network device.

The M-ACTION service is invoked by a CMISE-service-user to instruct a peer CMISE-service-user to perform a desired action. The actions performed are relative to each specific device. For example, an open system request could request a peer to send ICMP Echoes (pings) to various locations to test IP network connectivity. This concept is similar to an SNMP Set-Request message, which invokes an action on a network device. An open system can request many actions by another open system; Figure 9.2 shows one use of the M-ACTION service.

For example, a network management system could perform some fault isolation procedures automatically by sending an M-ACTION request to a peer open system, such as another network management system. In this hierarchi-

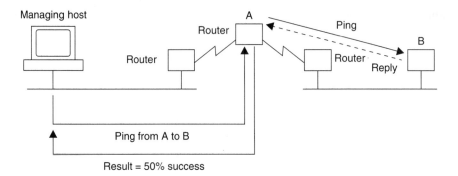

Figure 9.2 A typical M-ACTION service.

cal network management setup, if a server management system detects a problem in a certain region of the network, it could then delegate a fault management task to another client system, one that is responsible for the affected region.

The M-CREATE service is used by a CMISE-service-user to instruct a peer CMISE-service-user to create another instance of a managed object. The managed object represents the CMISE-service-user on the managed system. In CMIS each object that is managed has an associated instance. CMIS allows many instances of the same object but only one definition of the object. This is similar in concept to object-oriented programming, whereby each object has a definition called a *class*, and each use of this definition is called an *instance* of the class. One way to use the M-CREATE service is to allow managed objects to instruct one another about the presence of new objects. For example, on a management system a definition of an Ethernet bridge might exist. Each time a new bridge is added, the management system would create and use an instance of this definition. The management system could then inform other management systems (in a hierarchical or distributed environment) about the presence of the new bridge. This would be done by establishing a management association and using the M-CREATE service to create instances of the new bridge on the other systems.

The last of the management operation services is M-DELETE. The converse of M-CREATE, this service is used by a CMISE-service-user to ask that a peer delete an instance of a managed object.

Management Associations

A *management association* is the connection between two peer open systems for systems management. The process of connection relies on CMISE to interface with other protocols on the OSI protocol stack. Four possible types of associations can exist between peer open systems, as follows:

- Event

- Event/monitor

- Monitor/control

- Full manager/agent

Two peer open systems may establish any of these associations and still conform to the CMIS standard.

Event

An event association permits two open systems to send M-EVENT-REPORT messages. Two peer open systems may have an event association when they need to send to each other only management events. Two peer open systems would use management association services and management notification services for an event association.

Event/Monitor

This association is the same as the event association except that each system also may receive and issue M-GET messages. This type of association allows the peer open systems to query for management information and to receive network events. This association is useful for CMISE-service-users interested in the status of certain peer open systems but not allowed to change them. Two peer open systems would use management association services, management notification services, and a subset of management operation services for an event/monitor association.

In a common case a CMISE-service-user will have visibility of a peer open system that is not under its direct control (such as one owned by another organization). Although this peer open system is not administered by the management system, it might provide an important function requiring monitoring. An example is a router that connects the organization to the Internet. The router may be owned by an Internet service provider, but the status of this router and its current operation are important to the organization. Therefore, the network management system establishes an event/monitor association with the Internet router.

Monitor/Control

The monitor/control association allows for the communication of M-GET, M-CANCEL-GET, M-SET, M-CREATE, M-DELETE, and M-ACTION requests, although no event reporting is allowed. A CMISE-service-user may use a monitor/control association to change the configuration of a peer open system. In this case the receipt of notification services is not usually important, since the only task is to configure the peer open system. Two peer open systems would use management association services and a subset of management operation services for a monitor/control association.

Consider a CMISE-service-user that changes the configuration on a set of peer open systems. Each peer open system needs to get a new revision of an operating system downloaded to a hard disk. The CMISE-service-user establishes a monitor/control association to query the status of each destination peer open system (using the M-GET service) and to determine the free space on the destination hard disk. If the peer open system is functional and has enough disk space to receive the new operating system, it is downloaded (perhaps using a combination of M-SET and M-ACTION services). During this transaction, the receipt of notification services is not necessary, because this specific CMISE-service-user has no means of processing this service or informing a network engineer. Ideally, during this transaction, another CMISE-service-user on the network management system does have the ability to process management notification services and to inform the network engineer appropriately if an event occurs.

Full Manager/Agent

This association supports all of the CMIS services. If a network management system were managing a peer open system and needed to be able to perform any management task on it, the system could use a full manager/agent association.

Access Lists

In the same way that SNMPv1 uses community strings and SNMPv2 uses parties and contexts to verify that a system can access the management information, CMIS uses access lists. For each open system, these access lists explicitly state the access of other open systems. Although today the access control remains in an unspecified form, it is intended that a CMISE-service-user would check the access control before the invocation of any CMIS service.

9.3 CMIP

The missing piece in our discussion of the OSI network management protocols deals with the implementation of the concepts set out by CMIS. The protocol that implements CMIS is the Common Management Information

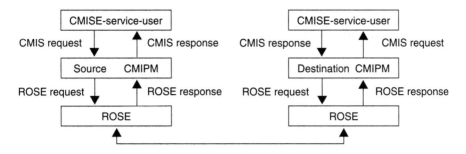

Figure 9.3 The flow of a CMIS service request between two CMISE-service-users.

Protocol (CMIP). The specification of this protocol explains in detail the manner in which the protocol should perform for each of the CMIS services.

The CMIP protocol requires a CMIP machine, or a CMIPM, to function according to a defined specification. A *CMIPM* is software that performs two functions: First, it accepts operations sent to it by a CMISE-service-user and initiates the appropriate procedure to accomplish the associated operation. Second, the CMIP machine uses ROSE to send messages across the network. Figure 9.3 shows the flow of a CMIS service request between two CMISE-service users.

The CMIPM uses a set of well-defined data units to implement the CMIS services. Each CMIS service uses a series of these data units. As an example, two CMIPM are called m-GET and m-Linked-Reply; m-GET gets a specific piece of MIB data from a CMISE-service-user, and m-Linked-Reply is used to respond to the m-GET and gives a way for a CMISE-service-user to correlate a reply message, which may take multiple packets. Thus when one CMIS-service-user issues an M-GET service, the result is an m-GET data unit sent and one or more m-Linked-Reply data units sent in return. Table 9.1 lists the CMIS services and their corresponding CMIP data units.

Table 9.1 CMIS Services and Corresponding Data Units

CMIS Service	*CMIP Data Units*
M-EVENT-REPORT	m-EventReport, m-EventReport-Confirmed
M-GET	m-Get, m-Linked-Reply
M-CANCEL-GET	m-Cancel-Get-Confirmed
M-SET	m-Set-Confirmed, m-Linked-Reply
M-ACTION	m-Action, m-Action-Confirmed, m-Linked-Reply
M-CREATE	m-Create
M-DELETE	m-Delete

CMIP only defines how to decipher the information in a packet; it does not state what a CMISE-service-user should do with any information requested from a managed object. Thus the CMIP specifications don't infringe on the functionality of the network management system, which can request any relevant information from a managed object and interpret that information in any manner.

9.4 PROBLEMS WITH CMIS/CMIP

Although the CMIS/CMIP protocol suite provides the networking community with a management protocol capable of performing many tasks, there are two critical problems. First, CMIS/CMIP requires a large amount of overhead. Second, it is difficult to implement. Both problems result from the fact that CMIS/CMIP is designed to run on a fully implemented OSI protocol stack. Because of the full-featured nature of the OSI protocols, they provide flexible functionality and use vast amounts of overhead. Some network devices may not have the memory or processing power to support the full OSI stack. For some vendors this makes the OSI stack difficult to implement because of hardware or software restrictions. There are many implementations of the OSI stack, but they are not widely deployed.

9.5 CMOT

The *Common Management Information Services and Protocol over TCP/IP (CMOT)* proposes to implement the CMIS services on top of the TCP/IP protocol suite as an interim solution until extensive deployment of the OSI protocol stack solution. RFC 1189 defines the CMOT protocol. Figure 9.4 shows the CMOT protocols on the OSI Reference Model.

The application protocols used by CMIS do not change with the implementation of CMOT. CMOT relies on the protocols CMISE, ACSE, and ROSE. However, instead of waiting for the implementation of the ISO Presentation Layer protocol, CMOT requires the use of another protocol on the same layer of the OSI Reference Model, the *Lightweight Presentation Protocol (LPP)*, as defined in RFC 1085. This protocol provides the interface to either of the two most common transport-layer protocols used today—UDP and TCP, which both use IP for network delivery.

A system that complies with the CMOT specification must have the functionality to establish one of the recognized associations—that is, event, event/monitor, monitor/control, or full manager/agent—with an open system. This system also must support only the type of association that is appropriate to the system.

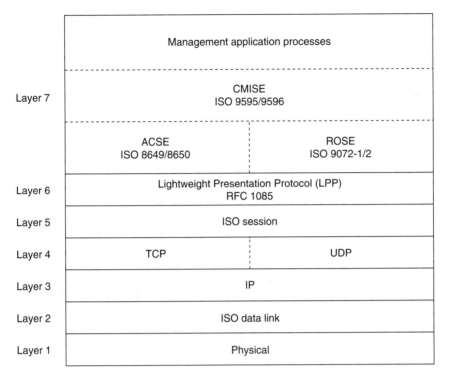

Figure 9.4 The CMOT protocols in the OSI Reference Model.

A potential problem with using CMOT is that many network management vendors don't want to spend time implementing another interim solution. Instead, numerous vendors have jumped on the SNMP bandwagon and have spent considerable resources in this effort. In fact, although the definition for CMOT exists, no significant work has been done on the protocol for quite some time.

9.6 LMMP

The IEEE 802.1b *LAN MAN Management Protocol (LMMP)* attempts to provide a network management solution for LAN environments. LMMP was formerly known as *Common Management Information Services and Protocol over IEEE 802 Logical Link Control (CMOL)*. Examples of network devices within a LAN environment include transparent and source route bridges, wiring hubs, and repeaters. This protocol, developed by 3Com Corp. and IBM, eliminates the need for the OSI protocols to implement the CMIS services. Because LMMP rides directly on top of IEEE 802 Logical Link Layer (LLC), it does not rely on any specific network layer protocol, such as IP, for network delivery.

By not requiring any network-layer protocol, LMMP is potentially easier to implement than CMIS/CMIP or CMOT. Yet without a network layer to provide routing information, LMMP messages cannot traverse routers. However, the implementation of proxy agents to convey the LMMP information beyond the boundaries of a local area network might overcome this problem.

SUMMARY

The OSI network management protocol suite, CMIS/CMIP, provides the functionality that might be necessary for a complete network management solution. There are three types of CMIS services: management association services, management notification services, and management operation services. Each peer open system can use a subset of these services, called associations. The four associations for CMISE-service-users are event, event/monitor, monitor/control, and full manager/agent. The protocol that implements the CMIS services is CMIP. CMIP uses data units to send messages between peer open systems.

Although CMIS/CMIP gives a wealth of functionality to accomplish network management, it relies on the implementation of the entire OSI protocol suite, which currently is not widely deployed. One reason for this lack of deployment is the complexity of the OSI protocol suite.

As an interim solution, CMOT provides the functionality of CMIS on the TCP/IP protocol stack. The main drawback to CMOT is that many vendors don't want to spend time implementing an interim-solution network management protocol. Currently, no work is being done on CMOT.

Instead of producing another interim network management protocol, IBM and 3Com have proposed LMMP, which incorporates the CMIS services directly on the IEEE 802 Logical Link Layer. By virtue of its definition, LMMP messages are limited to a single local area network segment.

FOR FURTHER STUDY

International Organization for Standardization, Open Systems Interconnection "Management Information Service Definition, Part 2: Common Management Information Service," International Standard Number 9595-2, ISO, Switzerland, May 1988.

_____. "Open Systems Interconnection, Management Information Protocol Definition, Part 2: Common Management Information Protocol," International Standard Number 9596-2, ISO, Switzerland, May 1988.

Rose, M., *The Open Book: A Practical Perspective on OSI*, Englewood Cliffs, NJ: Prentice-Hall, 1990.

Stallings, W., *SNMP, SNMPv2, and CMIP: The Practical Guide to Network Management Standards*, Reading, MA: Addison-Wesley, 1993.

PART 3

Management Information Bases

Chapter 10

A Look at RFC 1213 (MIB II) and RFC 1573

In This Chapter:

Chris slowly picked up the printout of MIB-II and softly whistled. A large percentage of devices on MegaNet supported this document, so it seemed like a logical place to start trying to look into the details of a MIB. All that needed to be done was to examine each object described in this document and then figure out how to apply each to solving the network management puzzle. Chris immediately saw how some of the information in MIB-II could help in certain network management tasks, such as documenting device configuration information, finding network addresses, and seeing how long a device had been active. But to do some of the things that Chris's manager

was asking for would require a bit more research. Fortunately, Chris
thought sarcastically, MIB-II had such user-friendly names to help:
ifInNUcastPkts, ipNetToMediaNetAddress, ipAdEntBcastAddr. . . .
Chris began to wonder where reading another language fell into the
job description.

In this chapter we examine each section of RFC 1213, "Management Information Base for Network Management of TCP/IP-based Internets: MIB-II,"
or simply MIB-II. We also examine each section of a related document, RFC
1573, "Evolution of the Interfaces Group of MIB-II." Our purpose is to help
network engineers and developers of network management applications decide how to use the information in them.

First, we define certain basic terms applicable to both MIB documents. We
then turn to various subtrees of MIB-II, including a discussion of MIB-II objects—that is, specific information accessible by the SNMP agent on a network device or computer system—and how to use these objects in network
management. For each MIB-II group, we list the objects that apply to the various types of network management and, where appropriate, discuss the objects and concepts presented by RFC 1573.

Throughout this chapter we discuss examining the rate of change in a MIB-
II object. The rate of change is defined as the amount a particular object
changes between time t and some later time $t + 1$, divided by the time difference $t + 1$ and t:

$$\text{Rate of object} = (\text{Value of object}_{t+1} - \text{Value of object}_t)/(t + 1) - t.$$

There are many ways you can compute this rate automatically. Some network
management systems use graphical features to compute the rate of a MIB object; others allow you to write a small program to compute rates. Also, you
could have a network management application store values of objects in the
relational database and use SQL to perform the rate calculations.

Although space restraints prevent our discussing all of these objects as they
apply to network management, we do examine as many as feasible. All of the
functions described in this chapter can be performed by the network engineer manually or, preferably, by the appropriate network management application. We prefer that the application, rather than the engineer, perform
the functions.

We recommend that you have a copy of RFC 1213 and RFC 1573 nearby
when reading this material (see Appendix A for instructions on obtaining
these RFCs). Definitions and explanations of the syntax used with a MIB are
available in RFC 1155, "Structure and Identification of Management Information for TCP/IP-based Internets (SMI)." These MIBs also contain infor-

mation about many protocols in the Transmission Control Protocol/Internet Protocol (TCP/IP) suite.[1] Much of the discussion in this chapter assumes your prior knowledge of these protocols and how they work.

10.1 MIB DEFINITIONS

The first section of RFC 1213 defines the types of objects available in the MIB. This RFC imports object types as defined in RFC 1155 and RFC 1212, "Concise MIB Definitions." In the RFCs a network device or computer system that has an SNMP agent is known as an *entity* and is the term we use in this chapter.

Both of the object types *NetworkAddress* and *IpAddress* refer to an IP address. Although the definition of NetworkAddress in RFC 1213 is generic, the MIB we discuss here applies only to IP entities.

A *counter* is an object that is a nonnegative integer that increases until it reaches some maximum value—for example, the total number of errors received on an interface. In MIB-II counters are 32-bit numbers, but as we saw in Chapter 8, SNMPv2 allows for the use of 64-bit numbers for counter objects.

A *Gauge* is an object that is a nonnegative integer that can rise and fall—for example, the current number of packets in the output queue of an interface. The *TimeTicks* object is a nonnegative integer that counts hundredths of a second since an event—for example, the amount of time a system has been operational.

RFC 1213 contains two new definitions: DisplayString and PhysAddress. A *DisplayString* specifies how to print ASCII strings. A *PhysAddress* defines how to format physical network addresses, such as medium access control (MAC) addresses.

10.2 THE SYSTEM GROUP

The system group contains data about the system in which the entity resides. Many of these objects are useful for fault management and configuration management.

Objects for Fault Management

The system group objects listed in Table 10.1 apply to fault management. The object identifier found in sysObjectID classifies the vendor with the entity, helpful data when you need to know the device's manufacturer.

---

[1] A good reference on these protocols can be found in various RFCs. Some of the other sources for this information are listed at the end of Chapter 1.

Table 10.1   System Group Objects for Fault Management

Object	Information
sysObjectID	The system manufacturer
sysServices	Which protocol layer the device services
sysUptime	How long the system has been operational

The object sysServices tells which level of the OSI Reference Model the device services. The value returned is a sum of values for each layer, using the formula $2^{(L-1)}$ where L is the protocol layer number. For example, a router that operates primarily at layer 3 would return a value of 4—$2^{(3-1)}$—whereas a host that runs transport-layer services (layer 4) and application layer services (layer 7) would return a value of 72—$2^{(7-1)} + 2^{(4-1)}$. This information is useful for debugging problems when the functionality of the device is unknown.

The sysUptime object tells how long a system has been functioning. A fault management application polling for this object can determine whether the entity has restarted: If the application sees a monotonously increasing sysUptime, the entity is known to be up; if the value of sysUptime is less than the previous value, the entity has restarted since the last poll.

If the value of sysUptime has decreased since the last poll of an object, the management application can assume either that the agent on the entity has been restarted or that the value of sysUptime has wrapped at the maximum value of $2^{32} - 1$. One possible way to determine which of these events has occurred is to see how long it has been since the last poll interval and the last known value of sysUptime, then to determine whether a wrap condition could exist. If a wrap condition could exist, the management application cannot determine which of the two events occurred. As we will see in Chapter 11, the Remote Network Monitoring Device MIB (RMON MIB) recommends polling objects frequently enough to be able to determine which of the two possible events has occurred.

RFC 1573 defines ifTestTable, a table of objects containing one row per interface on the entity. This table defines objects that allow a network management application to test an interface for a variety of faults. The exact tests for a specific interface are defined in the media-specific MIB for the interface. For example, the tests for a Token Ring interface are defined in "IEEE 802.5 Token Ring Interface Type MIB" (RFC 1743).

Objects for Configuration Management

The system group objects in Table 10.2 pertain to configuration management. For many entities, the software revision or operating system is available through sysDescr. This data can be useful both for managing the setup of the

Table 10.2   System Group Objects for Configuration Management

Object	Information
sysDescr	Description of the system
sysLocation	System's physical location
sysContact	Person responsible for the system
sysName	System's name

device and for troubleshooting. The objects sysLocation, sysContact, and sys-Name tell you, respectively, the physical location of the system, a person to contact for problems, and the name of the network device.

10.3 THE INTERFACES GROUP

The *interfaces group* objects offer data about each specific interface on a network device and are useful in fault, configuration, performance, and accounting management. The interfaces group contains a table of objects; each row in this table represents one interface on the entity.

In general, RFC 1573, "Evolution of the Interfaces Group of MIB-II," provides:

- A new table of objects for each interface on the entity

- A revised method for interface numbering

- Larger values for certain interface objects

- A methodology for handling interface sublayers

This section discusses each of these topics and how the new MIB objects in RFC 1573 relate to the functional areas of network management. In some instances the topics presented in RFC 1573 do not define new MIB objects but do alter the presentation of interfaces by the entity to a network management system or application.

The ifTable objects contain information about all the interfaces on an entity; an ifEntry is a row of information about a specific interface. One of the most significant changes recommended by RFC 1573 is the addition of a new interfaces group table, called the ifXTable (interface extensions table). The ifXTable, an extension of the objects found in the MIB-II ifTable, can be used in many areas of network management.

The number of ifEntry records is found in ifNumber. For example, if a device has three interfaces, the value of ifNumber will be 3, and there will be an array of three separate ifEntry records, one record for each interface.

The object ifIndex is an integer that is an index of the array of ifEntry groups. According to MIB-II, ifIndex is a value between 1 and ifNumber that remains constant until an entity restarts. The structure of the interfaces group is set out in Fig. 10.1.

RFC 1573 points out a potential problem with the MIB-II approach and suggests a few changes to the ifNumber and ifIndex objects. The problem with the RFC 1213 definition of ifNumber and ifIndex deals with devices that allow the dynamic addition or removal of interfaces. The dynamic addition of a dial-up link and the hot-swap of a piece of hardware are two common situations in which interfaces get dynamically added or removed from an entity. If an interface gets dynamically added to the entity, it is possible to increase both ifNumber and ifEntry at the same time. Yet if an interface was dynamically removed from the entity, ifIndex needs to remain constant, according to MIB-II. Also, if an ifIndex value that was previously in use by the entity was later reused for a new interface (without restarting the system), this could produce interesting results from the network management system's perspective, especially if the bandwidth or media types of the two interfaces did not match.

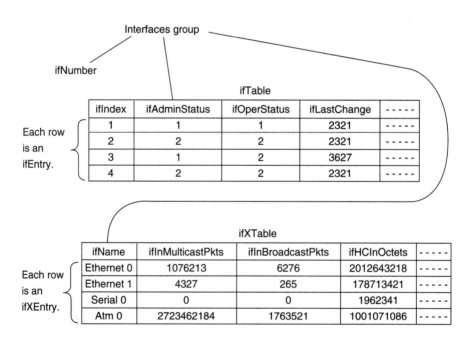

Figure 10.1 The interfaces group structure for a device with four interfaces. Querying ifNumber would yield a value of 4. Note that not all of the objects available in each ifEntry and ifXEntry are shown.

To solve this problem, RFC 1573 recommends that entities remove the requirement that ifIndex be less than ifNumber. Now ifNumber still gives the number of total interfaces on an entity and thus the total number of rows in ifTable. Also, ifIndex is still the index into ifTable. The entity is now allowed to assign a value of ifIndex larger than ifNumber for dynamically added interfaces. So a management system may encounter ifIndex values larger than ifNumber, given the presence of dynamically added or removed interfaces.

One small problem this solution causes is that it is no longer easy for a management system to correlate a physical interface on the entity to a row in ifTable (based on ifIndex). Therefore RFC 1573 proposes an object found in the ifXTable, ifName. This object contains the entity's local name for the interface in a particular ifEntry. So if the interface is known to the local device as "lan0," that text name would be found in ifName.

Objects for Fault Management

The interfaces group objects in Table 10.3 apply to fault management. From ifAdminStatus and ifOperStatus combined, the fault management application can determine the current status of the interface. Both objects return integers: 1 (up), 2 (down), 3 (testing), and 4 (unknown). Table 10.4 summarizes the possible meanings of these objects with respect to a single interface and can be interpreted as follows:

- If both ifAdminStatus and ifOperStatus return up, the interface is operational.

- If ifAdminStatus is up and ifOperStatus is down, the interface is in failure mode.

- If both ifAdminStatus and ifOperStatus are down, the interface has been administratively turned off.

- If both ifAdminStatus and ifOperStatus return testing, the interface is in testing mode (possibly loopback).

(All other combinations of the two objects are not applicable.)

Table 10.3   Interfaces Group Objects for Fault Management

Object	*Information*
ifAdminStatus	Whether the interface is administratively up/down/test
ifOperStatus	Whether the interface operational state is up/down/test
ifLastChange	Time when the interface changed operational state
ifTestTable	Test interface for faults

Table 10.4   Possible Meanings of Integers Returned

| | *ifAdminStatus* | | |
ifOperStatus	*Up (1)*	*Down (2)*	*Testing (3)*
Up (1)	Operational	N/A	N/A
Down (2)	Failure	Down	N/A
Testing (3)	N/A	N/A	Testing

If one of these four combinations is not returned by a query for ifAdmin-Status and ifOperStatus, the entity or device software might be working improperly. The object ifLastChange will contain the value of sysUpTime correlating to when the interface entered its current operational state.

RFC 1573 recommends a new state for ifOperStatus—dormant—which has a value of 5. This new state reflects that the interface is not operating but is waiting for some special event before transitioning to the up state. Some examples of this new, dormant state would be devices that have dial-backup, bandwidth-on-demand, or dial-on-demand features. The dial-backup feature refers to a device interface configured to become active only if the primary interface fails and is often used in disaster-recovery situations. An interface set up to become active only if the primary interface crosses a user-defined utilization percentage threshold has bandwidth-on-demand. This feature is often used to provide additional bandwidth to sites that rarely require it, such as an office that requires additional bandwidth only during a peak business period. Dial-on-demand describes a device that does not have any connection to the network but that becomes active and temporarily makes a connection (perhaps by dialing a modem) when some "interesting" packets arrive. This feature is often used for devices that transmit small amounts of data and do not justify a dedicated connection. Figure 10.2 shows the dial-backup, bandwidth-on-demand, and dial-on-demand features.

The dormant state of ifOperStatus changes Table 10.4 as shown in Table 10.5. If a network management application finds an interface with ifOper-Status equal to dormant, it should assume that the interface is waiting for an event to occur before transitioning to the up state.

RFC 1573 also defines the ifRcvAddressTable, which contains an entry for each address the entity will receive packets on for a particular interface. This information may alert the network engineer to configuration issues with the entity, especially if it is listening to too many or too few addresses.

An interface may receive packets that are broadcasts, multicasts, or unicasts (sent to the entity directly). An interface may listen to multiple multi-

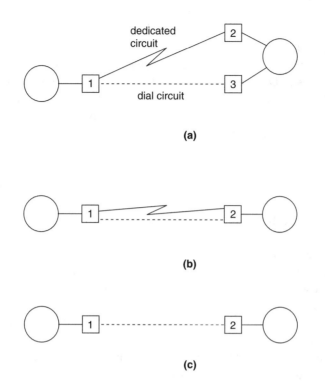

(a)

(b)

(c)

Figure 10.2   (a) dial-backup; for dial-backup, device 1 dials a
connection to device 3 only when the primary link to device 2 fails.
(b) bandwith-on-demand; for bandwidth-on-demand, device 1 dials
a connection to device 2 only when the primary link exceeds a user-
defined utilization threshold. (c) dial-on-demand; for dial-on-
demand, device 1 dials a connection to device 2 only when data
arrive that warrant the connection.

Table 10.5   Changes Resulting from Dormant State of ifOperStatus

| | *ifAdminStatus* | | |
ifOperStatus	*Up (1)*	*Down (2)*	*Testing (3)*
Up (1)	Operational	N/A	N/A
Down (2)	Failure	Down	N/A
Testing (3)	N/A	N/A	Testing
Dormant (5)	Dormant	N/A	N/A

cast addresses, depending on the network protocols running on the interface. For example, an interface may be listening for the multicast address assigned to DECnet Phase IV Hello messages (a message type used to communicate between hosts in DECnet Phase IV) if the interface is running this protocol. Many network protocols use specific multicast addresses to send messages to a select group of devices on a medium. If a network management application could access a table of multicast addresses and their related network layer protocols, the application could deduce the network-layer protocols the entity communicates.

Objects for Configuration Management

The interfaces group objects in Table 10.6 apply to configuration management. These objects give you information about the setup of an interface. The objects ifDescr and ifType name the interface and give its type, respectively. For example, if ifDescr returned the string "Ethernet0", ifType might return the number 6. The meaning of the number returned by ifType is defined in the MIB. To be more helpful to you, network management applications should map the number 6 to a string that gives you more information about the interface type, such as "Ethernet-CSMA/CD."

Table 10.6   Interfaces Group Objects for Configuration Management

Object	Information
ifDescr	Description of the interface
ifName	Name of the interface
ifType	Type of interface
ifMTU	Maximum datagram through the interface
ifSpeed	Bandwidth of the interface
ifAdminStatus	Administrative status of the interface (up/down/test)
ifHighSpeed	Bandwidth of a high-speed interface
ifPromiscuousMode	Whether the interface is in promiscuous mode
ifConnectorPresent	Whether this interface has a physical connector
ifLinkUpDownTrapEnable	Whether this interface generates traps
ifRcvAddressTable	Addresses this interface receives packets on

The object ifSpeed is a gauge that tracks the current interface speed in bits per second; for example, on an Ethernet interface ifSpeed typically returns 10000000, which represents 10 Mb/sec (10 megabits per second, or 10,000,000 bits per second). This object is helpful for finding the current speed for an interface that may change, such as one that can allocate bandwidth on demand for heavy bursts of traffic.

The object ifHighSpeed is a gauge found in the ifXTable of RFC 1573. This object is a 64-bit number and will be used only for interfaces with speeds of 4.2 Gb/sec (4.2 gigabits per second, or 4,200,000,000 bits per second) or faster.

The object ifAdminStatus tells you whether an interface is administratively active. By sending an SNMP Set-Request, you can use this object to remotely configure the interface on or off.

Also found in the ifXTable of RFC 1573 are the objects ifPromiscuousMode and ifConnectorPresent, which return the value of true and false. The object ifPromiscuousMode tells whether the current interface is receiving all packets on the medium, whether they are addressed to the entity or not. An interface may be set up to be in promiscuous mode for a variety of reasons, including network analysis. The object ifConnectorPresent can tell you whether this interface has a physical connector.

As we will see later, a physical interface can be represented by multiple conceptual rows in ifTable, called interface sublayers. If this is the case and if the status of the interface changes, multiple interfaces may send linkUp or linkDown traps (as required by an interface in SNMPv1 and SNMPv2). Because all but one of these traps will be redundant, RFC 1573 added the object ifLinkUpDownTrapEnable to let the network engineer configure whether an interface should send the linkUp and linkDown traps. RFC 1573 recommends that only the lowest sublayer of the interface generates traps. A configuration management application could query ifLinkUpDownTrapEnable to determine whether an interface and its sublayers are set up correctly.

Objects for Performance Management

The interfaces group objects listed in Table 10.7 apply to performance management. Performance management applications should be designed to watch the percentage of errors on an interface. The application must be able to find the total number of packets and errors on the interface. The application can determine the total number of packets received on the interface by totaling ifInUcastPkts and ifInNUcastPkts and the total number of packets sent on the interface by totaling ifOutUcastPkts and ifOutNUcastPkts:

Total packets received = ifInUcastPkts + ifInNUcastPkts
Total packets sent = ifOutUcastPkts + ifOutNUcastPkts

Table 10.7   Group Objects for Performance Management

Object	Information
ifInDiscards	Rate of input discards
ifOutDiscards	Rate of output discards
ifInErrors	Rate of input errors
ifOutErrors	Rate of output errors
ifInOctets	Rate of bytes received
ifOutOctets	Rate of bytes sent
ifInUcastPkts	Rate of input unicast packets
ifOutUcastPkts	Rate of output unicast packets
ifInNUcastPkts	Rate of input nonunicast packets
ifOutNUcastPkts	Rate of output nonunicast packets
ifInUnknownProtos	Rate of input unknown protocol packets
ifOutQLen	Total packets in the output queue
ifInMulticastPkts	Rate of input multicast packets
ifInBroadcastPkts	Rate of input broadcast packets
ifOutMulticastPkts	Rate of output multicast packets
ifOutBroadcastPkts	Rate of output broadcast packets
ifHCInOctets	Rate of bytes received, high-capacity interface
ifHCOutOctets	Rate of bytes sent, high-capacity interface
ifHCInUcastPkts	Rate of input unicast packets, high-capacity interface
ifHCOutUcastPkts	Rate of output unicast packets, high-capacity interface
ifHCInMulticastPkts	Rate of input multicast packets, high-capacity interface
ifHCOutMulticastPkts	Rate of output multicast packets, high-capacity interface
ifHCInBroadcastPkts	Rate of input broadcast packets, high-capacity interface
ifHCOutBroadcastPkts	Rate of output broadcast packets, high-capacity interface

RFC 1573 deprecates the use of ifInNUcastPkts and ifOutNUcastPkts, as these counters do not differentiate between two types of packets: broadcasts and multicasts. The objects ifInMulticastPkts, ifInBroadcastPkts, ifOutMulticastPkts, and ifOutBroadcastPkts were added to ifXTable. This changes the previous formulas (for those entities complying to RFC 1573) to:

Total packets received = ifInUcastPkts + ifInBroadcasts
+ ifInMulticasts
Total packets sent = ifOutUcastPkts + ifOutBroadcasts
+ ifOutMulticasts

The percentages of input and output errors on the interface are found with the following equations:

Percent input errors = ifInErrors/total packets received
Percent output errors = ifOutErrors/total packets sent

An application can use similar methods to monitor the number of packets discarded by the interface, using the objects ifInDiscards and ifOutDiscards. Errors or discards can result from a malfunctioning interface, media problems, buffering problems on the device, and so forth.

Once the errors have been discovered, you can begin resolving them. However, be aware that not all discards represent a problem. For example, a device may have a high percentage of discards because it's receiving many packets of an unknown protocol. The number of discards resulting from this situation is found in ifInUnknownProtos. Consider a network device that routes only IP. The device has an interface on an Ethernet, where many personal computers form a network of clients and servers that send messages between themselves as Ethernet broadcasts. Because the network device has to pick up the broadcasts, it consequently receives many packets it does not know how to process, thus causing the number of ifInDiscards to climb and the number of ifInUnknownProtos to grow proportionally. As you can see, in this situation a large number of ifInDiscards or ifInUnknownProtos may not indicate a problem.

A performance management application can use ifInOctets and ifOutOctets to compute the percent utilization on an interface. To perform this computation, two different polls would be required: one to find the total bytes at time x and another to find the total bytes at time y. The following equation computes total bytes sent and received between poll times x and y (in seconds):

$$\text{Total bytes} = (\text{ifInOctets}_y - \text{ifInOctets}_x)$$
$$+ (\text{ifOutOctets}_y - \text{ifOutOctets}_x)$$

Next, calculate total bytes per second:

$$\text{Total bytes per sec} = \text{total bytes}/(y - x)$$

Then find line utilization, as follows:

$$\text{Utilization} = (\text{total bytes per sec} * 8)/\text{ifSpeed}$$

In the equation for line utilization, the multiplication by 8 is necessary to convert from bytes to bits. The object ifSpeed is a number in bits per second.

Note that on an interface that operates at full duplex, such as a serial link, this equation will compute twice the interface utilization. For example, a serial link may operate at 64 Kb/sec (64 kilobits per second, or 64,000 bits per second) in full duplex. Thus if you totaled the input and output bytes of the interface, you would be computing utilization for a 128 Kb/sec link. One possible solution to this problem is to compute as separate numbers the total bytes input and output over the given time period. Then take the larger of these two numbers and divide by ifSpeed (or ifHighSpeed).

RFC 1573 makes some definitive recommendations concerning the size of counter objects for an entity's interface-specific counters:

- If the speed of an interface is less than 20 Mb/sec, the entity must use 32-bit counters for counting both packets and bytes.

- If the speed of an interface is between 20 Mb/sec and 650 Mb/sec, it must use a 32-bit counter for counting packets and a 64-bit counter for counting bytes.

- If the speed of an interface is greater than 650 Mb/sec, it must use 64-bit counters for both packet and byte counters.

This logic allows the use of 32-bit counters for most technology using SNMPv1, such as 10 Mb/sec Ethernet and 16 Mb/sec Token Ring, and a growth path into SNMPv2 for faster interface types.

To accommodate these recommendations, the following objects were added to ifXTable: ifHCInOctets, ifHCInUcastPkts, ifHCInMulticastPkts, ifHCInBroadcastPkts, ifHCOutOctets, ifHCOutUcastPkts, ifHCOutMulticastPkts, ifHCOutBroadcastPkts. In each case "HC" means "high capacity" and comes from the fact that each of these counters is a 64-bit number. An entity would use these objects according to the rules described previously. These objects have the same meanings as their MIB-II counterparts and do not remove the MIB-II objects. Even when the 64-bit counters are being used, a management system can still get the 32-bit counters. For example, the value of ifInOctets becomes the 32 least significant bits of ifHCInOctets. Note that for high-capacity interfaces, you will need to modify the formulas shown in this section to use the appropriate high-capacity objects.

The object ifOutQLen tells whether a device is having trouble sending data out on the interface. The value of the object will increase as the number of packets waiting to leave the interface increases. Trouble sending data out could result from errors on the interface or the device's not being to handle the packets as quickly as they are input. Although a large number of packets waiting in the output queue is not an immediate problem, its persistent growth might indicate congestion on the interface.

Used together, ifOutDiscards and ifOutOctets also may give an indication of network congestion. If a device is discarding many packets that are trying to leave the interface, as indicated by ifOutDiscards, and the total number of output bytes is decreasing, as shown by ifOutOctets, the interface might be congested.

Objects for Accounting Management

The interfaces group objects shown in Table 10.8 apply to accounting management. Using ifInOctets and ifOutOctets (or ifHCInOctets and ifHC-OutOctets), an accounting management application can determine the number of bytes sent and received on an interface. This data can be helpful to the network device that has a direct interface to a single billing entity. If traffic traverses this interface in transit to another billing entity, the model doesn't work well. However, if the interface does connect to a single billing entity without transit traffic, no calculations are necessary to find out how many bytes the billing entity sent to or received from the network. If the billing model uses packet counts instead of bytes, ifInUcastPkts, ifOutUcastPkts, ifInNUcastPkts, ifOutNUcastPkts, ifInMulticastPkts, ifOutMulticastPkts, ifInBroadcastPkts and ifOutBroadcastPkts (or ifHCInUcastPkts, ifHCOut-UcastPkts, ifHCInNUcastPkts, ifHCOutNUcastPkts, ifInMulticastPkts, ifOutMulticastPkts, ifInBroadcastPkts, and ifOutBroadcastPkts) give the data packet counts necessary to perform the billing process.

Other RFC 1573 Recommendations

So far the application of the new objects in RFC 1573 has been explained as the objects relate to the functional areas of network management. In addition, RFC 1573 defines the implementation of interface sublayers, handling virtual circuits, and handling bit, character, and fixed-length interfaces.

Interface Sublayers

On many entities a single physical interface may have characteristics of medium-specific MIBs that reside below the network layer of the OSI Reference Model. An example of this may be X.25 running over LAPB (Link-Access Protocol, Balanced) on a V.35 connector. In this example X.25 is the network-layer protocol, LAPB is the data link–layer protocol, and the phys-

Table 10.8   Interfaces Group Objects for Accounting Management

Object	*Information*
ifInOctets	Total bytes received
ifOutOctets	Total bytes sent
ifInUcastPkts	Total unicast packets received
ifOutUcastPkts	Total unicast packets sent
ifInNUcastPkts	Total nonunicast packets received
ifOutNUcastPkts	Total nonunicast packets sent
ifInMulticastPkts	Total multicasts received
ifOutMulticastPkts	Total multicasts sent
ifInBroadcastPkts	Total broadcasts received
ifOutBroadcastPkts	Total broadcasts sent
ifHCInOctets	Total bytes received, high-capacity interface
ifHCOutOctets	Total bytes sent, high-capacity interface
ifHCInUcastPkts	Total unicast packets received, high-capacity interface
ifHCOutUcastPkts	Total unicast packets sent, high-capacity interface
ifHCInNUcastPkts	Total nonunicast packets received, high-capacity interface
ifHCOutNUcastPkts	Total nonunicast packets sent, high-capacity interface
ifHCInMulticastPkts	Total multicasts received, high-capacity interface
ifHCOutMulticastPkts	Total multicasts sent, high-capacity interface
ifHCInBroadcastPkts	Total broadcasts received, high-capacity interface
ifHCOutBroadcastPkts	Total broadcasts sent, high-capacity interface

ical layer is a V.35 connector. For each of these layers of the OSI Reference Model, a unique medium-specific MIB exists. To handle these multiple layers, RFC 1573 recommends that an individual row in ifTable represent each sublayer and that a new MIB table, the ifStackTable, identify the upper and lower sublayers of the interface. The ifStackTable also has a mechanism to help identify the medium-specific MIB for each sublayer.

Virtual Circuits

Certain wide area network technologies allow for multiple logical connections over a single physical interface, called *virtual circuits*. X.25, Frame Relay, and ATM are all technologies that support virtual circuits. Because a virtual circuit is a logical connection over a single physical interface, RFC 1573 strongly recommends that all virtual circuits be represented by a single row in ifTable. This recommendation makes sense in nearly all situations, because the value of the MIB objects in ifTable would be identical for each virtual circuit, leaving the entity to keep multiple copies of the same information. Network management applications will have to query the media-specific MIB for a given technology to get information about virtual circuits. For example, if an application determines that an interface is running Frame Relay, it could then query the objects found in the "Management Information Base for Frame Relay DTEs" (RFC 1315) for virtual circuit objects.

Bit, Character, and Fixed-Length Interfaces

Many of the objects found in ifTable are applicable to every type of network interface. However, many other objects are applicable only to packet-oriented interfaces. With the definition of MIBs that work on a character level (such as V.35, RS-449) and with newer technologies that use fixed-length packets (such as ATM cells), it may no longer make sense to maintain packet-oriented objects for these interfaces (or interface sublayers). RFC 1573 provides different subsets of the ifTable objects (called groups) as follows:

- ifGeneralGroup: applicable to all interfaces

- ifFixedLengthGroup: for character-oriented or fixed-length interfaces

- ifHCFixedLengthGroup: for character-oriented or fixed-length high-speed interfaces

- ifPacketGroup: for packet-oriented interfaces

- ifHCPacketGroup: for high-speed packet-oriented interfaces

- ifVHCPacketGroup: for very-high-speed packet-oriented interfaces

The separation of the ifTable objects into these groups makes it possible for an interface to maintain only objects that make sense for its technology.

The objects in ifGeneralGroup apply to all interfaces (such as ifType and ifSpeed). Of the remaining groups, only one will be applicable to an interface.

The ifFixedLengthGroup has objects for character-oriented or fixed-length interfaces (such as ifInOctets and ifInErrors). The ifHCFixedLengthGroup contains the same objects as the ifFixedLengthGroup and adds the relevant 64-bit counters, such as ifHCInOctets. This group is designed to be used on character-oriented or fixed-length interfaces that run at 20 Mb/sec or faster.

The ifPacketGroup contains objects for packet-oriented interfaces (such as ifInOctets, ifInUcastPkts, and ifMtu). The ifHCPacketGroup contains the same objects and the necessary additional objects to handle interfaces with speeds greater than 20 Mb/sec and less than 650 Mb/sec (such as ifHCInOctets, ifInUcastPkts, and ifMtu). The ifVHCPacketGroup is also the same as the ifPacketGroup but has the objects needed to handle interfaces with speeds greater than 650 Mb/sec, (such as ifHCInOctets, ifHCInUcastPkts, and ifMtu).

10.4 THE ADDRESS TRANSLATION GROUP

No longer a separate group, address translation objects have been incorporated into other protocol groups. In this chapter we examine the use of address translation information in network management as it appears in each of those groups.

10.5 THE IP GROUP

IP is a network protocol that uses a connectionless mode of service to deliver datagrams. The *IP group* provides information about IP on the entity. This information is subdivided as follows:

- Objects that give data about errors and the types of IP packets seen.

- A table of information about the IP addresses on this entity.

- IP routing table for the entity.

- The mapping of IP addresses to other protocol addresses. This section supersedes the features of the address translation group.

The structure of the IP group is shown in Fig. 10.3. These sections offer objects that can apply to fault, configuration, performance, and accounting management.

Objects for Fault Management

The IP group objects listed in Table 10.9 pertain to fault management. All objects in the ipRouteTable can be useful for fault management, such as tracking routing problems and devices that advertise incorrect routing informa-

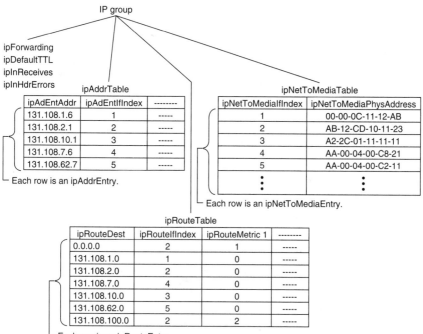

Figure 10.3 The IP group is divided into four areas. Note that not all the objects for each table are shown.

tion. These objects enable the fault management application to query the IP routing table for a device and discover routes through a network. Further, ipRouteType and ipRouteProto can tell how the routing information was learned.

Suppose, for example, that a user cannot connect from *Kirk* to *Spock* on *MegaNet*. The network setup for this scenario is shown in Figure 10.4. You could first examine the network map on the management system to ensure that all network devices are up and running. Next, because there are several possible routes from *Kirk* to *Spock*, you would want to find which one was being used. Accordingly, the fault management application could use ipRouteDest, ipRouteNextHop, and ipRouteIfIndex to query *Kirk* and ask for

Table 10.9 IP Group Objects for Fault Management

Object	*Information*
ipRouteTable	IP routing table
ipNetToMediaTable	IP address translation table

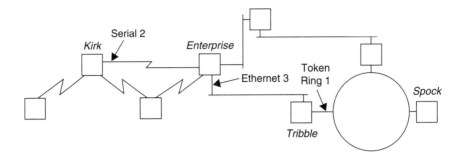

Figure 10.4 The network setup between *Kirk* and *Spock*.

the next hop to *Spock*, which happens to be to the machine *Enterprise* through interface Serial 2. The object ipRouteDest is used to find the correct routing entry to reach *Spock*, ipRouteNextHop gives the address of the next hop, and ipRouteIfIndex gives the outbound interface on the entity. The number returned by ipRouteIfIndex is correlated to the ifIndex from the interfaces group. The string "Serial 2" could then be found in ifDescr.

Your next step would be to ask *Enterprise* for the same information. You learn that *Enterprise* routes to *Spock* by sending data through the device *Tribble* by means of the interface Ethernet 3. Next, you discover that *Tribble* sends data directly to *Spock* by means of interface TokenRing 1. By performing this process, you will have learned that *Kirk* does have a valid route to *Spock*.

Other IP group data that could help you solve this problem are the objects listed in ipNetToMediaTable. These objects tell the mapping of IP addresses to another protocol address. A common example is an ARP (Address Resolution Protocol) table that maps IP addresses to MAC addresses. Returning to our example, let's say that as part of solving the problem, the fault management application queried *Tribble* for ipNetToMediaIfIndex, ipNetToMediaPhysAddress, and ipNetToMediaNetAddress in each row of the ipNetToMediaTable. It happens that one row of the table does contain an entry for *Spock*, found on interface TokenRing 1. You now know that *Tribble* has communicated with *Spock*.

A bit confused, you next might call the system administrator for *Spock* to find out whether any hardware or software on the system was recently changed. You learn that the token ring interface on *Spock* was changed this morning. Hence the ipNetToMediaTable (or ARP cache, in this case) is out of date on *Tribble*; the IP address to the Token Ring MAC address mapping is for the old interface board, which no longer exists. Therefore you could decide to fix the trouble with *Tribble* by clearing the ARP cache. Then the next time *Tribble* needs to contact *Spock*, *Tribble* will send an ARP and discover the correct translation between the IP address of *Spock* and the new Token Ring MAC address.

Objects for Configuration Management

The IP group objects in Table 10.10 apply to configuration management. Some network devices are set up to forward IP datagrams, such as routers. A configuration management application query to a device for the ipForwarding object can inform you about the functionality of the entity. For example, if the application queried a device for the system group object sysServices and found that a device services the network layer (layer 3), you might then want to learn whether the device forwards IP datagrams with ipForwarding. In this case an Appletalk router may return a value of sysServices indicating that it services the network layer, but ipForwarding may show you that the device does not route the IP.

As we saw in Chapter 4, knowing the network address, subnet mask, and broadcast address assigned to a device is invaluable for configuration management. The ipAddrTable gives information about the current IP addresses on the entity. Each row in the ipAddrTable is called an ipAddrEntry. Within each ipAddrEntry the ipAdEntAddr and ipAdEntIfIndex tell the IP addresses and related interface, respectively. You can use ipAdEntIfIndex to correlate the ipAddrTable entry to an interfaces group ifTable entry. The ipAdEntNetMask gives the subnet mask, and ipAdEntBcastAddr tells the broadcast address. Note, however, that the MIB defines these objects as read-only, so for configuration management purposes an application or engineer can query for this information but cannot alter it.

The ipRouteTable does define many of its objects as read-write. For configuration management purposes, the application could enter new routes with ipRouteDest and change the route type with ipRouteType. Further, configuration of the routing metrics is possible by setting ipRouteMetric1, ipRouteMetric2, ipRouteMetric3, ipRouteMetric4, and ipRouteMetric5. The setting of these objects allows the network engineer to control the routes IP packets take throughout the data network. You may wish to control these

Table 10.10 IP Group Objects for Configuration Management

Object	*Information*
ipForwarding	If the device is set up to forward IP
ipAddrTable	IP addresses on the device
ipRoute Table	IP routing table

routes for technical reasons (route around a path experiencing errors) or policy-based reasons (route through a network that costs less money to use).

Objects for Performance Management

The IP group objects listed in Table 10.11 pertain to performance management. Because of the large number of objects, we don't discuss each of them here but do summarize some of the key objects.

Using IP group objects, a performance management application can measure the percentage of IP traffic input and output by the entity. For example, the total packets received by the entity is available by computing the sum of ifInUcastPkts and ifInNUcastPkts for each interface and then dividing ipInReceives by this sum to find the percentage of IP datagrams received. Note that if the entity being queried supports RFC 1573, you will need to substitute the sum of ifInMulticastPkts and ifInBroadcastPkts for ifInNUcastPkts in this example. A similar computation could be done by using the object

Table 10.11   IP Group Objects for Performance Management

Object	Information
ipInReceives	Rate of input datagrams
ipInHdrErrors	Rate of input header errors
ipInAddrErrors	Rate of input address errors
ipForwDatagrams	Rate of forwarded datagrams
ipInUnknown Protos	Rate of input datagrams for an unknown protocol
ipInDiscards	Rate of input datagrams discarded
ipInDelivers	Rate of input datagrams
ipOutRequests	Rate of output datagrams
ipOutDiscards	Rate of output datagrams discarded
ipOutNoRoutes	Rate of discards due to lack of routing information
ipRoutingDiscards	Rate of routing entries discarded
ipReasmReqds	Rate of datagrams received needing reassembly
ipReasmOKs	Rate datagrams successfully reassembled
ipReasmFails	Rate of fragmentation reassembly failures
ipFragOKs	Rate of successful fragmentations
ipFragFails	Rate of unsuccessful fragmentations
ipFragCreates	Rate of fragments generate

ipOutRequests for datagrams sent by the entity. Note that the object ipOutRequests counts only the number of datagrams sent by this entity, not the datagrams forwarded. By looking at the rate of change in the objects ipInReceives and ipOutRequests, you can find the rate at which this entity is receiving and sending IP datagrams.

The entity counts the number of times it has had to discard a datagram. The datagram may be discarded on input—the ipInDiscards object—or on output—the ipOutDiscards object. The discarding of a datagram may occur because of a lack of system resources or any other reason that did not permit the proper processing of the datagram.

Other error conditions can occur because a datagram comes into the entity with an invalid IP header—counted by the entity—the object ipInAddrErrors. A large percentage of IP packets that result in errors could lead to performance issues for an application using IP for delivery. The application can calculate the percentage of errors from IP datagrams as follows:

$$\text{Percent IP input errors} = (\text{ipInDiscards} + \text{ipInHdrErrors} + \text{ipInAddrErrors})/\text{ipInReceives}$$
$$\text{Percent IP output errors} = (\text{ipOutDiscards} + \text{ipOutHdrErrors} + \text{ipOutAddrErrors})/\text{ipOutRequests}$$

The interfaces group objects can also be used to compare the total number of packets output on all interfaces in relation to the rate of IP output errors. This can tell you whether a large percentage of the packets output from the entity have resulted in IP output errors.

Some IP group objects can calculate errors that result from IP fragmentation. Computing percentages and rates of datagrams fragmented and their associated errors can prove insightful: It might be useful to know that a device is sending or receiving a large percentage of fragmented IP datagrams. Also, a large percentage of IP datagrams that result in fragmentation errors could have performance implications for an application using IP for network delivery. Fragmentation can occur when an IP packet traverses a network technology that supports only smaller packet sizes than the source system's interface. This can occur if an FDDI host is set to transmit frames at 4500 bytes (a size allowed on an FDDI ring) and the frame needs to route through an Ethernet (maximum frame size of 1500 bytes) to reach the destination. Although fragmentation is a standard part of IP, performing fragmentation often results in a slower forwarding performance of intermediate network devices, such as routers and switches.

The object ipRoutingDiscards can tell you whether the entity is discarding valid IP routing entries because of a lack of resources. The rate at which IP routing entries are discarded can help you find out whether the entity does not have enough resources to provide the necessary performance for the network. For example, if an entity has to buffer a large number of datagrams, this can consume memory. If the entity runs out of buffers, it may discard routing entries to make more buffers. But the routing entries that were discarded may be necessary to forward the buffered datagrams. Then the entity may have to rebuild routing entries it previously discarded, which takes more resources, or discard buffered datagrams because of a lack of routing information.

The object ipOutNoRoutes counts the number of times the entity did not have a valid route for a datagram. If the rate of this object increases, the entity may be unable to forward a datagram to the destination. This object increases for datagrams sent and forwarded by the entity. For example, if the entity is forwarding datagrams to a destination and then a network fault occurs, resulting in the entity's losing the route to the destination, this object will most likely increase until the source system realizes that the destination is no longer reachable through this entity.

If the entity has to process a large number of datagrams for which it does not have a locally supported upper-layer protocol, measured by the object ipInUnknownProtos, this may also cause a performance concern. Typically at this point the entity has received the datagram, checked it for errors, and determined that the destination was for a local IP address. If the entity now has to discard the datagram because it is destined for an unknown upper-layer protocol, resources are wasted. If this happens often or at a high rate, which can be tracked by checking the ipInUnknownProtos object over time, a performance problem may result.

Suppose, for example, that the human resources department using *MegaNet* has a collection of news servers that offer international news to the organization's employees. An employee can connect a personal computer (PC) client application to a news server and then can read news articles, search the archives for news items, save news articles locally, and so forth. An application written by the organization uses Network Basic Input/Output System (NetBIOS)[2] over IP to carry packets between the news servers and the clients. The upper-layer protocol that guarantees that the IP datagrams arrive reliably is NetBIOS and is installed only on the client PCs and news servers. If an employee tries to connect a PC application to a different server (not running NetBIOS over IP) that does not support NetBIOS, the object ipInUnknownProtos will increase. If many PCs repeatedly try to connect to a server that does not support NetBIOS, this may cause a performance problem.

---

[2] NetBIOS is a de facto standard application programming interface for the LAN environment. NetBIOS was originally introduced by IBM, but today many variants exist.

The object ipForwDatagrams tells the forwarding rate of the device with respect to IP datagrams. If the system is polled twice, once at time x (in seconds) and then again at time y (in seconds), the following formula shows the IP packet forwarding rate per second:

$$\text{IP forwarding rate} = (\text{ipForwDatagrams}_y - \text{ipForwDatagrams}_x)/y - x$$

The rate of IP packets received by the system is found as follows:

$$\text{IP input rate} = (\text{ipInReceives}_y - \text{ipInReceives}_x)/y - x$$

By having the application monitor these rates, you can determine whether the system is forwarding IP packets quickly enough to satisfy network requirements. The ipInReceives object gives the total number of IP packets received by the entity. If the entity then is forwarding these packets, the IP forwarding rate should be equal to the IP input rate. To make this calculation more accurate, subtract the rate of IP input errors and IP packets delivered to this system. Doing this means that you compare the forwarding rate only to the rate of IP packets received that were either not errors or for this entity.

Objects for Accounting Management

The IP group objects in Table 10.12 pertain to accounting management. The objects ipOutRequests and ipInDelivers tell the total number of IP packets an entity has sent and received, respectively, information that can be important for billing network users. For accounting purposes, use ipInDelivers; it gives the number of IP packets delivered to upper-layer protocols without error.

10.6 THE ICMP GROUP

ICMP (defined in RFC 792) is a protocol that carries error and control messages for IP devices. The *ICMP group* contains objects that give information about ICMP on the entity. All of its objects, listed in Table 10.13, apply to per-

Table 10.12   IP Group Objects for Accounting Management

Object	Information
ipOutRequests	Number of IP packets sent
ipInDelivers	Number of IP packets received

Table 10.13 ICMP Group Objects for Performance Management

Object	Information
icmpInMsgs	Rate of input messages
icmpInErrors	Rate of input errors
icmpInDestUnreachs	Rate of input Destination Unreachable messages
icmpInTimeExcds	Rate of input Time Exceeded messages
icmpInParmProbs	Rate of input Parameter Problem messages
icmpInSrcQuenchs	Rate of input Source Quench messages
icmpInRedirects	Rate of input Redirect messages
icmpInEchos	Rate of input Echo messages
icmpInEchoReps	Rate of input Echo Reply messages
icmpInTimestamps	Rate of input Timestamp messages
icmpInTimestampReps	Rate of input Timestamp Reply messages
icmInAddrMasks	Rate of input Address Mask Request messages
icmpInAddrMaskReps	Rate of input Address Mask Reply messages
icmpOutMsgs	Rate of output messages
icmpOutErrors	Rate of output errors
icmpOutDestUnreachs	Rate of output Destination Unreachable messages
icmpOutTimeExcds	Rate of output Time Exceeded messages
icmpOutParmProbs	Rate of output Parameter Problem messages
icmpOutSrcQuenchs	Rate of output Source Quench messages
icmpOutRedirects	Rate of output Redirect messages
icmpOutEchos	Rate of output Echo messages
icmpOutEchoReps	Rate of output Echo Reply messages
icmpOutTimestamps	Rate of output Timestamp messages
icmpOutTimestampReps	Rate of output Timestamp Reply messages
icmpOutAddrMasks	Rate of output Address Mask Request messages
icmpOutAddrMaskReps	Rate of output Address Mask Reply messages

formance management. Because of the large number of objects that apply to performance management, we don't discuss them individually here. We do, however, summarize several of the objects.

The entity must process every ICMP packet received; doing this can negatively affect overall entity performance. Although during periods of normal network traffic, the processing power consumed may be minimal, at busier times sending large numbers of ICMP packets could require enough resources to noticeably hamper an entity's performance. Further, some ICMP packets received, such as an Echo, require an Echo Response packet to be built, which consumes more processing power.

For the application to calculate the percentage of ICMP packets received and sent, it first must know the total number of packets received and sent by the entity. As we saw earlier, this is done by finding the total of packets input and packets output from each interface. We then would divide this sum by icmpInMsgs and icmpOutMsgs to arrive at the percentage of total ICMP packets received or sent. By having the application poll multiple times for these objects, you can discover the rate at which ICMP packets go in and out of the entity. Note that although an entity is receiving or sending many ICMP packets, it does not necessarily mean that a performance problem exists, but your having these statistics might help you solve a future, related problem.

Consider a setup in which a user complains about the slow performance of a remote login session to a *MegaNet* workstation called *Einstein*. In response, you could check the fault management tool to see whether a fault exists between the user and *Einstein*. Not finding a fault, you then could use the performance management application to graph the processor load on *Einstein*. Discovering that the processor load is very high, almost 70 percent, with spikes reaching above 90 percent, you then could check the accounting management application to find the number of users and processes on *Einstein*. Discovering only a small number of each, you next could produce a graph showing the packet rate entering and leaving *Einstein*. The packet rate is high, reaching almost to the maximum performance of the interface board. Looking more closely, you find that many of the packets are ICMP. Again you check the system processes, this time finding one that seems to be continuously sending ICMP Echo packets (pings) to every system on *MegaNet*. The purpose of this action is to verify the reachability of every system on the data network from *Einstein*; however, by doing so, the process is consuming enough system resources to cause a performance problem on *Einstein*.

ICMP group objects also can show the number of each ICMP packet type. Knowing the rate of icmpInEchos, icmpOutEchos, icmpInEchoReps, and icmpOutEchoReps, you could isolate performance problems such as that with *Einstein*. An entity receiving a large number of icmpInRedirects could indicate routing table and performance issues on the network. Likewise, an entity sending a large number of icmpOutRedirects may mean that the entity is changing routing table values and is telling a source to route packets on another path. Further, if an entity is sending or receiving many IP errors, the application could use icmpInErrors and icmpOutErrors to determine whether ICMP packets are causing the problem.

Another type of ICMP message, a Redirect, may also give you hints concerning network performance issues. A Redirect packet is sent to the source of an IP datagram when the receiving entity has to route the IP datagram out of the same interface on which it was received. The receipt of many ICMP Redirect messages can imply that the source entity is sending IP datagrams to the incorrect place to be routed and that these datagrams should be sent to a different location. This commonly happens when an entity has a choice of IP routers to route IP datagrams through. In Fig. 10.5 *Scroll* may be set up to route all IP datagrams off the local Ethernet through router *Foobie*. Yet the best path to the destination is through *Bletch*, resulting in *Foobie's* sending *Scroll* a Redirect. In theory, *Scroll* should change its route to the destination and send subsequent IP datagrams through *Bletch*, but often hosts do not perform this function. If the host continues to send IP datagrams for the destination to *Foobie*, an ICMP Redirect message will result from each.

You can find out the rate at which a host is receiving ICMP Redirect messages by using the object icmpInRedirects and determining whether a performance problem on the network is the result of the source host's sending to the incorrect initial router.

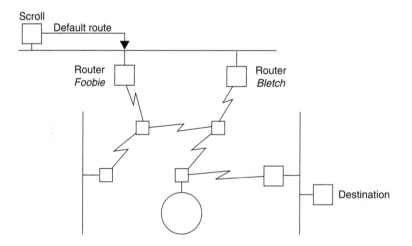

Figure 10.5   Scroll is configured to use Foobie as the default route off the Ethernet, yet the best route to the destination is through *Bletch.* This setup results in *Foobie* sending *Scroll* an ICMP Redirect.

10.7 THE TCP GROUP

TCP is a transport protocol that provides reliable connections between applications. As a transport layer, TCP deals with flow control, network congestion, and the retransmission of lost segments. TCP group objects can help in configuration, performance, and accounting management. As with the IP group, this group is subdivided into general objects about the TCP on the system and a table of values for each current TCP connection. This table changes with the start or end of a TCP connection. The structure of the TCP group is shown in Fig. 10.6.

Objects for Configuration Management

The TCP group objects in Table 10.14 apply to configuration management. The configuration of the TCP retransmission algorithm and its associated timers can drastically affect the performance of the applications that use this protocol for transport. If different systems use different retransmission schemes, network congestion or unfair distribution of bandwidth could result. For example, a system that uses a constant retransmission timer may tend to consume unnecessary bandwidth in comparison to one that uses Van Jacobson's algorithm.[3] By having the application query for tcpRtoAlgorithm, tcpRtoMin, and tcpRtoMax, you could learn whether the current configuration of the TCP works well in your system's network environment.

Modifying these objects may require some work or even be impossible. On some systems modification of the TCP retransmission timers requires rebuilding the operating system. Often, however, the TCP retransmission algorithm is an integral part of the operating system of a device and cannot be

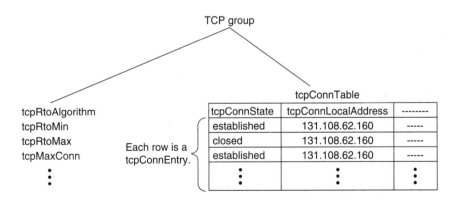

Figure 10.6 The structure of the TCP group. Note that not all the objects in each section are shown.

Table 10.14 TCP Group Objects for Configuration Management

Object	Information
tcpRtoAlgorithm	TCP retransmission algorithm
tcpRtoMin	Smallest TCP retransmission timeout
tcpRtoMax	Largest TCP retransmission timeout
tcpMaxConn	Total TCP connections allowed
tcpCurrEstab	Number of current TCP connections

altered. Changing the retransmission timer algorithm on a system usually requires installing a new TCP protocol stack.

The object tcpMaxConn can help you configure a network to handle the necessary number of remote TCP connections. If the total of all possible TCP connections does not satisfy user demand, another system might be needed. Or, if the system allows expansion, you might find that you have to add the resources to permit more TCP connections. Note that the current number of connections, found in tcpCurrEstab, can influence your decision on the total number of needed TCP connections.

The existing number of TCP connections to a system can also affect the system's performance. If a system that can handle 10 remote login sessions tries to serve 100 such sessions, performance most likely will be hurt.

Objects for Performance Management

The TCP group objects in Table 10.15 pertain to performance management. An attempt to establish a TCP connection can fail for a variety of reasons; for example, the destination system may not exist or the network may have a

Table 10.15 TCP Group Objects for Performance Management

Object	Information
tcpAttempt Fails	Number of failed attempts to make a connection
tcpEstabResets	Number of resets from established connection
tcpRetransSegs	Number of segments retransmitted
tcpInErrs	Number of packets received in error
tcpOutRsts	Number of times TCP tried to reset a connection
tcpInSegs	Rate of input TCP segments
tcpOutSegs	Rate of output TCP segments

---

[3] For further information on the TCP and retransmission issues, refer to the paper by Van Jacobson, titled "Congestion Avoidance and Control," cited at the end of this chapter.

fault. Knowing the number of rejected attempts at making a connection can help you quantify network reliability, with fewer rejections possibly indicating a more reliable network. Likewise, a situation in which TCP ends many established sessions in a reset condition might also reflect an unreliable network. The objects tcpAttemptFails and tcpEstabResets can help measure this network rejection rate.

The object tcpRetransSegs gives the number of TCP segments the system has re-sent. The retransmission of a TCP segment does not directly reflect a performance problem; however, the number of retransmissions can tell you whether the entity is having to send multiple copies of data in an effort to ensure reliability.

If the system is receiving TCP segments in error, the value of tcpInErrs will increase. Trouble receiving segments and an increase in this object might be caused by the source system's encapsulating the segments incorrectly, a network device's forwarding the segment in error, or any number of other reasons. In most situations the value of this object will rise as a result of some other error on the system.

The object tcpOutRsts gives the number of times the entity has reset a connection. The entity would attempt to reset a connection as a result of network unreliability, a user request to do so, or a resource problem; the exact reasons for sending a reset can be unique to an entity. By understanding TCP on the entity, you will be better able to understand the use of this object.

Having the application poll tcpInSegs and tcpOutSegs over time can enable you to check the rate of TCP segments as they enter and leave the entity. This rate may affect the performance of the entity or an application relying on TCP for transport.

Objects for Accounting Management

The TCP group objects in Table 10.16 apply to accounting management. An organization may want to know the number of TCP connections to and from a system in order to evaluate current usage of network resources. Such an evaluation could lead to the purchase of additional systems or a system reconfiguration. The objects tcpActiveOpens and tcpPassiveOpens give the total number of times a connection was made from or to the system, respectively.

The objects tcpInSegs and tcpOutSegs together count TCP segments in and out of the entity, respectively. Such information can be significant in network billing.

The object tcpConnTable gives the state of current TCP connections, the local TCP port and address, and the remote TCP port and address. These

Table 10.16   TCP Group Objects for Accounting Management

Object	Information
tcpActiveOpens	Number of times this system has opened a connection
tcpPassiveOpens	Number of times this system has received a request to open a connection
tcpInSegs	Total number of TCP segments received
tcpOutSegs	Total number of TCP segments sent
tcpConnTable	Current TCP connections

values pertain to the current state of the TCP on the entity and may change at any instant. Nevertheless, by having the accounting management application poll for the object tcpConRemAddress, you can determine the current remote system addresses of a TCP connection. (Note that the information obtained is only the remote system address, not the remote user.) If the application were to poll an entity for this object every fifteen minutes, system administrators could determine which remote systems use their resources and for what duration. (Of course, the granularity of the duration shown is only as fine as the polling interval.) The application then could generate bills for using the local entity for those users owning the remote systems and using the local entity.

The object tcpConnTable also contains information about the source and destination TCP port for each current connection. Many popular TCP applications use well-defined ports, making it possible to track which application is making or receiving the TCP connection. The port number differentiates between a remote login application, such as telnet, and a file transfer application, such as FTP. This data can be useful for accounting purposes to determine the reason for TCP connections to and from an entity.

Objects for Security Management

Information in the tcpConnTable also can be used in security management to track which remote systems access resources through TCP. This data can form the basis of reports to show that the entity has not allowed any connections from foreign or unrestricted systems. The polling interval would greatly influence the effectiveness of such a report—an intruder may need only a few seconds to gather its information before breaking the connection. If a poll of the table did not occur within those few seconds, all record of the intrusion would be lost.

10.8 THE UDP GROUP

Like TCP, UDP is a transport-layer protocol. UDP is a simple transport layer, providing an unreliable, connectionless mechanism for datagrams to be sent or received by an application. Therefore the *UDP group* contains only a limited number of objects. Those objects are subdivided as information about the UDP on this entity and entries about the current UDP applications accepting datagrams on the entity. The structure of the UDP group is shown in Fig. 10.7.

Because UDP does not establish connections, the UDP table does not give data about the current connections—they would never exist. Instead, the table tells about each existing local port and related network address.

UDP group objects can help in performance and accounting management. This functionality is similar to that of the TCP group objects for the same areas of network management.

Objects for Performance Management

The UDP group objects in Table 10.17 apply to performance management. Processing UDP datagrams can affect the performance of the entity, so polling for udpInDatagrams and udpOutDatagrams over time can yield valuable data about the input and output rate of datagrams.

The object udpNoPorts tells you when an entity is receiving datagrams for an unknown application (or a known application not currently running). If the rate of these datagrams is significant, a performance problem on the entity could result. An entity can commonly receive datagrams in this manner when a UDP application uses IP broadcast packets to deliver information. Upon seeing an

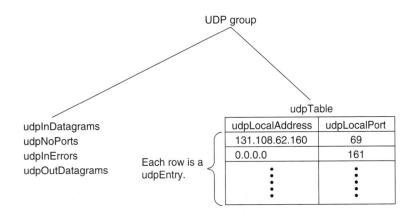

Figure 10.7 The structure of the UDP group.

Table 10.17 UDP Group Objects for Performance Management

Object	Information
udpInDatagrams	Rate of input datagrams
udpOutDatagrams	Rate of output datagrams
udpNoPorts	Rate of datagrams that were not sent to a valid port
udpInErrors	Rate of UDP datagrams received in error

IP broadcast, every IP device picks up the broadcast packet and delivers it to UDP. Only those systems with the application running and the proper UDP port receive the packet; all others report this packet in the udpNoPorts object.

For example, the Trivial File Transfer Protocol (TFTP) (defined in RFC 783) uses UDP to allow a device to send or receive a single file without using a password. A TFTP server offers a file by listening on a UDP port for a TFTP client asking for the file. In many cases a TFTP client will send an IP broadcast to find a TFTP server on the network. Systems that have such a server listening will receive the broadcast and send the file to the client, if possible. All other IP hosts that are not listening on the TFTP port will increment their udpNoPorts object.

As in IP and TCP, udpInErrors can tell you about specific errors on the network. Since UDP is designed to be a simple protocol, it performs only cyclic redundancy checks (CRC) on the data portion of the datagram. A UDP datagram may contain a CRC error for many reasons, including software or link errors or a faulty network device. A system receiving many datagrams that count as udpInErrors could contribute to the poor performance of an application in receiving information. For example, SNMP uses UDP for transport. If the network management system is having trouble receiving SNMP datagrams from a remote system, the local udpInErrors counter could indicate that the datagram containing the SNMP information possibly did not make it across the network successfully.

Objects for Accounting Management

The UDP group objects in Table 10.18 pertain to accounting management. You can use udpInDatagrams and udpOutDatagrams to determine how many UDP datagrams an entity has sent and received. In this way you can learn the demand for UDP and the applications that use it on the entity.

The udpTable contains objects similar to those found in the tcpConnTable. This table is a collection of udpEntry entries, each of which contains the objects udpLocalAddress and udpLocalPort; udpLocalAddress gives the local

Table 10.18   UDP Group Objects for Accounting Management

Object	*Information*
udpInDatagrams	Total number of UDP datagrams received
udpOutDatagrams	Total number of UDP datagrams sent
udpTable	Current UDP ports accepting datagrams

IP address for the listening port, and udpLocalPort gives the port number. However, because UDP is not a connection-based protocol, the entries in the udpTable remain valid for the time that the application listens on a port. This facility enables you to monitor which services the network offers on an entity basis. You could check where these services exist on the network to find out whether the appropriate network resources exist.

Objects for Configuration Management

Monitoring of available network services falls into the realm of configuration management. By checking with the udpTable, you can determine whether the entity's applications are set up correctly. For example, if an entity is known to have an application that offers remote printing on a known UDP port, you could easily verify this configuration information by using the udpTable.

Objects for Security Management

Security management also can use the information in the udpTable. In the same way that a security management application can poll for tcpConnTable information to check for unauthorized access, the application can check to ensure that an entity does not run an unsecured application using UDP. Suppose, for example, that the payroll department at *MegaNet* has decided that the application *Find-Employee-Salary* is to be run only on one specific machine; the application receives and sends datagrams to find an employee's salary on a specific UDP port. The security management tool could check the udpTable on all systems to check whether this local port exists, thus helping to control access to sensitive information.

10.9 THE EGP GROUP

EGP (defined in RFC 904) is a protocol that tells an IP network device about the reachability of other IP networks. EGP doesn't give the entire route to another network, but it does enable a device to know in which direction a network exists. IP networks can be grouped into logical areas called *autonomous systems*. An autonomous system is usually one network and its associated subnets or a collection of networks and subnetworks under the same administration. Two network devices in two different autonomous systems can share reachability information through EGP.

As shown in Fig. 10.9, *EGP group* objects are subdivided into objects providing configuration, performance, and accounting management information about EGP on this entity and a table of entries containing information about a unique EGP neighbor. Information in this table is useful in fault, configuration, performance, and accounting management.

The network devices that communicate with EGP between autonomous systems are called EGP neighbors. Each EGP process has a one-to-one relationship with each neighbor. Each EGP neighbor speaks a "hello" protocol that periodically informs other neighbors that it is still active. When the system queries for the neighbor's reachability information, it is performing an EGP poll.

For example, Fig. 10.8 shows two networks, A and B, each with an EGP neighbor communicating to the other network. EGP data may allow a device within network A or network B to know the best way to get to the other network. However, the device will not know how to reach a specific destination or subnetwork; it will know only the direction of all of the other networks.

Objects for Fault Management

The EGP group objects in Table 10.19 pertain to fault management. Each of these objects resides in the EGP neighbor table. The state of an EGP neighbor can provide information about how routing information is injected into an autonomous system. The fault management application could use egpNeighState to find the current state of an EGP neighbor. If a neighbor is up, it should

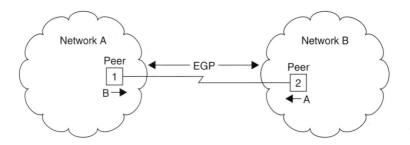

Figure 10.8 EGP peer 1 knows about the reachability of network B, and EGP peer 2 knows about the reachability of network A.

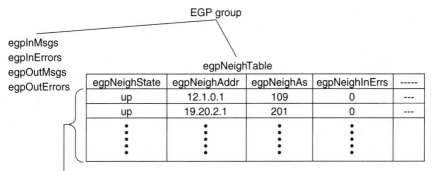

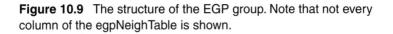

Each row is an egpNeighEntry.

Figure 10.9 The structure of the EGP group. Note that not every column of the egpNeighTable is shown.

be sending information about the reachability of networks to the local EGP process. Knowing when a neighbor enters the up state can tell you about new routing information that may enter the autonomous system. Similarly, knowing when a neighbor stops communicating and enters the down state could be helpful in solving a routing problem. As we saw in Chapter 9 with SNMP, when a neighbor enters the down state, the entity sends a trap message.

Objects for Configuration Management

The EGP group objects in Table 10.20 apply to configuration management. The object egpAs gives the autonomous system number for the local EGP entity. All the other listed objects tell about the configuration of a specific EGP neighbor. This information, polled by the configuration management application, can keep you informed about the setup of EGP and the routing information entering or leaving the current autonomous system.

The application can use egpNeighEventTrigger to start or stop communication with an EGP neighbor. This object enables you to control the EGP process on the system. Note that setting the object does not start EGP on the entity but rather restarts communication with an existing neighbor. This is

Table 10.19 EGP Group Objects for Fault Management

Object	Information
egpNeighState	State of each EGP neighbor
egpNeighStateUps	When an EGP neighbor enters an up state
egpNeighStateDowns	When an EGP neighbor enters a down state

Table 10.20   EGP Group Objects for Configuration Management

Object	Information
egpNeighState	State of each EGP neighbor
egpNeighAddr	The EGP neighbor IP address
egpNeighAs	The EGP neighbor autonomous system
egpNeighIntervalHello	The EGP hello interval
egpNeighIntervalPoll	The EGP poll interval
egpNeighMode	The EGP polling mode
egpNeighEventTrigger	Permits the starting or stopping of communication
egpAs	The local EGP autonomous system

the only object in the EGP group that can be set by the network engineer with an SNMP Set-Request. For example, consider a network device that has two EGP neighbors, each providing reachability information to many IP networks. The primary EGP session is up and passing reachability information into the local autonomous system; the secondary EGP session is idle. Although the primary path out of the local autonomous system is preferred because of cost and security considerations, at some point the primary EGP communication fails. Upon discovering this failure, you would probably attempt to restart communication. If this effort failed, you then could use the egpNeighTrig-gerEvent object to start the secondary EGP session.

Objects for Performance Management

Failure of the EGP communication in the example given in the previous section might have resulted from a failure on a circuit. In this case the error rate for EGP information received might have increased before the failure. A performance management application, monitoring this error rate, could have informed you if the rate increased. The EGP group objects in Table 10.21 apply to performance management.

As we saw in Section 10.3, to find a rate using an object requires multiple polls of the object. The performance management application could poll multiple times for an object and then divide the difference in the values of the object by the time elapsed between polls. This obtains the rate of change for an object.

The objects egpInMsgs and egpOutMsgs enable you to watch the rate of EGP messages entering and leaving the entity. Usually this rate will be insignificant, but during periods of network instability between EGP neighbors, it could climb. When this happens, processing EGP messages may consume

Table 10.21 EGP Group Objects for Performance Management

Object	Information
egpInMsgs	Rate of messages received
egpInErrors	Rate of errors received
egpOutMsgs	Rate of messages sent
egpOutErrors	Rate of messages not sent because of error
egpNeighInMsgs	Rate of messages received from this EGP neighbor
egpNeighInErrs	Rate of errors received from his EGP neighbor
egpNeighOutMsgs	Rate of messages sent to this EGP neighbor
egpNeighOutErrs	Rate of messages not sent to this EGP neighbor because of error
egpNeighInErrMsgs	Rate of EGP error messages received from this EGP neighbor
egpNeighOutErrMsgs	Rate of EGP error messages sent to this EGP neighbor

too many resources and so cause slow performance on the entity. Further, the EGP messages themselves may take up bandwidth on a serial link, thus causing poor or delayed transmission of data traversing the same link.

An increase in egpInErrors and egpOutErrors may coincide with the increase in the number of messages sent and received by the entity. If a message is received in error and a valid response isn't sent, the source EGP neighbor may retransmit the message. When resource limitations prevent the entity from sending valid EGP messages, egpOutErrors will increase. Consequently, when the rate of egpInMsgs nears the rate of egpOutErrors, the entity probably is suffering difficulty in building and sending EGP messages. A lack of entity resources, such as memory or processing power, could cause this phenomenon.

If EGP is causing performance issues on the entity or on an attached serial link, you need to isolate which neighbor is creating the problem. Using egpNeighInMsgs, egpNeighInErrs, egpNeighOutMsgs, and egpNeighOutErrs, you can compute the rate of input and output messages and the errors for each neighbor.

By examining the rate of increase in egpNeighInErrMsgs and egpNeighOutErrMsgs, you can determine when EGP neighbors are receiving and sending valid EGP error messages. An increase in the rate of these error messages may indicate a misconfiguration or a change in the future performance of EGP on this neighbor.

10.10 THE CMOT GROUP

The CMOT group exists only for historical reasons. Previously it was seen as a protocol to help in the transition from SNMP to CMIS/CMIP. But since CMOT is no longer considered in this light, there are no objects in this group.

10.11 THE TRANSMISSION GROUP

The transmission group gives you information about the specific media underlying the interfaces on a system. When the Internet standards for managing the various types of media are defined, this group is a prefix for this information. As we saw in Chapter 9, various MIBs are defined for different media types, such as Token Ring and FDDI.

10.12 THE SNMP GROUP

The SNMP group gives information about, among other things, the SNMP errors and packets entering and leaving the entity. This last group in the MIB is helpful in all five areas of network management. Fault management applications watching for SNMP problems can use the number of SNMP errors and their frequency; performance management applications can calculate the rate of SNMP packets entering and leaving the entity. Accounting management applications can use these objects to find the exact number of SNMP packets sent to or received by the entity. Finally, some of the other SNMP objects can be helpful in accomplishing security and configuration management.

As we saw in Chapter 8, RFC 1450, "Management Information Base for version 2 of the Simple Network Management Protocol (SNMPv2)," defines objects similar to those in the SNMP Group of MIB-II for an entity running SNMPv2. The SNMPv2 Statistics group of RFC 1450 has statistics for SNMPv2 packets and errors, and the SNMPv1 Statistics group has some of the objects discussed next. RFC 1450 defines the SNMPv2 traps an agent supports and a new group of objects that are settable on the agent. The topics discussed will help you use RFC 1450 for the various areas of network management.

Objects for Fault Management

The SNMP group objects in Table 10.22 apply to fault management. Each object gives information about SNMP errors. RFC 1157 defines each of these errors. Although an agent's receiving or sending these errors might not indicate

Table 10.22 SNMP Group Objects for Fault Management

Object	*Information*
snmpInASNParseErrs	Total input ASN errors
snmpInTooBigs	Total input "tooBig" errors
snmpInNoSuchNames	Total input "noSuchName" errors
snmpInBadValues	Total input "badValue" errors
snmpInReadOnlys	Total input "readOnly" errors
snmpInGenErrs	Total input "genErr" errors
snmpOutTooBigs	Total output "tooBig" errors
snmpOutNoSuchNames	Total output "noSuchName" errors
snmpOutBadValues	Total output "badValue" errors
snmpOutGenErrs	Total output "genErr" errors

a problem with the network itself, they may tell you that an entity is not handling SNMP packets properly. The numbers and types of errors also can indicate that the entity is receiving SNMP packets with errors from network devices. The solutions to these errors often reside in the configuration of either the SNMP manager or the agent. If reconfiguration does not alleviate these errors, the problem might lie within the implementation of SNMP on the manager or agent.

Objects for Performance Management

The SNMP objects in Table 10.23 apply to performance management. Like any other entity activity, SNMP can affect system performance. If you want to know what percentage of resources an entity is using to handle SNMP, you can find the rate of SNMP packets' input and output by using snmpInPkts and snmpOutPkts. The other objects listed in the table enable you to find the type of SNMP packets the entity is handling. Monitoring the rates of these objects can suggest the cause of a high SNMP packet input or output rate. For example, a high rate of snmpInGetRequests and snmpOutGetResponses may indicate that a manager is currently gathering information from the entity.

Objects for Accounting Management

Some of the same objects useful for performance management also apply to accounting management, as shown in Table 10.24. Instead of using these objects to find the rate at which packets enter and leave the entity, as in performance management, accounting management applications can use them to

Table 10.23   SNMP Objects for Performance Management

Object	Information
snmpInPkts	Rate of SNMP packets input
snmpOutPkts	Rate of SNMP packets sent
snmpInTotalReqVars	Rate of Get/Get-Next-Requests input
snmpInTotalSetVars	Rate of Set-Requests input
snmpInGetRequests	Rate of Get-Requests input
snmpInGetNexts	Rate of Get-Next-Requests input
snmpInSetRequests	Rate of Set-Requests input
snmpInGetResponses	Rate of Get-Responses input
snmpInTraps	Rate of traps input
snmpOutGetRequests	Rate of Get-Requests output
snmpOutGetNexts	Rate of Get-Next-Requests output
snmpOutSetRequests	Rate of Set-Requests output
snmpOutGetResponses	Rate of Get-Responses output
snmpOutTraps	Rate of traps output

find a total number for each type of SNMP packet sent and received, information that can be useful for network billing.

If the network billing model calculates costs based on packets sent or received by a billing group, this data can help compute the total number of SNMP packets sent into and out of the billing group. For example, suppose the marketing department of *MegaNet* receives a bill each month for the number of packets it receives from the network. The marketing department network is divided from *MegaNet* by two network devices, both of which are managed by an outside organization responsible for the network. The community strings configured in the two network devices are known only by the outside managing organization, ensuring that no other users can query the devices through SNMP. Therefore, because the billing process computes costs based on packets received, the SNMP packets these two devices receive should not be included in the final bill for the marketing department. The

Table 10.24   SNMP Group Objects for Accounting Management

Object	Information
snmpInPkts	Total SNMP packets input
snmpOutPkts	Total SNMP packets sent
snmpInTraps	Total traps input
snmpOutTraps	Total traps output

objects snmpInPkts and snmpInTraps can give the number of packets that should be subtracted from that final bill.

Objects for Security Management

The SNMP group objects in Table 10.25 apply to security management, which involves tracking failed authentication attempts. The actions taken to do this might include checking for unsuccessful password entries for a computer login or for invalid community strings in SNMP. The object snmpInBad-CommunityNames counts the number of times a user or application, when attempting to communicate with SNMP on an entity, does not give the correct community string. As discussed in Chapter 8, when an entity receives an invalid community string, it also might send an SNMP authentication failure trap message to a manager.

The snmpInBadCommunityUses object counts the number of times an SNMP packet was received having a community string that did not allow the requested operation. In many network devices different community strings can be set up for different operations. For example, one community string might authorize the Get-Request and Get-Next-Request operations; another might allow Get-Request, Get-Next-Request, and Set-Request operations. An organization that manages a network device might know the community string that allows all SNMP operations—Get-Request, Get-Next-Request, and Set-Request—but could elect to allow for public use only the community string that allows access to Get-Request and Get-Next-Request operations. In this case it would do so to ensure that only employees in the organization could configure the network devices through Set-Request operations.

If the values of either of these two objects were to increase, the security management application could warn you with a message or pop-up window. This event also could be logged in the relational database for future analysis. Such an analysis could show that the events occur on a timely basis, which could lead you to conclude that perhaps a management station polling the device doesn't know the proper community string.

Table 10.25   SNMP Group Objects for Security Management

Object	*Information*
snmpInBadCommunityNames	Total number of packets with a wrong community string
snmpInBadCommunityUses	Total number of packets with community strings that did not allow the requested operation

Objects for Configuration Management

The group object that applies to configuration management is snmp-EnableAuthenTraps. By definition, an entity must be able to send an SNMP authentication failure trap when it receives an SNMP packet with an incorrect community string. However, because community strings are in ASCII, this procedure can pose potentially dangerous security problems. You can override the entity and set snmpEnableAuthenTraps to enable (send) or disable (don't send) the trap.

SUMMARY

The standard MIB for SNMP—RFC 1213—contains a wealth of information useful in managing a data network, all of which is available from many network devices. Because of the copious amounts of data in the MIB-II, deciphering which objects help in which areas of network management often can be overwhelming and difficult. This chapter took a close look at RFC 1213, examining each group within MIB-II and offering guidance about the specific objects useful for each functional area of network management. We also examined RFC 1573, which defines an evolution of one group in MIB-II, the interfaces group.

FOR FURTHER STUDY

Case, J., McCloghrie, K., Rose, M., and Waldbusser, S., RFC 1450, "Management Information Base for version 2 of the Simple Network Management Protocol (SNMPv2)," April 1993.

Case, J., Fedor, M., Schoffstall, M., and Davin, C., RFC 1157, "Simple Network Management Protocol (SNMP)," May 1990.

Jacobson, V., "Congestion Avoidance and Control," Proceedings of the ACM, SIGCOMM '88, Volume 18, Number 4, August 1988.

McCloghrie, K., and Rose, M., RFC 1156, "Management Information Base for Network Management for TCP/IP-based Internets," May 1990.

————., RFC 1213, "Management Information Base for Network Management for TCP/IP-based Internets: MIB-II," March 1991.

McCloghrie, K., and Kastenholz, F., RFC 1573, "Evolution of the Interfaces Group of MIB-II," January 1994.

Mills, D., RFC 904, "Exterior Gateway Protocol Specification," April 1984.

Postel, J., RFC 792, "Internet Control Message Protocol," September 1981.

Rose, M., and McCloghrie, K., RFC 1155, "Structure and Identification of Management Information for TCP/IP-Based Internets," May 1990.

———., RFC 1212, "Concise MIB Definitions," March 1991.

Sollins, K., RFC 783, "TFTP Protocol (revision 2)," June 1981.

Chapter 11

A Look at RFC 1757 (RMON MIB)

Chris stared in disbelief at the stack of devices piled on the floor, chairs, and tables. These devices, called probes, were to be installed on a number of critical network segments throughout MegaNet. *Each device was going to help in the overall task of network management, or so the salespeople had said. Somewhat at a loss for a place to work, Chris removed one of the probes from its box. The device seemed to have multiple Ethernet interfaces and a wealth of LEDs on the front panel. "It will sure look pretty mounted in the Data Center . . . ," Chris mused.*

In this chapter we examine each section of RFC 1757, "Remote Network Monitoring Management Information Base," RMON MIB. The RMON MIB was first published as RFC 1271 and then later revised as RFC 1757. The wealth of information about a network segment that RMON MIB contains is useful in all the areas of network management. This chapter will help network engineers and software developers understand and apply this information.

Now that you have an understanding of how to apply MIB objects, it is important to realize that many MIBs other than MIB-II are available to help accomplish network management. First, we define a remote network monitoring device and explain the goals of the RMON MIB. Then we deal with each group within the RMON MIB. For each group, we will list objects as they apply to the various areas of network management. Space constraints prevent us from discussing all possible RMON MIB objects, but we try to examine as many as possible.

This chapter contains many references to the RMON MIB, RFC 1757. We recommend that you have a copy of RFC 1757 available when reading this chapter (information on getting this document is available in Appendix A).

11.1   REMOTE NETWORK MONITORING DEVICES

The purpose of a remote network monitoring device is to help perform network management on a network segment. The device, or probe, sits on network segments and monitors the segments while gathering statistics. The probe can have interfaces on multiple segments and can gather data for each individually. The probe may have its own memory, processor, and network interface card dedicated to performing its tasks involved with managing the network. The remote network monitoring device is responsible for gathering the statistics defined in the RMON MIB.

The RMON MIB is standardized to operate only on Ethernet network segments. However, the standard does not preclude other network technologies. A proposed standard, RFC 1513, "Token Ring Extensions to the Remote Network Monitoring MIB," updates the RMON MIB for managing Token Ring segments. Also, many vendor-proprietary implementations of RMON probes do support various network technologies, including Token Ring and FDDI.

An organization could put a remote network monitoring device on each Ethernet network segment. If deployed in this manner, a central network manager can gather statistics described in the RMON MIB on every network segment. Buying a dedicated device for each network segment can be a costly proposition for many organizations. In some cases the benefits of having the remote network device for network management access may outweigh these costs. Many such products exist today, such as those from Frontier Software Corp., ARMON, Inc., and Axon, Inc.

Another solution is to purchase software that can perform the remote network monitoring on a nondedicated device. One can purchase software for many workstations that can add remote network monitoring to the workstation function (such as the HP NetMetrix product). However, performing remote network monitoring requires the device to have its interfaces in *promiscuous mode,* or listening to each frame on the network segment. This can result in a decrease in the performance on the workstations' network interfaces. Nearly all network devices suffer a performance impact if their interfaces are placed in promiscuous mode. For example, a router typically needs to examine only the header of a frame on an Ethernet to determine whether it needs routing. However, if the router is also an RMON device, it may need to examine the entire frame (for every frame) regardless of whether it was going to route it.

Yet another option for remote network monitoring is to put the probe functionality into an intelligent wiring hub, available today from most popular hub vendors, such as 3Com Corp., Cabletron Systems, and Bay Networks. The wiring hub connects to end systems and is a logical place to put the probe. Figure 11.1 shows different RMON probes on network segments.

An RMON probe does not have to implement each group in the RMON MIB to be standards compliant. In fact, unlike MIB-II, a probe could implement only a select group or groups and still conform to the RMON MIB standard.

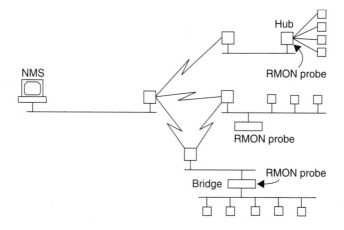

Figure 11.1 An RMON probe can reside in many different network devices or as a stand-alone unit.

11.2 RMON MIB GOALS

The RMON MIB has five goals:

- Offline operation
- Preemptive monitoring
- Problem detection and reporting
- Value-added data
- Multiple managers

A remote network monitoring device can provide *offline operation*, which can be beneficial when the device cannot be in continual contact with a central network management system. In some cases the probe cannot contact the central network manager because of a network fault or outage. In other situations, if a charge occurs for use of the network infrastructure, it can make sense for the probe to contact the central system only when a critical network event occurs, saving on network costs.

The probe can also help in *preemptive monitoring* on a network segment by continuously monitoring the segment and notifying the central management system in case of a failure. The probe can be set up to continuously run diagnostics and watch network performance. The results of these diagnostics can be sent to a log. If a problem does occur, the probe can provide information about the segment before and after the failure.

Problem detection and reporting can be accomplished by having a network manager configure the probe to recognize certain conditions on the segment, including error conditions. If such a condition occurs, the probe can log it and notify a network management system. This feature of the RMON device helps reduce the amount of network traffic between the central network management system and devices on the segment. Since the probe monitors the segment, it is not necessary for the network management system to monitor it as well.

The probe can provide *value-added data* for network management. The probe is a dedicated device, allowing it to spend time on interpreting information about the network segment. For example, the probe could find the segment hosts that generate the most errors or the most broadcast traffic. The probe could also compute which hosts communicate often and when. This information is often invaluable in solving network problems on the segment.

The final goal of the RMON device is to provide support for *multiple managers*. Many organizations have multiple network management systems that query the network. The RMON probe can respond to each of these managers and provide value-added data or problem detection for each separately. In most cases this will require the probe to allocate resources to handle communication to each manager independently.

11.3 THE STATISTICS GROUP

The statistics group contains objects that are measured for each Ethernet interface on the RMON device. The statistics for each Ethernet interface are kept separate from other interfaces. This feature allows the probe to provide data about multiple segments simultaneously. These statistics can be helpful in accomplishing fault, configuration, and performance management.

Each Ethernet interface will have a separate collection of statistics in a separate row of a MIB table called the etherStatsTable. Each row in this table is called an etherStatsEntry and is uniquely identified by a number given by the object etherStatsIndex, as shown in Fig. 11.2.

Objects for Fault Management

The statistics group provides many objects to help you isolate faults on a network segment or with the probe (see Table 11.1). The etherStatsDropEvents object tells how often the RMON probe itself ran out of resources to perform its activities. This number does not equal the number of packets dropped or not processed but instead the number of times the probe has seen this problem condition. If you see the etherStatsDropEvents object consistently increasing, you may wish to allocate more resources to the probe by putting more memory in the probe or taking some network interfaces out of a single dedicated probe. These network interfaces could be placed into new probes with their own dedicated resources.

Statistics group
etherStatsTable

etherStatsIndex	etherStatsDataSource	- - - - - - -
1	ifIndex.1	- - - - - - -
2	ifIndex.2	- - - - - - -
3	ifIndex.4	- - - - - - -
4	ifIndex.5	- - - - - - -
5	ifIndex.10	- - - - - - -
6	ifIndex.12	- - - - - - -

Each row is an etherStatsEntry.

Figure 11.2 The structure of the statistics group. Note that not all objects in each section are shown.

Table 11.1 Statistic Group Objects for Fault Management

Object	Information
etherStatsDropEvents	Number of times the RMON probe has run out of resources due to lack of resources
etherStatsBroadcastPkts	Isolates broadcast problems
etherStatsCRCAlignErrors	Isolates segments with packets having bad CRCs
etherStatsUndersizePkts	Isolates segments with packets having undersized packets
etherStatsOversizePkts	Isolates segments with packets having oversized packets
etherStatsFragments	Isolates segments with fragments
etherStatsJabbers	Isolates segments with jabbers

For each of the following objects, it is often important to monitor them if they change dramatically (increase by more than 2 percent) over time. This can be done without using a lot of resources on the probe or network bandwidth by polling for these objects over a long time period, such as every few hours. Then, if you notice an increase in any of the objects, you can use the probe to gather statistics to send the network management system an alarm. This technique optimizes the use of the probe and allocates its resources only when necessary to perform fault management.

A fault management application, given the network addresses of the RMON probes on the network as input, could perform this function automatically. In addition, the RMON MIB host group has objects that identify errors being sent by individual hosts on the segment. So if the probe noticed an increase in errors by examining the objects in the statistics group, it may be able to isolate the cause of the errors by using objects in the host group.

A *broadcast storm* on a network segment can dramatically affect its performance, often to the point of causing network down time. A broadcast packet needs to be processed by every host on the network segment. Some hosts perform poorly when they receive a lot of broadcast messages quickly, especially if the network interface card in the device interrupts the main processor of the system for each broadcast packet, as is fairly common. The object etherStatsBroadcastPkts can help you isolate when a broadcast storm occurs. If you see a dramatic rate of change in this object (such as a 50 percent or 100 percent increase), you should further investigate the traffic on this segment.

The etherStatsCRCAlignErrors object is useful in helping to isolate network segments that have CRC (cyclic redundancy check) errors. The CRC is a value placed within each frame by the source station on the segment. The value is computed based on the bits within the frame. The destination station takes the bits in the frame received and performs a similar calculation to the source. If the value computed by the destination is the same as the source, the frame is seen as valid. Otherwise, a CRC error occurs. The CRC value is also called a frame check sequence (FCS) on Ethernet. The computation of the CRC and FCS is not identical, but the overall algorithm and purpose of the two values are essentially the same.

A CRC error may occur for various reasons, most reflecting problems with the network segment. The CRC error may be caused by improper cable lengths, unterminated segments, or malfunctioning network hardware. The etherStatsCRCAlignErrors object also counts the number of packets that were of valid length (between 64 and 1518 bytes) but were improperly aligned on a byte boundary.

When the network segment has undersized or oversized packets, this can cause faults. Undersized packets can result from a problem with the medium. Oversized packets can result from hardware malfunctioning or a misconfigured station. The objects etherStatsUndersizePkts and etherStatsOversize Pkts can help you find out whether the segment is seeing many of these types of packets.

A fragmented packet is less than 64 bytes (the minimum frame size for Ethernet) and can be either misaligned on a byte boundary or have a bad FCS value. The object etherStatsFragments tells you the number of fragments seen on the network segment. Similar to undersized packets, fragments are often caused by a problem with the medium. If you see these errors on your network segment, you should first check the hardware on the segment.

A jabber packet is one greater than 1518 bytes (the maximum frame size for Ethernet) and can be either misaligned on a byte boundary or have a bad FCS value. The jabber signal on Ethernet is intended to let a station start transmitting on the wire without a frame to send, in an effort to stop another station from dominating the segment. The station that has been transmitting should see the jabber, sense a collision of traffic on the wire, and then wait before transmitting on the segment again. Excessive jabbers are sometimes caused by an interface board or transceiver continuing to send the jabber signal even though it is not necessary on the segment.

Objects for Configuration Management

Table 11.2 lists the statistics group objects that are useful in accomplishing configuration management. The etherStatsDataSource object tells you which physical interface on the probe applies to this etherStatsEntry. For example, if this row in the etherStatsTable applies to the first interface on the probe, the

Table 11.2 Statistics Group Objects for Configuration Management

Object	Information
etherStatsDataSource	Identifies the segment the probe currently monitors
etherStatsOwner	Identifies the manager that configured this row in the probe

value returned would be equal to ifIndex. 1, the object in RFC 1213 (MIB-II) that specifies the row in the ifTable that applies to the physical interface. The ifTable row specified by the ifIndex contains generic information about the physical interface. For example, by correlating the value returned by the object etherStatsDataSource and ifIndex, you can find the logical name of the interface (such as "Ethernet 1"), specified in the ifTable object ifDescr, for a set of RMON statistics.

The etherStatsOwner object tells you which network management system configured this row of the etherStatsTable. Network management systems can validate or invalidate a row of statistics. It is often useful to know which network management system configured this etherStatsEntry, to avoid redundant effort by two different systems or to figure out who is using the probes resources. A network management application could periodically inform a network engineer about which probes and interfaces it had set up. This information could be presented in report format for use in coordinating network management activities.

Objects for Performance Management

Table 11.3 lists the statistics group objects that are useful in accomplishing performance management. The total amount of traffic found on a network segment can affect performance. You can use the object etherStatsOctets with the following formulas to calculate segment utilization during the time period from x to y:

$$\text{Total bytes} = (\text{etherStatsOctets}_y - \text{etherStatsOctets}_x)/(y - x)$$
$$\text{Utilization} = \text{total bytes}/\text{ifSpeed}$$

Note that the result of these formulas is the current utilization of the entire segment, not of a single station on the segment. Later in this chapter, you will see that a historical utilization of the segment is calculated and stored automatically by the probe.

Table 11.3 Statistics Group Objects for Performance Management

Object	*Can Calculate*
etherStatsOctets	Total traffic rate
etherStatsPkts	Total packet rate
etherStatsBroadcastPkts	Broadcast packet rate
etherStatsMulticastPkts	Multicast packet rate
etherStatsPkts64Octets	64-byte packet rate
etherStatsPkts65to127Octets	65–127-byte packet rate
etherStatsPkts128to255Octets	128–255-byte packet rate
etherStatsPkts256to511Octets	256–511-byte packet rate
etherStatsPkts512to1023Octets	512–1023-byte packet rate
etherStatsPkts1024to1518Octets	1024–1518-byte packet rate
etherStatsCRCAlignErrors	CRC error rate
etherStatsUndersizePkts	Undersized packet rate
etherStatsOversizePkts	Oversized packet rate
etherStatsFragments	Fragment rate
etherStatsJabbers	Jabber rate
etherStatsCollisions	Collision rate

If you wish to know the current packet rate on the segment, you can compute a delta on the etherStatsPkts object. This information may be useful in solving performance issues if a station is sending packets at a rate that congests the destination or an intermediate network device.

Consider a situation in which you have a bridge on a network segment. A system, *Charlie*, on the same segment is communicating with a system, *Lucy* (see Fig. 11.3), on the other side of the bridge. A user on *Charlie* calls and complains of performance problems reaching *Lucy*. You use RMON probes to monitor the utilization on both network segments and find the utilization at 5 percent, a reasonable number. Next, you check the number of users and processes on each system and find both nearly idle. You check the load on the bridge and find its processor heavily utilized. Somewhat puzzled, you then check the packet rate on each of the network segments and find it surprisingly high, near 500 packets per second. You then use further statistics on the probe to find that all of these packets appear to be in the 65- to 127-byte range. Upon further inspection with a protocol analyzer (or RMON packet capture feature), you find that the packets are spanning tree packets sent to the bridge, causing it to recompute its forwarding table. During this recomputation, the bridge does not forward packets at the same rate as normal operation, and it is continuously recomputing. The many spanning tree packets are the result of a serial link in the bridged topology transitioning between an active and

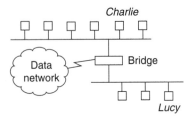

Figure 11.3 The network setup with *Charlie* and *Lucy* connected by a bridge.

an inactive state repeatedly. This leads to the performance problem between *Charlie* and *Lucy*. Observing the high packet rate on the segment helped in the diagnosis of this problem.

As we saw in the previous example, normal data packets on a network segment can cause performance problems. In addition, broadcast and multicast packets can cause unique problems. You can find the amount of current broadcast packets by using the etherStatsBroadcastPkts object. Broadcast packets are processed by every station on the segment and are forwarded by bridges. A high number of broadcasts can occur when devices repeat broadcasts they receive or when improper forwarding of packets results in packets looping throughout the network.

Multicasts are broadcasts sent to a specific subset of stations on the segment but not to every station. For example, the OSPF (Open Shortest Path First) routing protocol, used on IP networks, uses a multicast packet on Ethernet segments to send messages that need to be seen only by routers. All other stations on the segment do not receive or process the multicast packets (unless the station is in promiscuous mode and receiving each packet on the segment). Like broadcasts, excessive multicast packets can cause performance problems on the segment. You can examine the multicast packet rate on the segment with the object etherStatsMulticastPkts.

As shown earlier in this section, it is often useful to be able to examine the length of packets on the segment. Smaller packets need to be processed by network devices at a faster rate and are often associated with interactive data traffic. Larger packets can carry more data and may require more resources to process by all devices.

Consider a situation in which the *OrderFast!* company has an interactive order entry application on workstations throughout the world that talks to a mainframe computer. The data is sent from the workstations to the mainframe in small packets (64–100 bytes on average). The packets are small because each line the order entry personnel enters is sent in a new packet. The *OrderFast!* order entry people expect a response from the mainframe computer within a half second (500ms, i.e., milliseconds), because any delay longer than that results in "sluggish" performance that stops them from entering orders at the desired rate.

The *OrderFast!* data network consists of a variety of devices: routers, bridges, multiplexers, and hubs in a hierarchical topology. When the network was installed, it performed admirably, providing a 300 ms response time. However, like nearly all data networks, the use for the network grew over time. The *OrderFast!* marketing department developed an application that allowed phone solicitors to track calls on the same workstation platform as the order entry personnel. The marketing department wants to place another workstation for its application at every location where the order entry workstations exist and then to use the data network to gather information periodically throughout each day.

Before deploying these new workstations for the marketing department, network engineers need a method to determine how this traffic will affect the response time of the order entry application. They set up both workstations in a lab environment and used an RMON probe to monitor the types of packets each workstation put on the network segment. As expected, the order entry department application put 64- to 100-byte packets on the segment. Interestingly, the marketing application put large packets on the network, between 1100 and 1500 bytes. These large packets are efficient for large information transfers. By using the RMON probe, the network engineer determined the types of packets they will see on their data network. Now they can tune the *OrderFast!* network devices for both types of traffic, most likely prioritizing small packets to traverse the network more quickly than larger packets. This will help keep the network performing to accommodate the users' needs.

With the probe, you can examine the length of packets in six different size ranges (shown here with their associated RMON MIB objects in parenthesis):

- 64 bytes   (etherStatsPkts64Octets)

- 65 bytes to 127 bytes   (etherStatsPkts65to127Octets)

- 128 bytes to 255 bytes   (etherStatsPkts128to255Octets)

- 256 bytes to 511 bytes   (etherStatsPkts256to511Octets)

- 512 bytes to 1023 bytes   (etherStatsPkts512to1023Octets)

- 1024 bytes to 1518 bytes   (etherStatsPkts1024to1518Octets)

We have seen how the types of packets on a network segment can affect performance, but it is also true that any errors on the segment can have a similar effect. You can compute deltas on statistic group objects and see the errors on the segment. You can see the rate of CRC and alignment errors with the object etherStatsCRCAlignErrors, undersize packets with the object etherStatsUndersizePkts, oversize packets with the object etherStatsOversizePkts, fragmented packets using etherStatsFragments, jabbers with etherStatsJabbers, and collisions with etherStatsCollisions. Although the rate of a certain error is often useful, it is also useful to view the error percentage in relation to the total number of packets on the segment. You find the total errors on the segment between time x and time y with the following formula:

$$
\begin{aligned}
\text{Total-errors} = &\ (\text{etherStatsCRCAlignErrors}_y \\
&\ - \text{etherStatsCRCAlignErrors}_x) \\
&\ + (\text{etherStatsUndersizePkts}_y \\
&\ - \text{etherStatsUndersizePkts}_x) \\
&\ + (\text{etherStatsOversizePkts}_y \\
&\ - \text{etherStatsOversizePkts}_x) \\
&\ + (\text{etherStatsFragments}_y - \text{etherStatsFragments}_x) \\
&\ + (\text{etherStatsJabbers}_y - \text{etherStatsJabbers}_x)
\end{aligned}
$$

$$
\text{Error percentage} = \text{total} - \text{errors}/(\text{etherStatsPkts}_y - \text{etherStatsPkts}_x)
$$

Note that we did not include collisions as part of the error calculation for the segment. In fact, you could decide to do this, but since collisions can happen in an error-free segment, it may be more useful to compute the percentage of collisions seen on the segment:

$$
\begin{aligned}
\text{Collision percentage} = &\ (\text{etherStatsCollisions}_y - \text{etherStatsCollisions}_x)/ \\
&\ \text{etherStatsPkts}_y - \text{etherStatsPkts}_x) + \\
&\ (\text{etherStatsCollisions}_y - \text{etherStatsCollisions}_x)
\end{aligned}
$$

11.4 THE HISTORY GROUP

The *history group* enables a network engineer to take periodic statistical samples from a segment and store them within the probe for later retrieval and analysis. The objects in the history group consist of a configuration table to determine the sampling and a media-specific table that stores the samples once they are taken, as shown in Fig. 11.4.

The history group configuration table is called historyControlTable, and each row is called a historyControlEntry, which has seven objects. The first object, historyControlIndex, is an integer that uniquely identifies the historyControlEntry. The second object, historyControlDataSource, tells the source

History group

historyControlTable

historyControlIndex	historyControlDataSource	historyControlInterval	- - - - - -
1	ifIndex.1	20	- - - - - -
2	ifIndex.2	60	- - - - - -
3	ifIndex.3	60	- - - - - -
4	ifIndex.4	120	- - - - - -

Each row is a historyControlEntry.

etherHistoryTable

etherHistoryIndex	etherHistorySampleIndex	etherHistoryOctets	- - - - - -
1	1	78210	- - - - - -
2	1	81347	- - - - - -
3	1	100213	- - - - - -
4	1	116816	- - - - - -
5	2	7021	- - - - - -
6	2	16317	- - - - - -
7	2	21051	- - - - - -

Each row is a etherHistoryEntry.

Figure 11.4 The structure of the history group. Note that not all objects in each section are shown.

interface on the probe for data in this set of samples. This object contains a value, such as ifIndex.1. This value correlates to the value of ifIndex in RFC 1213.

The next two objects deal with the amount of storage the probe allocates for the set of samples. A network management system can request the probe to take a number of samples on the network segment. Each sample requires a *bucket*, or storage location. The object historyControlBucketsRequested is the number of buckets the network management system wants to store for this historyControlEntry. The number of buckets requested also gives the probe the maximum number of time intervals in this sample. This number can grow or expand as instructed by the network management system by the use of SNMP Set-Request messages. The object historyControlBuckets-Granted gives the number of buckets granted for this set of samples, because the probe may not have enough resources, such as disk space and memory, to fulfill a request. The probe makes an effort to grant as many buckets as requested by the network management system when setting up the historyControlEntry.

Next, the object historyControlInterval defines the time interval in seconds that the probe should sample the network segment. The sample period can be as short as a second or as long as an hour. When determining this time interval, it is important to choose an interval that will not result in an object overflow.

Each SNMP object has a maximum value of $2^{32} - 1$ in SNMP and a potential maximum of $2^{64} - 1$ in SNMPv2. If you monitor a value that increases rapidly, the set of samples may contain a period when the value of an object overflows. Typically this means that the number reaches its maximum value and then starts recounting at zero. For example, if you monitor the number of bytes on a 50 percent utilized Ethernet segment for over two hours, the bytes counter will wrap. This could easily happen if you set historyControlInterval to 60 and historyControlBucketsRequested to a number greater than 120.

The historyControlOwner object tells which network management system configured this historyControlEntry. This is useful for determining which management systems have allocated resources within the probe. The historyControlStatus object tells a management system whether this historyControlEntry is valid. Invalid entries may be kept for later use and may not be continually active.

A network management application could easily help a network engineer configure the sample rate of an object to make sure that it will not overflow. The application could ask the user which objects are to be polled how often. The application could then create a new historyControlEntry with these parameters and verify that the number of buckets the probe allocates is sufficient. If the probe does not have enough resources, the application could then show the user all of the existing rows in the historyControlTable and which network management system allocated the resources. The network engineer could then remove or make invalid any history entries not required, freeing up resources within the probe.

The etherHistoryTable section of the history group stores data the probe has gathered at each polling interval for the Ethernet medium. Today this is the only medium supported in the history group, although the potential for another medium does exist.

An etherHistoryEntry is a row of the etherHistoryTable. Each historical sample of Ethernet statistics is stored in a different row in the table. Each row has an etherHistoryIndex object that contains a value identifying which history the row belongs to. The value of etherHistoryIndex gives the historyControlIndex number for the history that relates to this specific sample. Thus many rows in the etherHistoryTable may have the same number in the object etherHistoryIndex. Each of these rows would be one interval of data for that history, where each interval is a single statistical sample.

Further, each etherHistoryEntry is uniquely identified by a number in the object etherHistorySampleIndex that starts at 1 and increments for each row in the table, without any correlation to a historyControlIndex. This number helps keep track of all the rows in the etherHistoryTable.

In a common situation a network engineer may decide to monitor the statistics in a segment every five minutes. After this information has been accumulated for a day, the information may be brought back to the network management system and stored in the relational database for future analysis. To accomplish this, the engineer would define a history that sets up the collection of the statistics every five minutes. The properties of this history are a row in the historyControlTable, a historyControlEntry. For this example assume that the history is assigned the historyControlIndex number 10.

Next, every five minutes the probe makes a new etherHistoryEntry (a new row in the etherHistoryTable). The etherHistoryIndex would contain the number identifying the row as belonging to the specific history, in this case 10. For each of these rows, the etherHistorySampleIndex object would contain a unique number identifying the row in the etherHistoryTable.

The probe also keeps track of the time when the objects in the row were filled with data in the object etherHistoryIntervalStart. This object records the value of sysUpTime when the probe starts sampling. This value, combined with the sample time, allows you to compute the total recorded time associated with the history. Further, if the probe can keep track of the time of day, it makes an effort to have a sample coincide with the first minute of the hour during the history. This sometimes results in the probe's not beginning to poll at the time the history is started by the user (by sending an SNMP Set-Request packet). The reason that the RMON MIB suggests this behavior is that when poll periods start at the beginning of an hour, it is easier to correlate information by network management systems from different probes. This also helps the network engineer by providing a point of reference when comparing different histories and generating reports.

Because all of the statistics in the history group are a record of what has happened on the network segment in the past, these objects are useful in the functional area of performance management.

Objects for Performance Management

Table 11.4 summarizes the history group objects useful in accomplishing performance management. By sampling these objects over time, you can produce a historical picture of the segment. An application could graphically show you the status of the network at any time period in the sample, based on a query to the relational database. Consider an application that instructs the probe to sample the network segment for all of these statistics every five minutes for one hour. After two hours, the application retrieves all of the information the probe has sampled and puts it in the relational database on the network management system. This will reduce the amount of management traffic sent between the devices on the segment and the network management system and not allocate vast quantities of resources

Table 11.4 History Group Objects for Performance Management

Object	Can calculate
etherHistoryOctets	Total traffic rate
etherHistoryPkts	Total packet rate
etherHistoryBroadcastPkts	Broadcast packet rate
etherHistoryMulticastPkts	Multicast packet rate
etherHistoryCRCAlignErrors	CRC error rate
etherHistoryUndersizePkts	Undersized packet rate
etherHistoryOversizePkts	Oversized packet rate
etherHistoryFragments	Fragment rate
etherHistoryJabbers	Jabber rate
etherHistoryCollisions	Collision rate
etherHistoryUtilization	Segment utilization

within the probe. Further, assume that this can occur continually over months or even years.

Now the network engineer can find out exactly the type of traffic, broadcast rate, errors, and utilization of the segment for every five-minute period since the probe began sampling. The engineer could produce graphs of the peak utilization periods, query the database for the period with the most errors, or compute the amount of broadcast traffic versus normal traffic. Because the application has access to this information, it could help diagnose trends on the segment. The network segment could have a trend of seeing more broadcast packets last week than this week, have a higher utilization since more users have migrated from terminal traffic to Ethernet-based applications, or see a trend showing a higher number of errors on the segment since a new device was added. The possibilities for analysis of this data are vast. It would be ideal for the application to provide some common analysis for the data collected and also offer a mechanism to allow the network engineer to look for arbitrary trends on the segment. This trend analysis is critical in accomplishing performance management on the network segment.

11.5 THE ALARM GROUP

The alarm group is useful for performance management. The objects in this group allow you to define two thresholds for a MIB object over a duration of time. The probe then samples this MIB object over the specified time interval and compares the value to the thresholds. The thresholds can be set up for any MIB object that corresponds to a numeric value, such as a gauge or a counter. For example, you may want to set up thresholds to watch for X number of errors seen in a ten-minute time period. If a threshold is crossed, the alarm group gives a way to generate an event.

Thresholds are defined as either rising or falling. A rising threshold is one that is crossed as the monitored value increases, whereas a falling threshold is crossed while the monitored value decreases. The advantage of having two threshold values is that it eliminates multiple alarms when a value bounces below and above the threshold value. We examined the need for this multiple threshold mechanism used in the alarm group in Chapter 6 during the discussion of the "More Complex Tool."

Objects for Performance Management

Table 11.5 summarizes the alarm group objects useful in accomplishing performance management. This group has a single table, called the alarmTable, which allows the network engineer to set up the alarm. Each row in the alarmTable is called an alarmEntry (see Fig. 11.5). Each AlarmEntry has a unique number associated with it, called an alarmIndex. The alarmInterval object specifies the interval of seconds that the probe should use to compare the sampled data to the thresholds. The alarmVariable object contains the ASN.1 object ID of the object being sampled.

You can set up the alarm to monitor the absolute value of the MIB object being sampled (for example, for a gauge object) or to monitor the delta of the MIB object being sampled (for example, for a counter object). You specify the

Table 11.5 Alarm Group Objects for Performance Management

Object	Information
alarmInterval	Specifies the interval for monitoring the sample object
alarmVariable	Specifies the MIB object to sample
alarmSampleType	Specifies how to interpret sample values
alarmValue	Gives current value of sample object
alarmStartupAlarm	Specifies how to interpret value when starting alarm
alarmRisingThreshold	Specifies the rising threshold
alarmFallingThreshold	Specifies the falling threshold
alarmRisingEventIndex	Specifies the event when rising threshold crossed
alarmFallingEventIndex	Specifies the event when falling threshold crossed

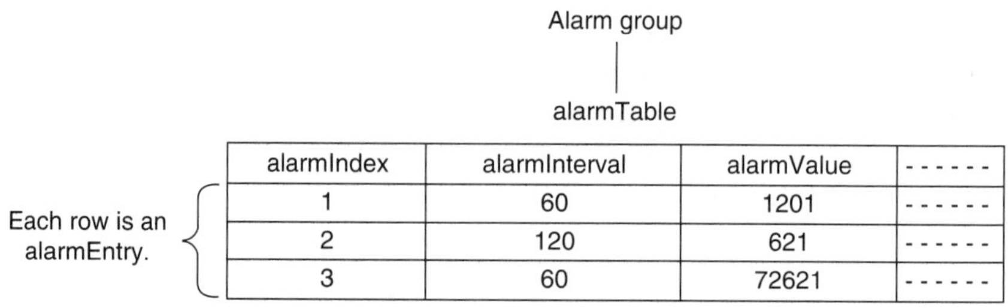

Alarm group

|
alarmTable

alarmIndex	alarmInterval	alarmValue	- - - - - -
1	60	1201	- - - - - -
2	120	621	- - - - - -
3	60	72621	- - - - - -

Each row is an alarmEntry.

Figure 11.5 The structure of the alarm group. Note that not all objects in each section are shown.

method of calculating the current value of the MIB object to be absolute values or delta values, using the alarmSampleType object. The object alarmValue gives the value of the alarm seen by the probe during the last sampling period.

The alarmStartupAlarm object describes how to handle the first sampled value after the alarm is started. An alarm can be generated if the first sample is equal to or greater than the rising threshold, the falling threshold, or both. The rising threshold value is found in the alarmRisingThreshold object; the falling threshold is found in the alarmFallingThreshold object.

An alarm can generate an event, based on the crossing of a rising or falling threshold. The object alarmRisingEventIndex specifies the event to generate when a rising threshold is crossed, whereas the object alarmFallingEvent Index specifies the event that corresponds to a falling threshold. An alarm-Entry also contains the management system that set up the alarm in the object alarmOwner and the current status of the alarm in the alarmStatus object.

In a common situation a network engineer may want to know whether the number of collisions on an Ethernet segment has increased by more than ten in a minute. To do this, the management system could instruct the probe to set the alarmInterval object to sixty seconds, the alarmValue to the object ether-StatsCollisions (from the statistics group), the alarmSampleType to check delta values, and the alarmRisingThreshold to the value of 10. The event to trigger if the threshold is crossed would be specified in the object alarm-RisingEventIndex.

11.6 THE HOST GROUP

The host group of the RMON MIB contains objects associated with each host known on the network segment where the probe resides. The probe discovers hosts on the network by keeping track of source and destination medium access control (MAC) addresses seen on the segment. The probe sees all packets on the segment because its interfaces are in promiscuous mode.

The objects in this group consist of a control table for discovery of hosts, a table of statistics about each host discovered, and a list of time-ordered host statistics (see Fig. 11.6). The control table sets up which interfaces host discovery is performed on by the probe. The table of statistics is kept on a per-hosts basis, and the time-ordered host table keeps those statistics ordered by time.

Objects for Configuration Management

Each section of the host group can be useful for the configuration management process. The control table can tell you about which network management systems have dedicated resources for host discovery on the probe. Also, the statistics about each host and time-ordered host statistics can help a net-

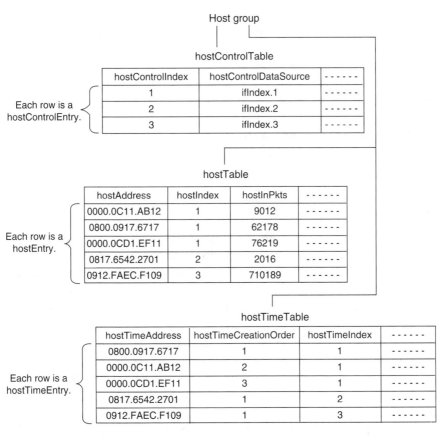

Figure 11.6 The structure of the host group. Note that not all objects in each section are shown.

work engineer determine the physical and logical configuration of the data network.

The control table, named the hostControlTable, is organized into rows, each called a hostControlEntry. There is a unique hostControlEntry in the host-ControlTable for each interface for which the probe is performing host discovery. Each hostControlEntry contains an object, called a hostControlIndex, to uniquely identify each row in the table. The hostControlDataSource object tells you which physical interface the probe is discovering hosts. The current size of the table is found in the hostControlTableSize object. The object host-ControlLastDelete gives the value of sysUpTime when the last entry was removed from the hostControlTable. The hostControlOwner object specifies the management system that allocated the resources on the probe for this host control table, and the hostControlStatus object indicates whether this entry is currently in use.

The objects in the hostControlTable are important for configuration management because they control the autodiscovery mechanism on the probe. A network management system can use this information to tell a network engineer about the autodiscovery status on each probe and allow the engineer to configure each probe as necessary.

There are two additional tables in the Host Group: the hostTable and the hostTimeTable. Each row in the hostTable is a hostEntry. A hostEntry gives the physical address of the host, a number to denote the order in which the row for this host was created, an index to identify this set of hosts, and counters specific to the host that show total packets' input and output, total bytes' input and output, total output errors, total output multicast, and broadcast packets. The hostTimeTable contains objects that contain the identical data, in a table of hostTimeEntry rows. The significant difference between the host-Table and the hostTimeTable is that the hostTimeTable is a sorted version of the hostTable, based on the time the host information was created by the probe. Essentially, this enables the management system to determine the order in which the probe discovered the hosts on the segment, allowing it to find the most recently discovered hosts, aiding the autodiscovery process for hosts.

Both the host table and the time-ordered host table have an object that gives the MAC addresses of the hosts on a segment, hostAddress and host-TimeAddress, respectively. This information, used in conjunction with a network-to-media table (an address resolution protocol cache), such as the ipNetToMediaTable from MIB-II, can give the network engineer the MAC address and network address of each device on each LAN segment on the data network.

For example, imagine that a network management system queries a probe to find the MAC addresses 00-00-0c-11-22-11, 08-00-09-00-23-54-ab, and 00-88-54-23-21-c4 on a segment, using the hostAddress or hostTimeAddress objects.

With this list of MAC addresses, the management system could find the vendor of each interface card on the segment (vendor codes for the first three bytes of the MAC address are well known and defined by the IEEE). The management system could also then query each device for its ipNetToMediaTable and discover the IP address associated with each MAC address. If the management system found a bridge or a router (using sysServices or sysObjectID, for example), it may discover a large table of MAC-to-network-level addresses.

Objects for Performance Management

Table 11.6 lists the host group objects that are useful in accomplishing performance management. Using these objects makes it possible to perform both short- and long-term analysis of traffic to and from a given host address. This analysis can help a network engineer identify hosts that are sending or receiving large portions of network traffic and can help isolate errors.

One practical application of this information is a pie chart showing traffic or error distribution on a host-by-host basis. A performance management application would have to query a probe to find the total traffic received (hostInOctets) and total traffic sent (hostOutOctets) by each host on the network segment. The total of all traffic on the segment could be found by computing the sum of these numbers or by using objects from the statistics (etherStatsOctets) or history (etherHistoryUtilization) groups. You can then compute the percentage of traffic for a single host as follows:

$$\text{Host percentage} = (\text{hostInOctets}_y - \text{hostInOctets}_x)$$
$$+ (\text{hostOutOctets}_y - \text{hostOutOctets}_x)$$
$$/ (\text{etherStatsOctets}_y - \text{etherStatsOctets}_x)$$

Similar percentages and pie charts could be produced for errors on the segment, helping a network engineer isolate those hosts sending errors.

Table 11.6   Host Group Objects for Performance Management

Object	Information
hostInPkts	Rate of input packets
hostOutPkts	Rate of output packets
hostInOctets	Rate of input bytes
hostOutOctets	Rate of output bytes
hostOutErrors	Rate of errors sent
hostOutBroadcastPkts	Rate of broadcast packets sent
hostOutMulticastPkts	Rate of multicast packets sent

Objects for Accounting Management

Table 11.7 lists the host group objects that are useful in accomplishing accounting management. The accounting management process involves counting packets and bytes per host. If the organization decides to perform accounting management based on packets received or sent, the objects hostInPkts, hostOutPkts, hostOutBroadcastPkts, and hostOutMulticastPkts give the necessary information per host.

In contrast, if the organization decides to base its accounting management scheme on bytes received or sent, the objects hostInOctets and hostOutOctets apply. If the accounting management application concludes that it needs to query each host on a segment, it is possible to query the RMON probe for all of the necessary statistics.

11.7 THE HOSTTOPN GROUP

The hostTopN group uses the objects in the host group to prepare reports for a set of hosts over a given time period. The reports are based on a base statistic specified by the network management system. The base statistic can be set to report on host statistics to find the top N for the number of packets received and sent, bytes received and sent, and errors, broadcasts, and multicasts sent. The management system also instructs the probe concerning the reporting interval and the number of hosts in each report. The variable number of hosts in each report is the source of the name of this group, because the value of N hosts can change for each report. Because the host-TopN group produces a specific report using statistics from the host group, all of the objects in this group apply to both performance management and accounting management.

Table 11.7 Host Group Objects for Accounting Management

Object	Information
hostInPkts	Number of input packets
hostOutPkts	Number of output packets
hostInOctets	Number of input bytes
hostOutOctets	Number of output bytes
hostOutBroadcastPkts	Number of broadcast packets sent
hostOutMulticastPkts	Number of multicast packets sent

For example, imagine that a network engineer wants to determine the top ten hosts for traffic volume on the entire data network for accounting management purposes. The engineer could gather the top ten hosts that receive and send bytes on each segment, using RMON probes. Next, the engineer could use a network management protocol to bring this information back to the SQL database on the network management system. Using SQL is a straightforward way to sort the data to produce a report showing the host that received the largest number of bytes on the network:

```
SELECT hostname,bytes-sent,bytes-received FROM rmon-data
SORT BY bytes-received
```

This SQL statement assumes that there is a database table called rmon-data that has columns for the name of the host (hostname), total bytes sent by the host (bytes-sent), and total bytes received by the host (bytes-received).

The hostTopN group contains two tables. The first, hostTopNControlTable, allows a network management system to set up a report, as shown in Fig. 11.7. The results of the report are then put into the hostTopNTable.

Each row in the hostTopNControlTable is a hostTopNControlEntry. Each hostTopNControlEntry contains an index, called a hostTopNControlIndex, to uniquely identify the report. Since each report could use a different host table (from the host group), there is another index, called the hostTopNHostIndex, to identify the proper host table from the host group. The value of hostTopNHostIndex correlates to the value of hostIndex in the host group.

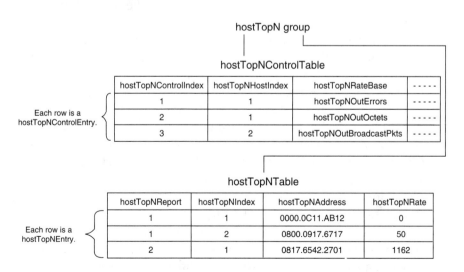

Figure 11.7 The structure of the hostTopN group. Note that not all objects in each section are shown.

To specify the statistic to use as the basis of the report, the manager sets the value of the hostTopNRateBase object. Each report can measure only one statistic. The time the probe started the report based on hostTopNRateBase is available by using the object hostTopNStartTime. The duration of time to examine statistics for the report is specified in the object hostTopNDuration; hostTopNTimeRemaining gives the duration of time left to gather this data.

The object hostTopNRequestedSize allows the management system to specify the number of N hosts in the report, and the object hostTopN-GrantedSize shows the actual number of N hosts granted by the probe for the report. A probe may not have the resources to handle the total N number of hosts in the report. The management system that started this report (and requested the allocation of resources) is available in the object hostTopNOwner. The object hostTopNStatus tells the current status of the report.

Consider that in using the statistics group, you found that a segment has a large percentage, say, 10 percent, of CRC errors. You could first see whether this is a current problem by checking the errors seen by the probe using statistics from the history group. If the problem is new, you could see which hosts were recently added to the network, using the time-ordered host table, the hostTimeTable.

To help you isolate which host may be sending frames with bad CRCs, you could query the probe for each HostEntry from the hostTable (from the host group) and check each individual host for the number of hostOutErrors. To optimize this process, you could set up a report by using the hostTopN group with the rate statistic set for hostOutErrors. If the problem is new to the segment, you would set the start time of the report to be the current time. If the problem appears in the historical statistics gathered by the probe, it may be useful to have the report start at an earlier time. A report showing the top ten hosts in terms of sending errors may be sufficient. Once the report is done, it will show you the top ten hosts on the segment in terms of sending errors.

The top N report the probe makes is put into the hostTopNTable. Each row in the hostTopNTable is a hostTopNEntry. The object hostTopNReport has an index that identifies the report to which this entry belongs. The probe may have multiple reports stored in the hostTopNTable at any given time. The next object in the hostTopNTable is the hostTopNIndex, which tells the location of this row in the report between 1 and N. The final two objects in a hostTop-NTable are the address of the host (hostTopNAddress) and the rate of change in the rate base statistics for the host (hostTopNRate).

In the previous example, in which the probe produces a top-ten report based on the rate of change for hostOutErrors, the hostTopNTable would have at least ten rows for this report. Each row would have a unique value in host-TopNIndex, placing this row in its relative place in the final performance management report.

11.8 THE MATRIX GROUP

The matrix group contains tables of objects that keep statistics on the number of packets, bytes, and errors sent between two addresses on a segment. The probe forms these tables by examining the source and destination MAC addresses in the packets on the segment. The probe keeps two tables: one from the source to the destination and another from the destination to the source. The information in the matrix group can help you determine traffic patterns on a segment, making this data useful in performance management, security management, and accounting management.

The matrix group is useful in performance management because it helps you determine the flow of traffic on the segment and track errors between hosts. You can use the matrix group objects to determine whether all of the traffic on the segment is destined for a particular host (such as a server) or series of hosts. You can find out the percentage of traffic leaving the segment, because the MAC address of the bridge, switch, or router will appear in the matrix. You can also find out whether one host has sent a lot of errors to another.

Next, a table of data that tracks conversations between addresses can help in security management. A network engineer can query this information periodically and see exactly which hosts on the segment have sent packets to a secure host. If the network engineer knows that a network device has forwarded or sent packets to the secure host, it will be more difficult to determine the exact source address. To overcome this difficulty, some network devices keep a matrix of network-layer addresses that does record the source network–level address of a packet.

The matrix group can help the network billing process in accounting management. The matrix of conversations recorded by the RMON probe gives data per segment, allowing for accounting by packets or bytes. If the network management system gathered this information, then producing a report showing how many packets or bytes a single host sent or received would be relatively easy. On a network segment where there is a network device, the matrix group information could tell the network engineer exactly which hosts were communicating off the segment and how many network resources (in terms of packets or bytes) they were consuming.

The matrix group is divided into three tables: a control table, a table of source-to-destination traffic, and a table of destination-to-source traffic. The matrixControlTable controls the operation of the matrix group. Each row in the matrixControlTable is a matrixControlEntry. A probe may have several matrixControlEntry rows in the matrixControlTable because the probe may have only some interfaces collecting the matrix group objects (see Fig. 11.8). The matrixControlIndex specifies a unique number for each matrixControlEntry. The matrixControlDataSource object identifies the interface that this

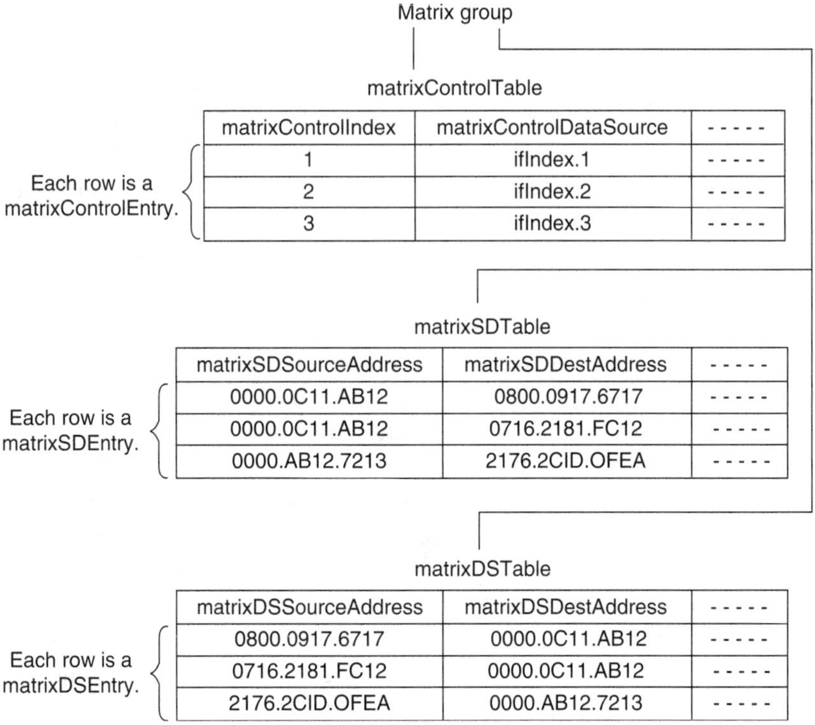

Matrix group

matrixControlTable

matrixControlIndex	matrixControlDataSource	- - - - -
1	ifIndex.1	- - - - -
2	ifIndex.2	- - - - -
3	ifIndex.3	- - - - -

Each row is a matrixControlEntry.

matrixSDTable

matrixSDSourceAddress	matrixSDDestAddress	- - - - -
0000.0C11.AB12	0800.0917.6717	- - - - -
0000.0C11.AB12	0716.2181.FC12	- - - - -
0000.AB12.7213	2176.2CID.OFEA	- - - - -

Each row is a matrixSDEntry.

matrixDSTable

matrixDSSourceAddress	matrixDSDestAddress	- - - - -
0800.0917.6717	0000.0C11.AB12	- - - - -
0716.2181.FC12	0000.0C11.AB12	- - - - -
2176.2CID.OFEA	0000.AB12.7213	- - - - -

Each row is a matrixDSEntry.

Figure 11.8 The structure of the matrix group. Note that not all objects in each section are shown.

matrixControlEntry controls. The current sizes of the source-to-destination table and the destination-to-source table are found in the object matrix-ControlTableSize. The object matrixControlLastDeleteTime gives the last time an entry was deleted from these tables. Finally, the matrixControlOwner object tells which management system set up this matrixControlEntry, and the matrixControlStatus object tells its current status.

The source-to-destination traffic table is called the matrixSDTable. Each row in this table is named a matrixSDEntry and contains the source address of the traffic (matrixSDSourceAddress), the destination of the traffic (matrixSDDestAddress), the number of packets sent from source to destination (matrixSDPkts), the number of bytes sent from source to destination (matrixSDOctets), and the number of errors sent from source to destination (matrixSDErrors). A matrixSDEntry also contains a number, called a matrixSDIndex, that uniquely identifies a set of rows in the table. The matrixSDIndex allows the probe to have data about multiple segments stored in the same table and still be able to identify the set of entries belonging to a specific segment. The destination-to-source traffic table is exactly the same as the source-to-destination table except that the objects have names with "DS" instead of "SD." Having both of these tables allows the probe to produce traffic matrix information for traffic being sent and received by a host.

In a common setup, users on a local area segment may complain to a network engineer that the performance of the segment is rather poor. The users may want to install a network device, such as a bridge, switch, or router, to partition the segment into smaller pieces to help performance. A network engineer could examine matrix group data to determine whether partitioning the segment with a device would really help performance. It would first be beneficial to determine whether hosts on the segment talk primarily among themselves or whether traffic heads mostly to another segment.

The network engineer could use the matrixSDTable (and corresponding matrixDSTable) to find this information. If a significant portion of traffic from the hosts on the segment does head to another segment, partitioning the segment into smaller pieces that have equal access to a network device that connects to the other segment may make sense. If a significant portion of the traffic stays on the segment and heads for a single host (such as a server), providing additional bandwidth to the server may make sense. In another case, if the traffic is spread fairly evenly among all of the hosts on the segment and the performance is poor, it may make sense to use a higher-speed medium or to provide multiple parallel paths among the hosts. Regardless of the network-design decision made to help the performance of the segment, the data from the matrixSDTable will be invaluable to the network engineer.

11.9 THE FILTER GROUP

The filter group enables a network engineer to instruct the RMON probe to look for specific packets on a segment. The probe is configured with a filter that tells it which packet to look for on the segment. When the probe sees a packet that matches (or does not match) the filter, it sends the packet to a channel (see Flowchart 11.1). A channel keeps a count of the number of packets that it has seen and can, optionally, generate an event when it sees a packet or capture the packet for further analysis. The filter group contains a table of filters and another table for channels.

This functionality is useful in the areas of fault management and security management. The filter group can aid the fault management task because the probe can observe specific packets or errors on the segment and then have a channel generate an event. Security management tasks can benefit from the filter group because a network engineer could set up a filter to look for a certain type of packet or packets from or to a specific user or host and, if it appears, have a channel send an event to the network management system.

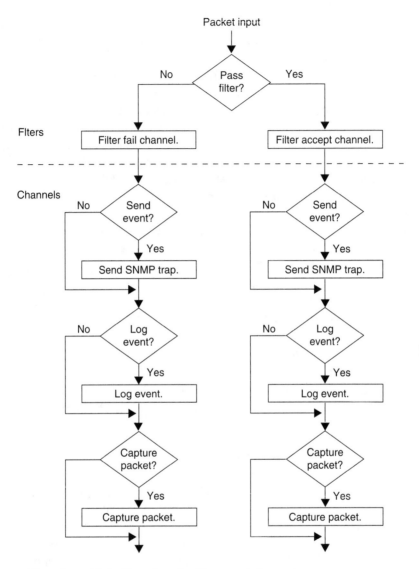

Flowchart 11.1 Flowchart for filters and channel.

Filters

A filter is the definition of the packets that the probe will observe. Two types of filters are available: a data filter and a status filter. The probe can look for packets that match a specific bit pattern, using a data filter, and observe packets based on their current status (valid, runt, giant, CRC error), using a status filter. You can set up very complicated filters, with multiple filters sending to a single channel. For example, you may want to look at packets that have a specific data pattern in them (such as a host name) or that are in error and come from a specific host address on the segment.

The Boolean logic flow for this filter is as follows:

$$[(\text{Data filters}_x) \cup (\text{Status filter}_x)] \cap (\text{Data filter}_{x+1})$$

This Boolean logic is for a packet filter to match a specific pattern (Data filter$_x$) or an error (Status filter$_x$) and a specific host address (Data filter$_{x+1}$).

The filters are set up in the filterTable. Each row in the filterTable is a filterEntry (see Fig. 11.9). Each filterEntry has a number, called a filterIndex, that uniquely identifies it. The object filterChannelIndex specifies the channel for this filter.

Data filters allow you to specify the offset in the packet where the filter begins to find a match by using the filterPktOffset object. The most common offset used may be zero, which tells the probe to start looking at the first bit of the packet. The data you want to match in the packet before sending it to the channel is specified in the filterPktData object. You can also apply a bit mask to the data. This provides a way to set bits that the filter does not care to examine (sometimes called "don't care" bits) by using the filterPktData-Mask object. The inverse of the bit mask can also be set by using the filter-PktDataNotMask object.

Status filters are set up differently from data filters. Status filters examine the status of the packet as the probe receives it. If the packet has an error, the

Filter group

filterTable

filterIndex	filterChannelIndex	filterPktData	- - - - - -
1	1	"Allan"	- - - - - -
2	1	"Karen"	- - - - - -
3	2	0x0800	- - - - - -

Each row is a filterEntry.

channelTable

channelIndex	channelDataControl	channelEventIndex	- - - - - -
1	on	1	- - - - - -
2	on	1	- - - - - -
3	off	3	- - - - - -

Each row is a channelEntry.

Figure 11.9 The structure of the filter group. Note that not all objects in each section are shown.

filter computes a sum based on error codes. The sum initially takes a value of zero. For each error found in the packet, $2^{error\ code}$ is added to the sum. The object filterPktStatus contains this sum. The error codes and the bits that represent them are dependent on the media type of the interface on the probe. As an example, on an Ethernet the following bits and associated errors are defined:

- Bit 0: Packet is longer than 1518 octets.

- Bit 1: Packet is shorter than 64 octets.

- Bit 2: Packet experienced a CRC or alignment error.

Thus an Ethernet packet that was a giant (longer than 1518 octets) and also a CRC error would result in the object filterPktStatus having a value of $2^0 + 2^2$, or 5. Like data filters, status filters allow bit masking with the filterPktStatusMask and filterPktNotMask objects.

Similar to other tables in the RMON MIB, the filterTable has the filterOwner object to say which management system set up this filter and the filterStatus to give the current status of the filter.

Channels

The second table in the filter group is the channelTable. Each entry in the channelTable is called a channelEntry, which in turn has a unique number, called a channelIndex, used to identify it. The interface of the probe this channel operates on is found in the object channelIfIndex.

A channel can accept a packet if it matches the filter or if it fails to match the filter. The channelAcceptType object needs to be set to one of these two conditions. A channel without a filter set for it will never accept a packet if it is set to accept all packets that match a filter. The same channel will, however, accept all packets if it is set to accept packets that fail to match a filter. For each packet accepted by the channel, the object channelMatches is incremented.

If the object channelDataControl is turned on, this channel can generate events or capture the packet when a packet enters the channel. Otherwise, if channelDataControl is set to off, the channel can accept only the packet and increment the channelMatches object.

You can have events in the events group turn a channel on or off. The concept here is that when a given event occurs, it may be desirable to have a channel open with filters looking for specific data or status packets on the segment. Imagine that for security management purposes, you have an event set up to watch for any packets having a source on the local segment and destined for a secure host (note that having the event set up will require another separate channel). When this event occurs, you may want a channel to generate a new event (such as an SNMP trap) to the management system and then begin to capture these packets. To accomplish this, you would need to set the channelTurnOnEventIndex object to correlate to the event that examines packets looking for those destined to the secure host. When this event occurs, the channel opens and channelMatches is incremented. As we will see later, you could then begin to have this channel capture these packets for further analysis. There is also a corresponding channelTurnOffEventIndex object to have a channel close when an event occurs.

In addition to having events open and close a channel, the channel itself can generate an event. The channelEventIndex object specifies which event the channel should generate when channelDataControl is on and the channel accepts a packet. The channelEventStatus object tells you that an event has been sent by this channel. The channelEventStatus object can tell you that the event is ready, sent, or always ready. Under normal situations, once the channel has sent an event, its status moves from ready to sent. A channel with a sent status will not generate another event until a management system moves the channelEventStatus back to ready. Optionally, you could lock the channelEventStatus to always ready, but this allows for many potential events to be sent and could have an impact on network resources. In a typical situation once an event has been sent, the management system will either reset the channelEventStatus back to ready after a short period of time or prompt the user to verify that this is the proper action to take.

The object channelDescription allows you to enter in a text description of the channel for documentation purposes. Finally, the channelOwner object tells which management system set up this channel, and channelStatus gives the current status of the channel.

11.10 THE PACKET CAPTURE GROUP

This group is used to set up a buffering scheme for those packets sent to one channel from the filter group. Because the packet capture group relies on channels, the probe needs to first implement the filter group. Like the filter group, this group can provide functionality to help in both fault management and security management. This functionality is available not because of the functions the probe supports for the packet capture group (capturing a packet for later retrieval) but because of the ability of the network management system and applications to download the packet and then decode it (see Flowchart 11.2).

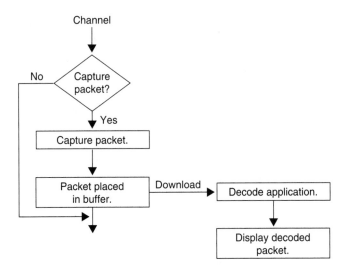

Flowchart 11.2 The flowchart for an application that uses the packet capture group.

This latter feature is where the benefit from this RMON MIB group will help network engineers. Here, therefore, we mention this RMON MIB group only briefly. Many companies offer software to decode packets that are sent to a channel and stored in the packet capture group. The level of packet decoding available varies, depending on the application, but on many products this feature generally gives the network engineer a good breakdown of the many fields in the packet.

The combination of an RMON probe with the packet capture group and software to decode captured packets appears to provide the same functionality as a network protocol analyzer. Although in some cases this may be true, in today's marketplace dedicated network protocol analyzers can usually capture packets at a higher rate and generally have more decoding features. Also, network protocol analyzers usually provide features other than packet decoding, such as traffic generation.

11.11 THE EVENT GROUP

The event group allows the definition of events. As we have seen, an event can be triggered from alarms and channels. An event can also trigger an action, such as opening or closing a channel. As we will see, an event can produce a log entry and may, optionally, cause the probe to send an SNMP trap to a network management system.

Events can help in fault management, performance management, and security management. The generation of events by the RMON probe can help eliminate the need to have a network management system periodically poll devices to discover network faults. If the probe generates an event based on an alarm that is watching the number of errors or traffic on the segment, this preemptive monitoring can aid in performance management. Likewise, if an alarm or filter is set up to watch for a security violation, the event can inform the network engineer of a security management issue. The log of events can also help produce an audit trail, which is important data in accomplishing security management.

The event group has two tables: one for events and one for log entries of events. In the first table, called the eventTable, each row is called an eventEntry, as shown in Fig. 11.10. An eventEntry has a unique number, specified by the eventIndex object, which identifies the event. A text description of the event for documentation purposes is found in the eventDescription object.

The eventType object specifies the type of notification the probe should invoke when the event triggers. The probe can do nothing, log the event, send an SNMP trap, or both log the event and send an SNMP trap. If the probe sends an SNMP trap when the event occurs, it uses the community string found in eventCommunity. The security mechanisms found in SNMPv2 are not in the RMON MIB yet but will be added at a later date. When the probe sends the event, it records the value of sysUpTime (from MIB-II) in the object

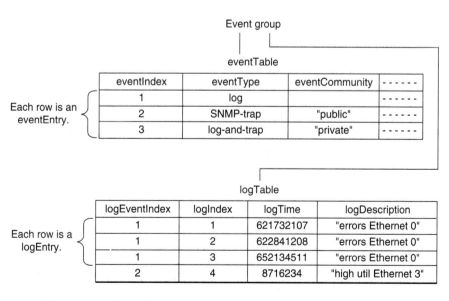

Figure 11.10 The structure of the event group. Note that not all objects in each section are shown.

eventLastTimeSent. This enables the network engineer to correlate events from the probe with other events, such as those generated by other network devices or by the management system.

The network management system that set up this event is identified in the object eventOwner. The current status of this event is stored in the object eventStatus.

The second table in the event group is the logTable. Each row in the logTable is called a logEntry, and each has a unique number, called a log-Index, for identification purposes. The object logEventIndex correlates a logEntry to the originating event. The logTime object records the value of sysUpTime at creation time, and logDescription provides a text description for the LogEntry.

Imagine that a performance management application is using an RMON probe to monitor the number of errors on an Ethernet segment. The application sets up the alarm group objects to trigger an alarm if the number of CRC, alignment, or framing errors on the Ethernet increases by more than fifty in a given minute. This rising alarm is then set up to generate an event that sends an SNMP trap to the management system that the application sees in the event log.

When this first event is received, the application sends a series of SNMP Set-Requests to the probe and sets up a status filter and an associated channel. The new channel is set up to capture the packets with errors to the packet capture buffers on the probe. The application then sets up another event with a different description and has the new channel trigger this new event. When an SNMP trap with the description of the new event is seen by the network management system and application, the application downloads the captured packets and decodes them for the network engineer. The application then resets the channel to capture more error packets in the future. The flow for this application is shown in Flowchart 11.3. In this example the first event notified the application that there was a performance problem on the segment. The application then allocated resources on the probe to examine the problem further and to capture relevant packets for later diagnosis.

SUMMARY

The RMON MIB, RFC 1757, contains a wealth of data for managing network segments. This data resides in any networking hardware that implements this MIB, which is called an RMON probe. Because of the many different goals of this MIB and the numerous amount of objects, this chapter took a close look at the exact MIB objects and their use in the functional areas of network management.

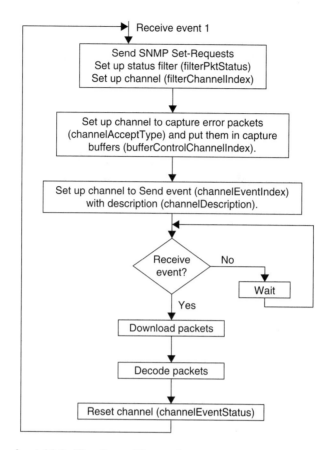

Flowchart 11.3 The flow of the performance management application, showing some relevant RMON MIB objects.

FOR FURTHER STUDY

Stallings, W., *SNMP, SNMPv2, and CMIP: The Practical Guide to Network-Management Standards*, Reading, MA: Addison-Wesley, 1993.

Waldbusser, S., RFC 1513, "Token Ring Extensions to the Remote Network Monitoring MIB," September 1993.

———., RFC 1757, "Remote Network Monitoring Management Information Base," February 1995.

PART 4

Productivity Tools for Network Management

Chapter 12

Productivity Tools

In This Chapter:

The set of features in the network management platform Chris used was definitely impressive, with tools to help in each area of network management. But tools that would help productivity are lacking. To produce a report, for example, Chris copies the data the network management platform stores over to a personal computer and then uses Microsoft Excel to turn the data into a report for management. Seems as though there are just a few things left to be added to the network management platform to make it a bit more complete. . . .

A network management system comprises a set of software tools to help the network engineer manage a data network. However, the system also can include many other helpful features that do not directly relate to a specific functional area of network management. The addition of certain tools can significantly enhance the productivity of the engineer and hence the efficiency of the system. For example, the engineer might need a way to manipulate and examine the objects in a MIB. After using MIB objects to gather information from a device, the engineer could use presentation tools to produce logs, graphs, and reports of the data. The engineer further could use problem-solving tools to analyze the data gathered from network devices and offer possible solutions.

In this chapter we look at three types of productivity tools beneficial on a network management system:

- MIB tools—a compiler, a browser tool, an alias tool, and a query tool

- Presentation tools—a centralized log, a report writer, and a graphics package

- Problem-solving tools—a trouble-tracking system, a set of tools for network design, and an expert system

Although it would be desirable for a system to possess a complete set of such tools, they can exist independently. In addition to the common tools we discuss, others might exist or could be developed for specific network environments. Already tools on the market incorporate many features we describe in this chapter. We recommend that when you are purchasing or developing a network management system, you consider including some or all of these productivity tools, depending on how you want the system to help you perform network management.

12.1 MIB TOOLS

The following tools can be helpful for manipulating MIB information on a network management system:

- A MIB compiler, which loads MIBs into the system, can help you obtain necessary data from the inevitably large variety of devices on the network. This facility also can enable you to relate MIB attributes to graphical elements on the network map.

- A MIB browser, an electronic means of browsing the MIB after it has been loaded in order to find specific information.

- A MIB alias tool for associating potentially confusing MIB object names to references that are more familiar to you.

- A MIB query tool to poll agents in the network devices in order to examine the values returned, which can help you decide whether polling for an object is useful.

MIB Compiler

A *MIB compiler* takes in a file in RFC 1155 format and converts it for use with the network management system. Customized versions of a MIB are usually preferred because they perform searches and lookups faster than an ASCII file can. You might need to use the MIB compiler to incorporate a new vendor-specific MIB or an update of an existing MIB file. This function should be simple to use. The system should also generate a customized version of the MIB that permits the network management system to query a device by using SNMPv1 or SNMPv2.

Perhaps the system has an input field that allows a user to specify the name of the ASCII MIB file. In this case the compiler could automatically read in this file and allow you to view the specific objects; an example of this tool is shown in Fig. 12.1. These objects can apply to any of the five functional areas of network management.

Nearly every network management platform on the market today has a MIB compiler. HP OpenView and IBM NetView/AIX use a small graphics window (similar to that shown in Fig. 12.1) that allows you to compile a MIB on the platform. SunConnect SunNet Manager has a utility, called mib2schema for SNMPv1 and v2mib2schema for SNMPv2, that performs this same function.

For example, suppose that you wanted to learn the current number of active stations on a wiring hub, information that is important for accounting and performance issues. This information is not available with the standard MIB. However, you could add the vendor-specific MIB for the wiring hub to the network management system and thus be able to retrieve this data.

In another case the wiring hub could allow for the activation and deactivation of a port by performing a SNMPv1 Set-Request on a vendor-specific MIB object. As we saw in Chapter 3, a fault management tool could use this

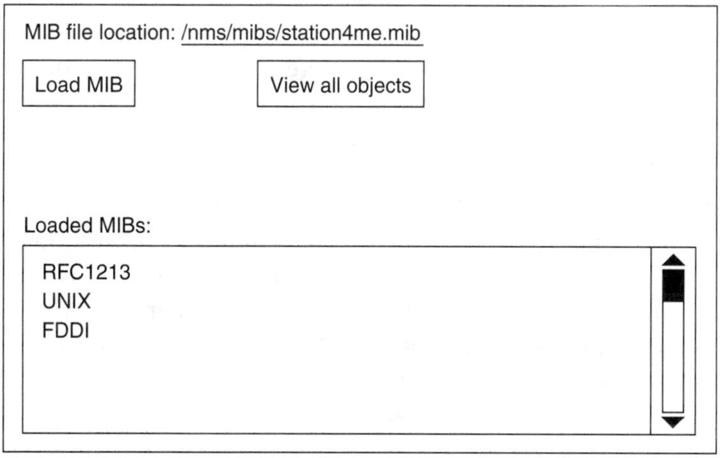

Figure 12.1 A tool that compiles MIBs into the network management system.

object to shut off a faulty port, and a configuration management tool could use it to set up the hub.

Although accessing vendor-specific MIB information is important, you often might find it useful to relate the objects to the network map. Suppose that in the same wiring hub MIB, an object shows the input error rate on each port. You could set up a process to gather this input error rate data and store it in the relational database for performance management. However, you could find it helpful to have the port and its associated representation on the network map display a graphic signal if a high input error rate occurs. The performance management application probably could not perform this function because, as written, it doesn't understand the vendor-specific MIB object. Building a relationship between a specific MIB object and a graphical element is a sophisticated way to use MIB information.

Let's look at still another example. Suppose that you want to set up the network management system to monitor the input error rate on a fiber distributed data interface (FDDI) on a file server. You decide that if the input error rate exceeds 2 percent, you would want the device on the network map to flash the icon depicting the file server. As you can see, setting up such arbitrary relationships between MIB objects and the network map can help your productivity: Having the network management system inform you when the input error rate on the FDDI ring exceeds 2 percent would free you to work on other tasks until you were alerted.

Still, this functionality might not provide all the necessary features you want. For example, you might want to associate multiple MIB objects and their decrease, increase, or change of state to a graphical element. Consider a situation in which you manage a network of T-1 multiplexers interconnecting LANs in many cities. Using objects in the standard MIB, such as those in the interface table, the fault management application could cause links with errors to flash on the network map. For T-1 links, an important piece of data from the multiplexers is a standard metric called *severely errored seconds*. This information is not available through the standard MIB but is available through the T-1 MIB.[1] Further, you decide that you want a link on the network map to flash when the severely errored seconds object reaches a defined threshold. To provide this functionality, the network management system first must learn about the T-1 MIB. Then you would need a means of telling the system to flash the appropriate link on the network map when the error rate of the T-1 multiplexers increases. Figure 12.2 shows an example of an application interface that associates MIB objects with map elements.

[1] The MIB referenced is RFC 1406, "Definitions of Managed Objects for the DSI and E1 Interface Types." The object that counts the current severely errored seconds is dsx1CurrentSESs.

Network map

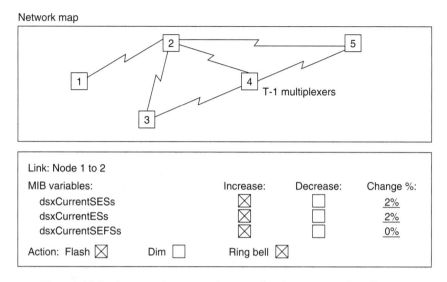

Figure 12.2 A network map and an application to associate T-1 objects to a graphical element.

MIB Browser

Once the network management system can use a MIB, you might find it helpful to have a means of browsing the MIB. A *MIB browser* shows the various groups in the MIB in a graphical manner, such as by displaying the MIB tree, and can search for MIB information about a specific function. For example, you can use a mouse to traverse the MIB tree and examine the individual objects. Or you might want to know what area of the MIB has information about error rates. In this case you could type in the string "errors" to prompt the browser to show all objects on this subject. This feature of the browser is similar to having an index for the MIB. A sample browser is shown in Fig. 12.3.

Many network management platforms have a MIB browser. Some let you query the MIB by using a mouse to produce a graphical tree of the MIB (HP OpenView, Cabletron Spectrum); others have utilities that customize the menu system of the platform to reflect the structure of the MIB (SunConnect SunNet Manager).

MIB Aliases

Once you have found the important objects from the new MIB, you might find it useful to associate the object name to a more familiar string. The *MIB alias tool* can provide this function. For example, the interfaces table in RFC 1213 contains an object named ifInOctets, which counts the number of octets

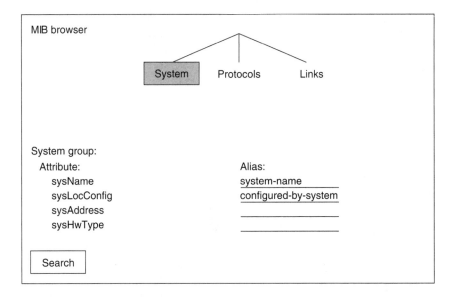

Figure 12.3 A MIB browser.

received in this interface. Since an octet is a byte, this object is counting the number of bytes input on the interface. However, because the association of octet with byte may not be obvious from the object name, the system allows you to associate this name to something that is more meaningful to you. In other words, you assign an alias to the term *octet*, such as Total-Input-Bytes, which might make more sense to the average user.

Because a MIB alias tool is useful and tends to make MIB object names understandable to users, this facility does exist on many network management platforms. However, with the wealth of MIB objects defined, it is often a very tedious task to alias the full set of objects a user may want to use.

MIB Queries

After browsing the MIB and setting up aliases, you next would probably want to look at the values returned by the agent on the network device. Often the description of an object in a MIB may be vague or need clarification. One way to do that is to query the device agent for objects from the new MIB and then examine the result. Therefore MIB tools should include a means of allowing you to perform a one-time query of a specific MIB object. By doing this, you can know whether the information the agent returns is relevant to the current task.

An extension of this facility would allow you to create your own custom MIB queries. A *custom query* is a collection of specific MIB objects found in any MIB the system understands. The custom query is intended to retrieve specific information from a device that the network management system either does not show or displays in a format you would like to change. Using a custom query, you can create your own view of MIB objects.

There are two common methods for building the custom query: pseudocode language and window-based generation. The pseudocode method allows you to build a file that contains commands for building the custom query. The advantage of this method is that it is usually easy to make a single custom query and then copy it for making other queries rapidly. Its disadvantage is that you have to learn the pseudocode language and syntax.

Using a window-based generation facility to build the custom query has two advantages: First, you don't have to learn pseudocode; second, you can obtain immediate feedback about how the output of the query will appear. In this method you are presented with a blank window. Query generation is performed by walking through menus and using a mouse to specify where on the window the output will go. For example, you could select MIB objects with the MIB browser and then denote where their output should appear on a blank window representing the custom query. The primary disadvantage of this method is that you usually have to traverse many menus to produce the custom query.

For example, suppose that the MIB for a workstation by the vendor *Station4Me!* allows you to query the agent for the number of users logged in and the processing time for their current session. Because this is vendor-specific MIB information, the network management system does not have a standard window for viewing this information. To resolve this problem, you could build a custom query that displays the necessary information and then use the custom query to learn the number of users and processing time for their current session on any *Station4Me!* workstation.

Many network management platforms on the market can query for specific MIB objects and create custom queries. Most use a graphical approach to building the query and then build this query into the menu system of the platform. In many cases if you create a custom query on the platform, a user who does not know the platform well may assume that your query is part of the standard platform feature set.

12.2 PRESENTATION TOOLS

The presentation of information to the network engineer is a crucial function of a network management system. Many applications on the system attempt to present their information in an easy-to-understand manner. Still, the following presentation tools, which all applications can use, can help increase overall system productivity:

- A centralized log for all system messages and network events, which can provide you with a means of tracking network activity as seen by the system.

- A report generator that can enable you to format the data into a text report.

- A graphics package to enable you to view data in a graphical format. This package could be offered by the system or through an interface to an existing graphics packages and would be able to present information in line, bar, and pie chart formats.

Centralized Log

A centralized log tool would show messages generated by the various applications and provide you with one location for monitoring system status. This tool would obtain its input both from the applications running on the network management system and from the network. If an application found a significant event, it could make an entry in the log, either automatically or as prompted by you.

Determination of whether an event is significant would depend on the application. For example, the fault management application that polls devices to determine their current connectivity most likely would consider the loss of communication to a device a significant event and would automatically make an entry about the event in the central log. On the other hand, the performance management tool that monitors statistics and thresholds could be set up so that you determine whether the crossing of a threshold is an event worthy of a log entry.

This log also could show network events, such as the receipt of an unsolicited message (an SNMPv1 trap) or the loss of connectivity to a device obtained through polling. The centralized log tool should also provide a means for searching for specific events between two specified time periods, as illustrated in Fig. 12.4.

As we have seen, the network management system could use an ASCII file or a relational database to store the central log. Either or both storage facilities could be useful for keeping the log information. Ideally, this would be a configurable option of the centralized log tool.

Network management platforms and applications tend to both have logging facilities. HP OpenView and IBM NetView/AIX have a series of logs that appear in a separate log window. Each log contains messages about a particular set of events. SunConnect SunNet Manager has a main log window that shows all network events. All platforms support a way to query the logs by host name. Also, most platforms store their log information in an ASCII file.

```
Name: Tokyo                           Additional criteria: Link #123-47
Start time: Mon 9:00 AM
End time: Wed 3:00 PM

 ┌────────┐
 │ Search │
 └────────┘

 Time:                Node:
 Mon      9:05 AM     Tokyo, link # 123-47    FAILED!
 Mon      11:15 AM    Tokyo, link # 123-47    up
 Tues     12:02 AM    Tokyo, link # 123-47    FAILED!
 Tues     12:12 AM    Tokyo, link # 123-47    up
```

Figure 12.4   A sample centralized log tool and a specific search.

Therefore some network management applications choose to take the entries from the log on the platform and put them in a relational database, where they can be sorted, searched, and correlated to other network events.

Report Writer

A report writer tool would allow you to produce custom reports. Although other tools on the system will produce their own reports, you might want to produce a specific report that is not available from the default system. A useful tool might provide a general facility to extract data from the database through SQL and then generate reports based on that data. Thus the report format you specify could contain any valid SQL statement, including mathematical formulas. The tool further could allow you to generate reports at a given time of day, week, month, or year.

You would need to tell the report writer tool what information to extract from the database and how to display it in the report. The tool could accept this input through a graphical interface. For example, you could be given a blank template and then use the mouse and keyboard to specify text and information retrieved from the database, as illustrated in Fig. 12.5. Using this method would allow you to see exactly what the report will look like before you generate it. This method is similar to that described previously for the window-based generation of custom MIB queries.

As we saw in Chapter 6, a common performance management report shows link utilization for the peak network usage times. You could set up the

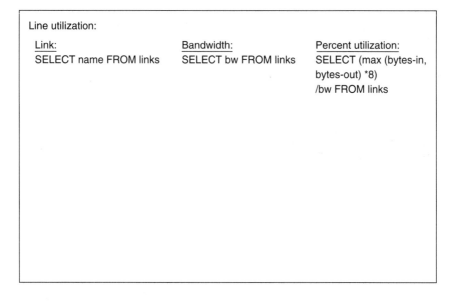

Line utilization:

Link:	Bandwidth:	Percent utilization:
SELECT name FROM links	SELECT bw FROM links	SELECT (max (bytes-in, bytes-out) *8) /bw FROM links

Figure 12.5   A sample line utilization report showing link names, bandwidth, and percent utilization. The engineer formats the report and selects the variables to retrieve from the database. The report writer uses this information to generate the desired output.

report writer to create a report displaying circuit names, bandwidth, and percent utilization. In this case you might want the system to generate this report early each morning to show the previous day's utilization.

Many report writers are available that work with relational database systems. If the platform uses a popular relational database from Oracle, Sybase, Ingres, or Informix, the company will most likely recommend a report writer. The various report writers are usually graphically based and allow you to build a custom report fairly easily.

Graphics Package

A generic graphics package can provide another way to present information. Many tools in most functional areas of network management benefit from having a graphics package for displaying data. Like the report writer, this package would retrieve information stored in the database and allow you to produce any desired graph. The graphics package should be able to produce the three common graph types—line, bar, and pie.

Ideally this package would operate by showing you a graph on the screen, enabling you to use the mouse to delineate a section of the graph, and then producing another graph of the delineated section. The package further should allow you to alter the graph, such as changing the color of the different plots or the labels or scaling of axes. Because graphical representation of data is extremely useful in network management, nearly all network management platforms support a graphics package to produce line graphs, but finding a package that supports pie and bar graphs is rare. Further, the graphics package should be able to save a snapshot of any graph in a format understood by the report writer, thus allowing reports to be generated that contain both text and graphs.

12.3 PROBLEM-SOLVING TOOLS

Intelligent problem-solving tools on the network management system can improve your productivity by tracking outstanding problems and guiding you toward problem resolution. The first of these tools, a trouble-tracking system, would allow you to track problems from discovery to resolution. The second set of tools may help you perform network design analysis in an attempt to avoid problems before the occur. The third tool, an expert system, would go further and, using a set of rules in combination with data about the network, could form evaluations and suggestions to help you resolve network problems. Even more advantageously, the ideal expert system could learn from previous problems and hence alter its rule base as needed.

Trouble-Tracking Systems

A trouble-tracking system can monitor network problems and open issues about not only fault management but also all other aspects of network management. For example, the system could track configuration changes, security modifications, performance requests and improvements, and accounting resources.

The system would operate by creating a new ticket for each unique problem or issue. Each ticket would record the data about the problem or issue and the actions taken toward handling it, from start to finish. Or, you or a network operator could create a ticket manually by entering all the known information about a problem. Certain information, such as the device name, the areas of the network affected, the person who administers the device, and so forth, usually would be required to initiate a new ticket.

Alternatively, if possible, the network management system could fill in this information. This action would be initiated by a network event reported by a management tool; for example, as we saw in Chapter 3, sophisticated fault management tools can take steps toward solving problems. Expert systems also can help the system automatically work toward problem resolution. However, if the system were not able to resolve the problem, a trouble ticket would be created that stated the problem and included the necessary information (device name, contact person, and so on) obtained from the relational database.

After the system created a ticket, it would be assigned to a network engineer. Assigning tickets helps ensure that problems are balanced fairly among engineers. Although the system could assign the problems automatically, most organizations would probably prefer to manually assign them; some engineers might have previous knowledge of particular problems or be better suited for certain types of tasks. Also, if problems are assigned by the system, it could be cumbersome to inform the system whenever an engineer takes a vacation or leaves the office for a few hours; failure to do this, however, could mean that the system would assign a problem to an absent engineer.

Each problem assigned to an engineer should have a classification entered automatically by the system or manually by an engineer. This classification can help you in the future when you are trying to categorize the problems that occur frequently. Some common classifications include link fault, network device fault, security breach, configuration error, performance problem, and accounting issue. A sample ticket entry is shown in Fig. 12.6.

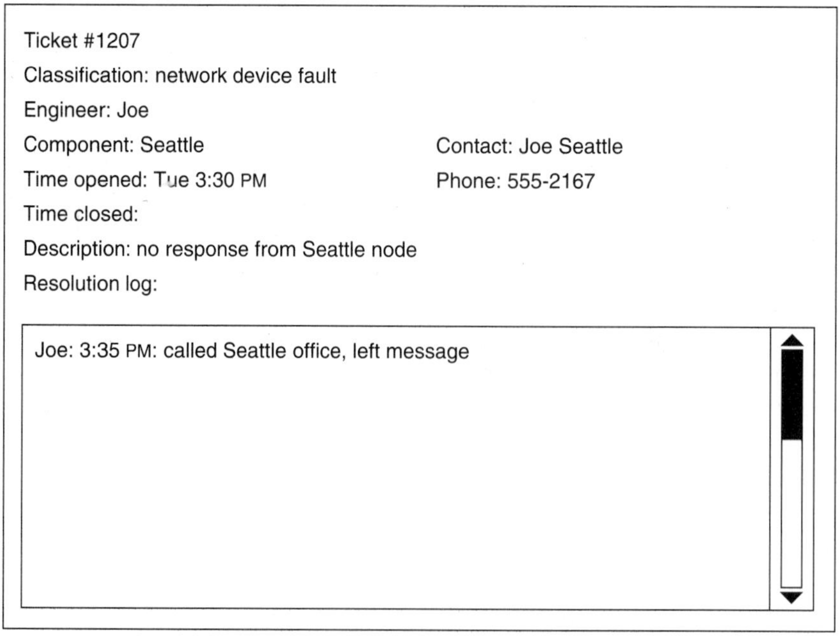

Ticket #1207
Classification: network device fault
Engineer: Joe
Component: Seattle   Contact: Joe Seattle
Time opened: Tue 3:30 PM   Phone: 555-2167
Time closed:
Description: no response from Seattle node
Resolution log:

Joe: 3:35 PM: called Seattle office, left message

Figure 12.6 A sample trouble ticket.

The trouble-tracking system would store all information about tickets in the relational database so that you could browse in the database for past problems relating to current issues. This browsing facility would need to be easy to use and should allow you to initiate an SQL search. For example, you might enter into the system the keywords "Paris," "London," and "circuit 123-654-3432" to search for past experiences about the circuit between Paris and London on circuit number 123-654-3432. The system then would perform the necessary SQL searches and produce a listing of all past tickets matching the given criteria.

A system that generated tickets automatically also could search the system database for similar problems. Thus you would receive not only the ticket but also a list of past problems that are similar to the current one, data that you can use for problem solving.

The trouble-tracking system further could use the searching ability of the database to gather data on the frequency and type of past problems. This information then could be fed to the report writer, thus making available reports that list how many problems in the past were due to a particular problem with a link fault, security breach, devices by a certain vendor, and so on. It also would be possible to generate a report of which problems consume the time and resources of network engineers. Further, you could use the graphics package to produce graphs showing this same data.

For example, suppose that you have upgraded the hardware of a network device, *Opus*, which is a front-end processor to a mainframe, *Milo* (see Fig. 12.7). This hardware upgrade also requires that software on *Milo* be reconfigured. Therefore two tickets, outlining two problems, would be entered into the system: the hardware configuration change of *Opus* and the software configuration change necessary on *Milo*. The first ticket is classified "hardware upgrade" and the second "configuration change." As engineers worked to solve these problems, they would record on their tickets each step taken. This data then would become available to help solve future similar problems on the affected device.

Trouble ticket systems are generally not part of a network management platform today and are usually applications that work in conjunction with the platform. Remedy Corporation makes a trouble-tracking system, called the Action Request System, which works with many popular network management platforms.

Network Design Tools

A set of network design tools can help you perform tasks that may avoid future problems on the data network. A network design tool learns the configuration of the network and then allows you to make changes to see how they affect traffic flow and performance.

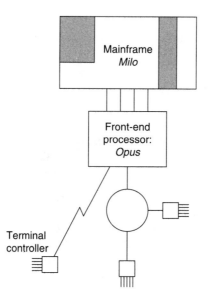

Figure 12.7 The front-end processor *Opus* serves terminal controllers with users setting up sessions with the mainframe *Milo*.

To learn the configuration of the network, design tools need input on the configuration of each network device. This information can be obtained from text files that describe the device configuration or from a network management protocol. For example, the tool could read the CONFIG.SYS file off each DOS-based personal computer or query each device for information in the system group of MIB-II. However, it would be rather time consuming to produce a tool that interpreted the text configuration file of every possible network device (even if the device had such a file). Furthermore many devices do not support a network management protocol, and even if they do, the information available in MIB-II may not be sufficient to learn the full configuration of the device. This means that the tool would have to learn how to use every possible vendor-specific MIB, another impractical task. Therefore many network design systems use a combination of approaches and also capture packet information off the current network as an additional aid in determining the network configuration. Some tools use RMON probes for this task (if they exist on the network).

If you are attempting to use a network design tool before you deploy the network, the methods described here to determine the current configuration of the network do not make much sense. Therefore some network design tools have sample devices that generically represent different types of network components. You can customize the sample devices to match the network devices you will deploy. This method often does not produce an exact representation of the network but is often close enough for rudimentary network design analysis.

The output of learning the configuration of the current network (or of the future network) is a graphical network map. With this map, you can add or remove network devices, move devices to new locations, and so on. Then the network design tool allows you to analyze the traffic patterns on the newly designed network, find security holes, and produce graphs and reports on potential network performance. The functionality of this analysis depends on the tool that you are using and is often enhanced by the use of an expert system. This analysis can help you produce a data network with fewer faults, configuration problems, and performance issues.

Some of the companies that make network design tools today are Make Systems, Comdisco Systems, Optimal Networks, and NetSys Technology. A network engineer needs to determine exactly which network devices to analyze, since most network design tools do not work with every possible network device.

Expert Systems

An expert system can take as input a current situation, evaluate the data, estimate the source of the issue, and suggest an action necessary for resolution. The expert system can perform these steps as part of an analysis of a network design or to help troubleshoot a problem. It does this by using a *rule set*, a set of if-then-else conditions that are considered sequentially. The tool follows these rules to draw conclusions and make suggestions given a certain set of situations. Based on the results of this procedure, the expert system then could test some of its own suggestions, which would eliminate the need for an engineer to perform each step toward solving a problem.

In general, a generic set of rules can provide you with a good start toward problem resolution. In practice, generic rules often generate generic suggestions, such as "check the modems," rather than correct answers to the problem. Although these suggestions might help novice network engineers, they are of little help to engineers who already know to perform the suggested action.

For example, if a link has failed, the expert system might know to make the following good, generic suggestions: Check the modems at each end, check the configuration and reachability of the network devices at each end, and call the circuit vendor. However, if the rules were more specific, such as "If circuit 123-654-3432 fails, suggest to call Allan at (415) 555-8877," the expert system would know to check the signals on each modem or test connectivity to the network devices and then suggest a call to the responsible network engineer. Based on the results of the tests, the system next could use the trouble-tracking system to create a new ticket detailing the steps the expert system has already performed.

Key to an expert system is its ability to use past experience or historical data to alter its rule base, thus streamlining its actions to reach a correct conclusion quickly. For example, suppose that a Token Ring has a performance problem. The expert system might present to you a list of possible solutions, as follows, given in order of most probable solution (see Fig. 12.8):

- Ring physically open

- Station on ring malfunctioning

- Medium attachment unit (MAU) failure

- Ring violates cable specifications

Here the expert system would begin by evaluating each possibility on the network and then would check each possible solution in turn. Finding that the first three solutions are not true, it could suggest to you that the fourth possible solution—the ring is violating cable-length specifications—might be the cause. Subsequently it would open a trouble ticket for the problem.

However, you discover that the performance problem in fact results from the fact that a network device forwarding packets between the locally attached ring and a serial link has become overwhelmed with traffic on the ring.

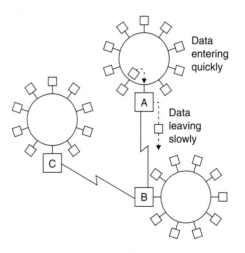

Figure 12.8 The slow forwarding rate of device A causes performance problems when under heavy load.

The network device cannot forward frames as quickly as the ring can pass them, thus causing the performance problems. You then could enter the solution—upgrade the network device—into the trouble ticket. This information also would be entered into the expert system in a format that allows it to alter its own rule set. Consequently the next time a performance problem occurred on this ring, the expert system would cycle through the first three checks and then try to test the performance of the network device before issuing a trouble ticket. If the network device were the problem in this subsequent performance problem, the expert system would have the correct solution and could point you directly to the answer.

Although expert systems hold considerable promise for solving routine problems for network engineers, they take a fair amount of time to run a simple test and draw conclusions. In most environments a proficient network engineer often can be on the way to solving a problem well before an expert system offers a suggestion. When advances in the technology allow for complex expert systems to be quick and efficient, they could very well influence the engineer's job in all facets of network management.

SUMMARY

Productivity tools can help the network engineer in a variety of ways. Three types of tools are available: MIB tools, presentation tools, and problem-solving tools. MIB tools enable an engineer to use all possible agents on the network. Presentation tools provide methods by which the engineer can display—as logs, reports, and graphs—information gathered by the network management system. Problem-solving tools can help by tracking problems to resolution and providing system-generated "educated guesses" useful in solving problems.

MIB tools include a compiler to load MIB information into the system, as well as tools that allow the engineer to browse the MIB, to rename confusing object names to user-defined names that are more easily understood, and to perform single queries of network agents.

Presentation tools include a centralized log of files stored in a text file or a database management system that can present information from all network components. Other presentation tools are a generic report writer and a graphics package.

Problem-solving tools helpful to a network engineer are a trouble-tracking system, a network design tool, and an expert system. The trouble-tracking system assigns current problems to an engineer and allows for searching through historical information. An expert system uses a rule set to offer solutions to common network problems and is able to learn from previous solutions.

FOR FURTHER STUDY

Nadeau, R., *Mind, Machines and Human Consciousness: Are There Limits to Artificial Intelligence?* Chicago: Contemporary Books, 1991.

Payne, E., and McArthur, R., *Developing Expert Systems: A Knowledge Engineer's Handbook for Rules and Objects*, New York: Wiley, 1990.

Wiederhold, G., *Database Design*, New York: McGraw-Hill, 1983.

Appendix A

Obtaining RFCs

Request for Comments (RFCs) are documents to communicate ideas for development in the Internet community. Some RFCs become Internet standards. To obtain copies of RFCs, contact Government Systems, Inc., (GSI) as follows:

- Telephone:
  (800) 365-3642
  (703) 802-4535
  (703) 802-8376 (FAX)

- Postal mail:
  Attn: Network Information Center
  14200 Park Meadow Drive, Suite 200
  Chantilly, VA 22021

- Electronic mail:
  nic@nic.ddn.mil

You also can use anonymous FTP to obtain RFCs from locations throughout the world. Log in to a machine, using the username *anonymous* and the password *guest*. After logging in, change to the proper directory and use the command **get** to retrieve the file you desire. To end your session, enter **quit**. Your session should appear similar to the following, with your input in boldface type:

```
% ftp nic.ddn.mil
Connected to nic.ddn.mil.
Name (nic.ddn.mil:allan): anonymous
331 Guest login ok, send "guest" as password
Password:
230 Guest login ok, access restrictions apply.
ftp> cd rfc
250 CWD command successful.
ftp> get rfc1213.txt
ftp> quit
%
```

The following machines are some of the places on the Internet where you can find RFCs:

- nic.ddn.mil (192.112.36.5)
- nis.nsf.net (35.1.1.48)
- nisc.jvnc.net (128.121.50.7)
- wuarchive.wustl.edu (128.252.135.4)
- venera.isi.edu (128.9.0.32)
- info.diku.dk (130.225.96.4)
- funet.fi (130.230.1.1)
- mcsun.eu.net (192.16.202.2)
- sunic.sunet.se (192.36.125.2)

Appendix B

Obtaining Technical Standards

The American National Standards Institute (ANSI), International Organization for Standardization (ISO), International Telephone and Telegraph Consultative Committee (CCITT), and Institute of Electrical and Electronic Engineers (IEEE) publish networking standards and recommendations. You can obtain these standards, usually for a fee, from several organizations by postal mail.

- For copies of ANSI standards, contact ANSI at the following mailing address:
  1430 Broadway
  New York, NY 10018
  (212) 642-4932 and (212) 302-1286

- For copies of ISO standards, contact the ISO at the following mailing address:
  1 Rue de Varembe
  Case Postale 56
  CH 1211 Geneva 20
  Switzerland

- For copies of CCITT standards, contact the CCITT at the following mailing address:
  2 Rue de Varembe
  CH 1211 Geneva 20
  Switzerland

- To obtain copies of IEEE standards, contact the IEEE at the following mailing address:
  IEEE Service Center
  445 Hoes Ln
  P.O. Box 1331
  Piscataway, NJ 08855

Various private organizations also offer copies of many standards. Two such organizations are the following:

- Global Engineering Documents
  2805 McGaw Avenue
  Irvine, CA 92714
  (800) 854-7179

- Omnicom/Phillips Publishing Incorporated
  P.O. Box 59665
  7811 Montrose Road
  Potomac, MD 20854
  (800) OMNICOM

Appendix C

Network Management System Sample Request for Proposal (RFP)

When building a network management system, most organizations turn to a vendor (or set of vendors) to provide them with the necessary software and hardware. Many vendors have various products, including network management platforms and applications. As an aid to help choose which products to purchase, an organization will often issue an RFP.

This appendix provides a sample RFP for your use. In this appendix, we assume that you want to purchase a network management system comprising a platform and applications.

I. PLATFORMS

A. Hardware

List any specific hardware requirements and considerations. In general, it makes sense to find a network management system that is compatible with your current environment. Ideally, you would want to use the hardware that you already have installed and are familiar with. However, managing large networks may require a system dedicated to network management.

- What manufacturer's hardware is supported or required?

- What are the hardware requirements in regards to CPU, disk space, memory, and peripherals?

- What is the average price of the typical hardware configuration necessary to run the software?

- Does the platform software require a dedicated system?

B. Software

List any specific software requirements and considerations. This would include operating systems (which sometimes are tied to the hardware platform) and graphical user interfaces. You also need to identify the network protocols that are on the network.

- What operating systems are supported or required to run the software?

- What network protocols do the management applications support?

- Does the software provide a graphical user interface?

- Does the software provide a network map (flat or hierarchical)?

- Does the software provide a database management system for storage of data collected from the network?

- If there is a DBMS:

  Can it be used to set up relationships between data?

  What language is used to query the database?

  Can it generate custom tables and reports?

- Does the software provide a customizable menu system?

- Does the software provide an event log?

- Does the event log provide event correlation or a way to determine the direct impact of a fault?

- Does the software have a documented application programming interface (API)?

- What type of security features are available to prevent unauthorized access to the network data?

C. Architecture

Let the corporate structure and management of your company guide you. If your company is highly centralized and all the technical network resources are in one location, choosing a platform that has the same structure would be advisable.

- What is the basic architecture of the platform (centralized, distributed, hierarchical, or a hybrid)?

- Does the platform support the OSF DME?

II. STANDARDS

First and foremost, the network management software must be able to manage devices running your network protocols. The most common network management protocol is SNMP, but you may have applications that require CMIS/CMIP, or moving to those protocols may be part of your corporate plan. The ability to add vendor MIBs is fairly important, particularly if you plan on building a heterogeneous network.

A. Management of Network Protocols

This list would include the network protocols that are used on your network.

- TCP/IP
- OSI CLNS/CLNP
- Novell IPX
- Apple Appletalk
- Banyan Vines

B. Network Management Protocol Support

- SNMP
- SNMPv2
- CMIS/CMIP

C. MIB Support

- MIB-I RFC 1156
- MIB-II RFC 1213
- RMON RFC 1757
- Supported vendor MIBs
- Can other MIBs be added?

III. APPLICATIONS

The importance placed on each area of network management is determined by each company. Most network management packages cannot do everything, so it is im-

portant for the network engineer to work with management to set clear goals and to then look for the package that will best fit.

A. Fault Management

- What polling method is used to determine connectivity/reachability of devices?

- Can the system log events and network traps?

- How are faults reported (audio, visual, text)?

- What other fault management features are available?

B. Configuration Management

- Does the software allow storage of configuration files?

- Can configurations be accessed and changed through the software?

- Can the software log changes to the configurations of devices?

- What other configuration management features are available?

C. Performance Management

- Can the software display real-time graphs and statistics of device and link performance?

- Can the software gather data for future performance analysis?

- What types of analysis can be done with the performance data?

- What other performance management features are available?

D. Security Management

- Can the software determine the implications of security filters on current network traffic?

- Can the software log network security violations?

- How are network security violations reported?

- What other security management features are available?

E. Accounting Management

- Can the software gather accounting data from network devices and hosts?

- Does the software use the general accounting model defined in RFC 1672?

- What other accounting management features are available?

IV. PRODUCTIVITY TOOLS

List additional tools that would be valuable in doing network management of your particular network.

A. MIB Tools

- Does the software provide a MIB compiler?

- Does the software provide a MIB browser?

- Does the software provide a MIB query tool?

- Does the software provide a MIB alias tool?

B. Presentation Tools

- Does the software provide a centralized log for all system messages and network events?

- Does the software provide a generic report generator?

- Does the software provide a graphics display package for data?

C. Problem-Solving Tools

- Does the software provide a trouble-tracking system?

- Does the software provide a network design tool?

- Does the software provide an expert system?

Glossary

A

abstract syntax   A data structure description that does not depend on hardware structures and encodings.

access point   A piece of network hardware or software that allows access to the data network.

accounting management   The process of gathering statistics about resources on the network, establishing metrics, checking quotas, determining costs, and billing network clients.

ACSE (association control service element)   The application service element that handles association establishment and release.

address   The location of a network device or service; for example, an IP address or socket for a program.

address resolution   The process of mapping one address to another (that is, ARP) or a name to an address (that is, name resolution).

agent   A set of software in a network device that is responsible for handling requests by a particular protocol, such as SNMP.

alarm   A sound or message used to grab the attention of a network engineer.

alert   *See* alarm.

algorithm   A method used to solve a problem.

anonymous FTP (anonymous File Transfer Protocol)   An FTP subset that allows users limited access to certain files and commands.

ANSI (American National Standards Institute)   Within the United States, the body that coordinates voluntary standards groups.

Apple Appletalk   A network protocol suite used primarily by Apple, Inc., computers.

application   A software package, such as a network management system or tool, distinct from system software.

API (application programming interface)   A programmatic interface to a set of software libraries.

Application Layer   The seventh layer of the OSI Reference Model; responsible for application communication.

architecture   The method or style used in building an object, such as the software of a network management system or hardware of a network device.

ARP (Address Resolution Protocol)   A protocol for mapping IP addresses to Ethernet/IEEE 802.2 addresses; documented in RFC 826.

ASCII (American National Standard Code for Information Interchange) A 7-bit character set used for information exchange.

ASN.1 (Abstract Syntax Notation One)   The OSI language for describing abstract syntax.

ATM (asynchronous transfer mode)   The ITU-T (formerly CCITT) cell relay standard for multiple applications using fixed-sized cells.

ATM (automated teller machine)   A machine that performs certain banking and credit card transactions, such as cash withdrawals.

audit trail   User activity recorded for review as part of discovering security breaches.

authentication   The process of establishing the identity of a network user.

autodiscovery   A method used by a network management system to dynamically find the devices attached to a data network.

automapping   A method used by a network management system to dynamically produce a logical map of a data network.

autonomous system   The piece of a data network usually under the control of a single organization and that usually runs a single interior routing protocol.

availability   The percentage of time the data network is accessible for use and operational.

B

bandwidth   The rate at which information is transmitted.

Banyan Vines   A network protocol suite used by personal computers running the operating system from Banyan, Inc.

baud rate   The number of symbols per second that can be transmitted.

billing   The process of charging users for the use of the data network and its associated services.

bit   A unit of information that denotes one of two possible states, true or false; represented by a 1 or 0.

bitmapped display   A computer screen capable of setting the characteristics of each bit displayed.

bps (bits per second)   The number of bits transmitted in one second.

bridge   A network device that operates at the Data Link Layer and connects LANs.

brouter   A network device that performs both bridging and routing simultaneously.

buffer storage   Storage space on a network device for storing packets as they are processed or waiting to be transmitted.

byte   A series of bits treated as a single unit.

C

capacity planning   The process of determining the future requirements of network resources.

carrier signal   A continuous wave that is modulated with information on a serial connection.

CCITT (International Telephone and Telegraph Consultative Committee)
An international organization that defines standards and recommendations for the connection of telephone equipment. Now known as the ITU-T (International Telecommunication Union Telecommunication Standardization Sector).

centralized architecture   An architecture centered on one system.

centralized log   A storage location where all the tools and applications on the network management record information.

channel   A communication path.

channel bank   Terminal equipment for a transmission system used to multiplex individual circuits.

ciphertext   Encrypted data.

circuit   A communications link between two or more points.

cleartext   Unencrypted (therefore readable) data.

client   A system that uses the services of a server.

CLNS (Connectionless Network Service)   An OSI network layer service.

cluster controller   A network device used to connect terminals to a mainframe computer.

CMIPM (Common Management Information Protocol Machine)   Software services that accept CMIS operations and initiate the appropriate procedures to accomplish the associated operation.

CMIS/CMIP (Common Management Information Services/Common Management Information Protocol)   The OSI network management services and protocol.

CMISE (Common Management Information Service Element)   An application service element responsible for deciphering the meaning of network management protocol information.

CMISE-service-user   An application that performs network management using the CMIS services.

CMOL (Common Management Information Services and Protocol over IEEE 802 Logical Link Control)   A network management protocol that implements CMIS services directly on top of the IEEE 802 Logical Link Layer. CMOL is now known as LMMP.

CMOT (Common Management Information Services over TCP)   An implementation of the CMIS services over TCP; documented in RFC 1189.

community string   An ASCII string used for authentication by SNMP.

computer server   A computer that performs processing for client computers.

concentrator node   A network device that connects many subsidiary network devices.

configuration management   The process of obtaining information from network devices and using it to manage their setups.

congestion   The point at which time bandwidth utilization causes network performance problems.

connectionless   A service in which the network delivers data between two systems independent of other simultaneous communication.

CPU (Central Processing Unit)   The main piece of hardware on a system that performs data processing.

critical network event   A network event that warrants the immediate attention of a network engineer.

CSU (Channel Service Unit)   A digital interface device that connects network devices to the local digital telephone loop.

D

database   A large, multipurpose collection of data on a system, organized so that it can be retrieved, searched, and updated rapidly.

datagram   A piece of data, sent to a network, that provides connectionless service.

Data Link Layer   The second layer of the OSI Reference Model; responsible for addressing, transmission, error detection, and framing on a channel.

data network   A communications network made of network devices for the purposes of transferring data between systems.

DBMS (database management system)   *See* database.

DCE (distributed computing environment)   A framework for distributed computing proposed by the OSF.

DEC   Digital Equipment Corporation.

deencryption   The process of deciphering an encrypted message.

DES (Data Encryption Standard)   The standard cryptographic algorithm developed by the U.S. National Bureau of Standards.

destination host   The host that is the destination of a transaction.

device   A system that can access a data network. *See* host, system.

digit   A number between 0 and 9 inclusive.

Digital DECnet   A protocol suite used primarily by computers developed and supported by the Digital Equipment Corporation.

diskless client   A system that does not have any local storage facility and relies entirely on the network to connect to a file server.

distributed architecture   An architecture spread among many systems.

DME (distributed management environment)   A framework for distributed management proposed by the OSF.

DoD (Department of Defense)   A branch of the U.S. government responsible for the nation's defense; responsible for developing the DoD protocols, such as TCP/IP.

DOS (disk operating system)   An operating system commonly run on personal computers.

DS-1 (Digital System 1)   An abbreviation used to denote the 1.44 Mbps (U.S.) or 2.108 Mbps (Europe) digital signal carried on a T-1 facility.

DS-3 (Digital System 3)   An abbreviation used to denote the 44 Mbps digital signal carried on a T-3 facility.

DSU (data service unit)   A device used in digital transmission for connecting a CSU to a network device.

E

EGP (Exterior Gateway Protocol)   A routing protocol for passing reachability information between autonomous systems; documented in RFC 904.

electronic mail   A software service that allows one user to send a message to another user.

encryption   The scrambling of data through the use of an algorithm.

encryption key   A piece of information that serves as a basis for encryption.

enterprise network   A data network that serves an entire enterprise and its associated telecommunication needs.

entity   Any network system that has an SNMP agent.

Ethernet   A networking protocol developed originally by Xerox Corporation for use on LANs.

event   An occurrence on the data network that might warrant the attention of a network engineer.

expert system   A system that has the ability to learn and aids in problem solving by using a rule-based system.

F

fault   A problem on the data network.

fault management   The process of identifying network faults, isolating the cause of the fault, and, if possible, correcting the fault.

FDDI (fiber distributed data interface)   A standard specifying a 100 Mbps token-passing network using fiber-optic cable.

FEP (front-end processor)   A network device that provides network interface capabilities for a network device.

fiber-optic cable   A network medium that conducts modulated light transmission.

file   An ordered collection of data.

file server   A system with disk space used by multiple clients.

file system   The storage space on a host.

file transfer   An application that moves files from one network device to another.

filter   A process that limits information based on certain criteria.

finger   An application that allow users to learn whether other users are logged into the local and remote systems.

firefighting   A situation in which network engineers spend most of their time continually solving problems and not working toward the future development of the data network.

firewall   A device or combination of hardware and software used to enforce security between two networks.

flow control   A technique for ensuring that a transmitting host does not overrun a receiving host with data.

fragment   A piece of a packet that has been broken into smaller units.

Frame Relay   A wide area protocol used between network devices based on virtual circuits.

FTP (File Transfer Protocol)   An IP application protocol for transferring files between network devices.

full duplex   A capability for the simultaneous transmission of data in both directions.

G

gateway   A network device that can perform protocol conversion from one protocol stack to another.

Gbps (Gigabits per second)   One billion bits per second.

graph   Method used to display data in a pictorial manner, such as in a bar, line, or pie shape.

graphics package   Software that converts data into graphs.

GUI (graphical user interface)   The user interface to an application that uses graphics instead of only text.

H

half-duplex   The capability of transmitting data in one direction at a time.

hardware   The physical components of a computer.

hardware address   A Data Link Layer address for a network device. *See* MAC address, physical address.

HEMS (High-Level Entity Management System)   A network management protocol that was considered for Internet standardization; documented in RFC 1076.

hop count   A routing metric used to find the distance between two network devices.

host   A computer system on a data network. *See* device, system.

host authentication   A process whereby the destination host identifies the source host of a transaction by its name or address.

hub   A network device that is the center of a star-topology network.

I

IAB (Internet Activities Board) A group that oversees the work in networking technology and protocols for the TCP/IP internetworking community.

IBM International Business Machines.

IBM SNA (IBM Systems Network Architecture) A network architecture developed by IBM.

ICMP (Internet Control Message Protocol) A Network Layer protocol that carries messages to report errors relevant to IP packet processing; documented in RFC 792.

IEEE (Institute of Electrical and Electronic Engineers) A professional organization that defines network standards.

IETF (Internet Engineering Task Force) A subgroup of the IAB, chartered to identify and coordinate solutions in the areas of management, engineering, and operations of the Internet.

Information Superhighway A marketing and political term representing the collection of connected public networks; the Internet.

interface A connection between two network devices or hosts.

Internet A term used to refer to the world's largest internetwork, which connects thousands of networks around the world. It is usually referenced as "the Internet."

internet A term used to describe a group of interconnecting devices that make up a network. Should not be confused with the Internet.

internetwork A collection of networks interconnected by network devices that generally act as a single network.

Internet worm A program written by Robert Morris, Jr., that used various techniques to spread itself throughout the Internet in November 1988.

inventory An itemized list of current items, such as network devices.

IP (Internet Protocol) A Network Layer protocol that contains addressing and control information for packets to be routed; documented in RFC 791.

IPng (Internet Protocol next generation) The next version of IP, currently being developed by the IETF. Also known as IPv6 (IP version 6).

IRTF (Internet Research Task Force)   A subgroup of the IAB, chartered to work on research problems concerning the TCP/IP network community and the Internet.

ISO (International Organization for Standardization)   An international body that develops, suggests, and names standards for network protocols.

ITU-T (International Telecommunication Union Telecommunication Standardization Sector)   *See* CCITT.

K

Kbps (kilobits per second)   One thousand bits per second.

Kerberos   The implementation of a key authentication service written by MIT Project Athena.

key   In a packet, a unique piece of information that authenticates the data in a transaction.

key authentication   A process whereby the destination host requires the source host of a transaction to present a key for the transaction.

key server   A server that validates requests for transactions between hosts by giving out keys.

L

labeled node   In the MIB tree, a piece of information that has an object identifier and a short text description.

LAN (local area network)   A high-speed network covering a limited geographic area, such as a single building.

LAPB (Link Access Procedure, Balanced)   A bit-oriented data link protocol.

leased line   A transmission line set up by a communications carrier for the private use of a customer.

link   A communications channel between source and destination and including all intervening network devices.

link driver   A network device that ensures reliable transmissions of digital signals over long distances.

LLC (Logical Link Control)   An IEEE sublayer of the Data Link Layer that handles framing, flow control, and errors.

LMMP (LAN MAN Management Protocol)   A network management protocol, previously called CMOL, that implements CMIS services on top of IEEE 802 Logical Link Layer for use in LAN environments.

log file   A file that maintains a record of information output by applications and that may be useful for later examination.

loopback   A way a machine communicates to itself; used to test the network interfaces.

LPP (Lightweight Presentation Protocol)   A protocol on the OSI Presentation Layer that does not provide the full functionality of the complete OSI Presentation Layer, thus making it easier to implement; documented in RFC 1085.

M

MAC (media access control)   The lower portion of the Data Link Layer as defined by IEEE; concerned with media access issues.

MAC address   A Data Link Layer address for a network device. *See* physical address, hardware address.

mainframe   A large computing system.

managed object   A network device that can be managed by a network management protocol.

management association service   A class of CMIS services that controls the interaction between peer open systems.

management notification service   A class of CMIS services that provides information about network events.

management operation service   A class of CMIS services that provides the ability to manage network devices.

MAU (Medium Attachment Unit for IEEE 802.3; Multistation Access Unit for IEEE 802.5)   In IEEE 802.3, a Physical Layer network device that performs collision detection and the transfer of bits to and from the network. In IEEE 802.5, a wiring concentrator that attaches multiple stations to the network.

Mbps (megabits per second)   One million bits per second.

MD5 (Message Digest 5)   An algorithm that generates a 128-bit number specific to a message and its contents.

media   The physical substance through which pass transmission signals, such as coaxial or fiber-optic cable.

message   A logical collection of information in the Application Layer.

MIB (Management Information Base)   A database of managed objects accessed by network management protocols.

MIB-I (Management Information Base I)   The first MIB defined for managing TCP/IP-based internets; documented in RFC 1156.

MIB-II (Management Information Base II)   The current standard MIB defined for managing TCP/IP-based internets; documented in RFC 1213.

microwave link   A communications link based on electromagnetic waves.

minicomputer   A computer that is larger than a personal computer but smaller than a mainframe, usually distinguished by processing power and peripheral support.

MIT   Massachusetts Institute of Technology.

modem (modulator-demodulator)   A device that performs bidirectional conversion from digital signals into a form for communication over analog communication facilities.

MTBF (mean time between failures)   The average time between failures of an object, such as a network device.

MTU (maximum transmission unit)   The maximum size of a packet (in bytes) that can be handled over an interface.

multiplexer   A network device used to switch circuits.

N

name resolution   The process of resolving a system name to a network address through the use of a name server.

name server   A system that responds to queries to map system names to network addresses.

network   *See* data network.

network access point   A location, such as a port or software program, by which users obtain access to the network.

network address   A Network Layer address that refers to a logical, not physical, network device.

network billing   The process of billing users of a data network to recover expenses or obtain profit.

network component   *See* network device.

network device   A generic term referring to any device that can access a network.

network engineer   A person responsible for one or more of the following tasks on a data network: installation, maintenance, and troubleshooting.

network inventory   A collection of information about network devices, circuits, people, vendors, and so forth, useful for accomplishing network management.

Network Layer   The third layer of the OSI Reference Model; handles routing.

network management   The task of controlling a complex data network so that it can be used in a useful and proficient manner. Network management is divided into five categories: fault management, configuration management, security management, performance management, and accounting management.

network management architecture   The architecture of a network management system describing the framework for applications that perform network management.

network management protocol   A protocol designed to perform network management.

network management system   A bundle of software that provides features and functionality to help network engineers.

network operator   A person who helps performs tasks to help operate the network on a day-to-day basis.

network protocol   A protocol that operates at the Network Layer.

network resource   A network device that provides a service for users.

network simulation   The process of simulating how a network will act and perform.

network topology The physical arrangement of network devices and media within a data network.

NIC (Network Information Center) A center that serves the Internet community by providing user assistance, documentation, and other services.

node *See* network device.

Novell IPX (Novell Internetwork Packet Exchange) A network protocol suite used by personal computers running the operating system from Novell, Inc.

NSAP (Network Service Access Point) An OSI Network Layer address.

O

object A software-defined entity having its own properties, methods, and internal workings.

object (MIB) In a MIB tree, a piece of information that is either an intermediary node or a leaf node containing a value.

OID (object identifier) A series of integers separated by periods that denote the exact traversal of a MIB tree to a labeled node.

open system A system running the OSI protocol stack.

operating system On a computer, the application, such as UNIX or DOS, that performs intrinsic functions, such as file and storage system access.

operating system security Within an operating system, the security mechanisms that limit the actions of users and protect information.

OSF (Open Software Foundation) An organization that explores technologies for use throughout the computer industry.

OSI (Open Systems Interconnection) An international network protocol suite developed by ISO and ITU-T (formerly CCITT) for use on multivendor equipment.

OSI Reference Model A network architectural model developed by the ISO and ITU-T (formerly CCITT); used universally for understanding and teaching network functionality.

P

packet   A logical collection of data.

packet filter   In a network device, a configuration that limits the flow of a packet, based on certain criteria.

password   A series of characters to uniquely identify a user.

PC (personal computer)   A computer system, such as an IBM PC or Apple Macintosh, used by a single user.

performance management   The process of analyzing the characteristics of a data network to monitor and increase its efficiency.

physical address   The Data Link Layer address of a network device. *See* hardware address, MAC address.

Physical Layer   The first layer of the OSI Reference Model; defines the mechanical, physical, and electrical interface to a network and its associated medium.

physical security   The physical security of network devices, such as locked doors and keyboards.

polling   The process whereby one device queries other devices for information.

port   An interface to a networking device.

Presentation Layer   The sixth layer of the OSI Reference Model; controls the syntax of information passed between two Application Layer programs.

print server   A system with a printer used by multiple clients.

promiscuous mode   A mode whereby a device listens to every frame on a segment.

protocol   A formal description of a set of rules and conventions that describe how network devices exchange information.

protocol analyzer   A network device used to capture packets on a network and analyze their contents.

protocol translator   A network device or software package that converts one protocol into another.

proxy agent   An agent that can gather information about other systems and then relay this information to a management station via a protocol, such as SNMP.

public data network A network set up by a government or private organization to provide widespread communications to the public, sometimes for a fee.

Q

query A message that inquires of the status of an object or device.

quota The amount of a network's resources allowed for a user or group.

R

RAM (random access memory) A type of computer memory in which the access time is independent of the address.

reachability The process of establishing whether one system can communicate with another.

rejection rate The amount of time a network cannot transfer information because of a lack of resources and performance.

remote bridge A bridge that connects physically separate network segments via a WAN link.

remote login An application allowing users to log in to a system via the network.

repeater A Physical Layer network device that regenerates and propagates bits between two network segments.

reports Text, and possible graphics, showing the results of a process or the listing of numerical information.

report writer A set of software tools that help in the writing and formatting of reports.

response time The amount of time it takes for a piece of information to enter the network and be processed and then have a response leave the network.

RFC (Request for Comments) Documents to communicate ideas for development in the Internet community and that might become Internet standards.

RFP (Request for Proposal) A paper put out by organizations listing vendor requirements for a given technology that they are interested in purchasing.

RMON (remote network monitoring) MIB   A MIB that defines a set of all objects available for an RMON probe.

RMON probe   A device that is designed to help perform network management on a network segment.

ROM (read-only memory)   A type of computer memory that can be read but not changed.

ROSE (Remote Operations Service Element)   An OSI application protocol used to access remote open systems.

route   The path between two systems on a data network.

router   A network device that can decide how to forward packets through a network by examining Network Layer information.

RPC (remote procedure call)   Procedure calls that are sent from a client to a server, with the results sent back to the server.

RTT (round-trip time)   The time required for information to travel from the source system, through all intermediate network devices, to the destination system, and back to the source system.

S

satellite link   A link that uses geostationary orbiting satellites to provide communications links between two network devices.

SDLC (Synchronous Data Link Control)   An IBM synchronous Data Link Layer protocol used on serial links.

security management   The process of protecting access to sensitive information found on systems attached to a data network.

security violation   A breach in security that results in unauthorized users accessing sensitive information.

sendmail   A UNIX application that provides electronic mail service through the use of SMTP.

sensitive information   Any data on a system that an organization decides to secure, such as business data, customer information, and research and development schedules.

serial interface   A network interface that connects to a serial link.

serial link   A link in which the bits of a data character are transmitted, in order, over a single channel.

server   A generic term used to refer to a host that offers some service to client hosts.

session   A related set of communications transactions between two network devices.

Session Layer   The fifth layer of the OSI Reference Model; coordinates session activity between applications, such as remote procedure calls.

SGMP (Simple Gateway Monitoring Protocol)   A network management protocol that was considered for Internet standardization and later evolved into SNMP; documented in RFC 1028.

SMI (structure of management information)   Rules used to define managed objects in a MIB; documented in RFC 1155.

SMTP (Simple Mail Transfer Protocol)   An Internet protocol providing electronic mail services.

SNMP (Simple Network Management Protocol)   A network management protocol used for managing IP network devices; documented in RFC 1157.

SNMPv2 (Simple Network Management Protocol version 2)   A network management protocol used for managing network devices; documented in RFC 1448.

socket   A software data structure that provides a communications access point within a network device.

software   A set of computer programs.

source host   The host that is the source of a transaction.

source route bridge   A network device that performs source routing in a situation in which the entire route to a destination is predetermined prior to sending data.

spanning tree   A subset of a network topology without loops.

spanning tree algorithm   An algorithm for preventing loops in a bridged network through the use of a spanning tree.

SQL (Structured Query Language)   A standard language developed by ANSI for accessing databases.

SQL query   A request for information within a database using SQL.

standard   An officially specified or commonly used collection of rules or procedures.

subnet mask   A 32-bit address mask used in IP to calculate a specific subnet.

switch   A network device that operates at the Data Link Layer and connects LANs and devices.

system   A generic term used to describe a network device or computer on a data network. *See* host.

T

T-1   A telephone term to describe a digital carrier facility for the transmission of data at 1.544 Mbps.

T-3   A digital WAN service that provides transmission of data at 44 Mbps.

TCP (Transport Control Protocol)   A Transport Layer protocol that provides reliable transmission of data on IP networks; documented in RFC 793.

TCP/IP   The two most popular Internet protocols that provide Transport Layer and Network Layer service.

technology   A method or process for handling a technical problem.

telecommunications   A generic term describing communications over a telephone network and that involve computer systems.

terminal   A computer device that can display text and graphics but that has no processing power.

terminal server   A network device that connects asynchronous devices to a WAN or LAN.

text message   A message or other output that does not require graphics for viewing, such as a line of text on an ASCII terminal.

TFTP (Trivial File Transfer Protocol)   A simplified version of FTP that performs the transfer of files from one host to another (usually without the use of a password); documented in RFC 783.

threshold   A point at which a significant event may occur.

throughput   The rate of information arriving at, and possibly going through, a point in a network system.

timeout   An event that happens when one network device expects to hear from another within a specified amount of time but does not.

Token Ring   A token-passing LAN developed by IBM. Standardized as IEEE 802.5.

Transport Layer   The fourth layer of the OSI Reference Model; responsible for reliable network communication between hosts.

trap   Unsolicited message sent by an SNMP agent to a management station to alert about a specific network event.

trend analysis   An analysis of information over a period of time, with an emphasis on predicting future data points.

troubleshooting   The process of diagnosing and fixing problems.

trouble-tracking system   A software package designed to help network engineers track the resolution of current and past network problems.

twisted pair   A transmission media consisting of two insulated or noninsulated wires arranged in a regular spiral pattern.

U

UDP (User Datagram Protocol)   A connectionless transport protocol used on IP networks; documented in RFC 768.

UNIX   A popular operating system for computers.

user   A person who utilizes a network device or computer system.

user authentication   A process whereby the destination host uniquely identifies the source user of a transaction, usually through the use of a password.

user interface   The interface the user sees when communicating with a software tool or application.

utilization   The amount of use of a network device, link, or system.

V

vendor   An organization that sells network devices or systems.

virtual circuit   A logical circuit established to produce reliable communication between two network devices.

virtual LAN   A logical collection of devices that may be in physically disparate locations.

W

WAN (wide area network)   A data network that spans a large geographic area.

wiring closet   A room designed for data and voice networks that often serves as a central location for network devices.

workstation   A midsized computer system designed for a small number of users.

X

X11   *See* X Window System.

X11 Motif   A set of standard software libraries that provide a consistent look and feel for X11 applications.

X.121   An X.25 Network Layer address.

X.25   An ITU-T (formerly CCITT) standard that specifies packet format for the transfer of data in a public data network.

X.400   An ITU-T (formerly CCITT) recommendation that defines a standard for the transfer of electronic mail.

X.500   An ITU-T (formerly CCITT) recommendation that defines a standard for distributed maintenance of directories and files.

X Window System   A distributed windowing system that is vendor and machine independent; originally developed by MIT for UNIX workstations.

Xerox XNS (Xerox Network Systems)   A network protocol suite used by personal computers developed by Xerox PARC.

Index

Abstract syntax, 307
Access point, 307
Accounting management
  benefits of, 126–128
  description of, 12–13, 125–126, 307
  host group of RMON MIB objects for, 262
  interfaces group objects for, 209
  IP group objects for, 219
  on network management system, 136–142
  reporting accounting information and, 142–143
  SNMP group objects for, 237–239
  steps in, 128–135
  TCP objects for, 225–226
  UDP objects for, 228–229
ACSE (association control service element), 182–184, 307
Address, 307
Address resolution, 307
Address translation group, 212
Agent, 307
Alarm, 307
Alarm group of RMON MIB
  description of, 256–257
  objects for performance management, 257–258
Alert, 307
Algorithm
  definition of, 307
  spanning tree, 324
American National Standards Institute (ANSI), 299, 307
Anonymous FTP (File Transfer Protocol), 307
API (application programming interface)
  description of, 20, 308
  interfacing with platform through, 27
Appletalk, 42, 82, 308
Appletalk Echo, 40
Application, 308
Application layer, 308
Application security, 76
Architecture
  centralized, 22–23, 309

definition of, 308
distributed, 25–26
hierarchical, 23–25
ARP (Address Resolution Protocol), 308
ASCII, 62, 286, 308
ASN.1 (Abstract Syntax Notation One), 154–155, 308
ATM (asynchronous transfer mode), 50, 68, 308
ATM MIB (IBM), 159
ATMs (automated teller machines), 4–5, 308
AT&T StarSentry, 21, 25
Audit trail
  definition of, 308
  security management and, 100
  use of, 97
Authentication
  definition of, 308
  host, 86–88, 90
  key, 91–92, 316
  SNMPv2 and, 172–174
  user, 88–90, 326
Autodiscovery
  description of, 19, 308
  function of, 60–61, 64
Automapping
  description of, 19, 308
  network configuration shown by, 61
Autonomous system, 308
Availability, 121, 308

Bandwidth, 309
Bandwidth-on-demand, 202, 203
Banyan Vines, 40, 309
Baud rate, 309
Billing
  accounting management and, 130
  on bases of bytes, 132–134
  complex tools for, 137–139
  definition of, 309
  fee based on amount of network resources consumed, 131–135
  one-time installation fee and monthly fee, 131
Bit, 309